Transnational Crime, Crime Control and Security

Transnational crime and security are key modalities of governance in a globalizing world. World-wide, there is a tendency to treat every imaginable source of harm as a potential source of insecurity, and therefore as a crime. The catastrophic imagination is fueled by the precautionary logics of a world system troubled by systemic risk. As these logics become pervasive, security measures are invoked in an effort to control the imagined sources of harm, and the consequences are not always clear-cut. Further, the terminology of transnational crime, threat, risk and (in)security (and the phenomena to which they refer) is substantively deterritorialized, raising further theoretical and practical difficulties. Research and scholarship concerning these issues touches upon crucial features of the world system. This series offers wide inter-disciplinary scope for scholarship exploring these central aspects of global governance and governance globally.

Richard Kjellgren

Internet-Mediated Exploitation in the Scottish Online Sex Market

A Case Study in Computational Criminology

palgrave
macmillan

Richard Kjellgren
Salvation Army Centre for Addiction
Services and Research,
Faculty of Social Sciences
University of Stirling
STIRLING, UK

ISSN 2947-4264 ISSN 2947-4272 (electronic)
Transnational Crime, Crime Control and Security
ISBN 978-3-032-09274-8 ISBN 978-3-032-09275-5 (eBook)
https://doi.org/10.1007/978-3-032-09275-5

This Palgrave Macmillan imprint is published by the registered company Springer Nature Switzerland AG
The registered company address is: Gewerbestrasse 11, 6330 Cham, Switzerland

This book is dedicated to my mum and dad. Thank you. For everything.

Acknowledgements

Thanks to all respondents who made my research possible by sharing their perspectives and insights; you were extraordinarily generous with your time amid an ongoing global pandemic. Special thanks to my primary contact at Police Scotland's Human Trafficking Unit, who provided excellent support throughout the research process.

I am very grateful to my PhD examiners, Professor Ella Cockbain, Dr Ben Matthews and Professor Alasdair Rutherford. Their feedback and encouragement greatly enhanced the quality of my PhD, on which this book is based. They are, in addition, scholars and colleagues of the highest quality, and I am extremely grateful for having had the opportunity to, and continuing to, learn from you.

I am also indebted to Josie Taylor and colleagues at Palgrave Macmillan and Springer Nature, for support and patience through the publication process.

To my PhD supervisors, Professor Niall Hamilton-Smith and Dr Dave Griffiths: you have provided unwavering support from the days of my undergraduate degree, throughout my MSc and to the final days of my PhD. You have always gone above and beyond and supported my development from an overly enthusiastic undergraduate to a full-fledged researcher. The best way I can imagine of repaying this debt is to strive to be as supportive and collegiate as you are to my future students and colleagues.

To my colleagues at SACASR and the Faculty of Social Sciences in Stirling, and particularly Dr Catriona Connell and Professor Tessa Parkes: thanks for always inspiring me, leading by example and supporting me to become a better researcher.

I also want to thank Dr Johan Holm for inspiring me to pursue higher education and for igniting my sociological imagination and to Dr Morgan for her kindness, wisdom and insight.

To my family and friends: I am eternally grateful to all of you, and your support, whether you know it or not, has been crucial to all the work that I do, giving me courage, inspiring hope and encouraging me when I need it the most.

To Podrick, my scruffy terrier: you're a true pal.

There are few words that can express the gratitude I owe to Christina. There simply is no other human being that compares to your warmth, generosity and kindness. Thank you, absolutely and categorically, for everything.

Finally, to my mother, who never had the opportunity to see how happy my new life in Scotland would make me: tack för allt, bästa mamma. Du har varit med mig under hela denna resa. För alltid saknad, men aldrig glömd.

Competing Interests The author has no competing interests to declare that are relevant to the content of this manuscript.

Ethics Approval This research received ethical approval from the University of Stirling's General University Ethics Panel on 8th October 2020 (reference number: GUEP/20/21/1007).

Contents

List of Figures

Network Influences on Extreme Service Advertisement

Key Messages and Conclusions: Future Directions in the Computational Criminology of Internet-Mediated Exploitation

List of Tables

Methods in Practice: Designing an Effective Workflow in Computational Criminology

Exploitation and the Policing of Contemporary Sex Markets in Scotland

Complexity, Similarity and Tie Formation in Advert Networks

Network Influences on Extreme Service Advertisement

Introduction

Context

In an increasingly networked society (Castells 2010), human behaviour becomes more likely to be mediated by online technologies. Much of our daily communication occurs online, and crime has not been exempt from the wider digitalisation occurring throughout society. Indeed, many crimes and experiences of victimisation are likely to involve an element of technology (Stratton et al. 2017). Online technologies are perhaps particularly important in the context of contemporary organised crime: new technologies have affected how criminal networks facilitating more complex forms of crime operate in covert and risky settings (Leukfeldt et al. 2019). One such crime is human trafficking, which is the focus of this book.

Human trafficking has previously been highlighted as one of the most complicated crimes to investigate (Pajón and Walsh 2018), the complexity of the crime being attributable to several features. Human trafficking is a processual crime (Malloch and Rigby 2016), consisting of three stages: recruitment, transportation and exploitation. It is also an essentially relational crime; the process of exploitation is predicated upon

R. Kjellgren, *Internet-Mediated Exploitation in the Scottish Online Sex Market*,
Transnational Crime, Crime Control and Security,
https://doi.org/10.1007/978-3-032-09275-5_1

social relations, and patterns of victimisation and opportunities for offending are embedded within social networks (Verhoeven et al. 2013). Others have also highlighted how human trafficking is fundamentally spatio-temporal (Cockbain et al. 2022), often involving the movement of victims across vast distances, and exploitation can occur over prolonged periods (Cockbain and Brayley-Morris 2018). This case study is specifically focused on sex trafficking, and what makes this a particularly complicated crime is that it involves the policing of a market that is comprised of both autonomous, independent sex workers, and also individuals who are victims of exploitation (Vajzovic 2019; Sanders et al. 2021).

The term 'victim' is heavily contested in the fields of sex work, exploitation and trafficking, and often associated with what Agustín (2007) has termed the 'rescue industry', and actors seeking to further criminalise sexual labour (e.g., All-Party Parliamentary Group on Prostitution and the Global Sex Trade [APPG] 2018). Sex workers are often labelled as 'victims' of exploitation or trafficking, even though they would never themselves use such terms to describe their experiences. Conversely, others involved in the sex market may identify with the term 'victim', and in such instances, it may be equally inappropriate to describe individuals as 'sex workers', if their entry into and labour within the sex market was characterised by a lack of choice. To reflect these complexities, the term 'sex worker' is used more generally to describe individuals who are working in the sex market, and the term 'victim' is used specifically to refer to instances where respondents in the qualitative interviews described someone's experiences as exploitative, or involving any form of criminal victimisation (e.g., violence, coercion or force).

Exploitation within the sex market tends to be mediated by online technologies, which both change how organised crime groups within these spaces operate, and the role and utility of open-source intelligence (OSINT) in policing contexts (Crocker et al. 2017). Historically, within Scotland—and more broadly, the United Kingdom (UK)—the policing of sex markets has largely been focused on more public aspects, including street-based sex work, with an emphasis on nuisance, public order, morality and third-party control (Scoular et al. 2019). With the sex market becoming increasingly internet-mediated (Sanders et al. 2018), traditional policing approaches are inadequate to respond to contemporary harms and exploitation (Scoular et al. 2019). Notwithstanding the digital element, contemporary policing has more recently been influenced by broader changes in the understanding of sex work as a distinct form of labour (Sanders et al. 2021), as opposed to more radical feminist views equating sex work with sexual violence or exploitation (e.g., APPG 2018).

Recent guidance from the National Police Chiefs' Council (NPCC) proposes an approach to policing that focuses on harm reduction and recognises the nuance of experiences encompassed within the sex market (Vajzovic 2019). This, for instance, involves a focus on responding to where the threats of harms, violence and exploitation are greatest, and the importance of building trust with the wider sex worker community to better address their needs (Vajzovic 2019). Nevertheless, the UK encompasses a large number of distinct police forces and divisions, and there is substantial variability in how sex markets are policed locally (Sanders et al. 2021). This also includes how intelligence is gathered and collated; there is often limited intelligence on human trafficking, though intelligence-led policing is nevertheless important to control this crime more effectively (Atkinson and Hamilton-Smith 2022). Of specific relevance to this research is the role of OSINT, which in this context primarily consists of online escort adverts posted on adult services websites (ASWs). How such intelligence is generated and utilised similarly also varies between forces (Sanders et al. 2018; Scoular et al. 2019).

Whereas contemporary discourse tends to emphasise technology as essential to facilitate sex trafficking (e.g., Farley et al. 2014; McKinley 2017), our current understanding of the role that online technologies play in this context is, at best, partial and fragmented (Milivojevic and Segrave 2017). The intersection of technology and trafficking has aptly been termed the 'trafficking-technology' nexus; however, beyond small-scale qualitative samples or anecdotal evidence, we do not yet have a clear understanding of how this supposed nexus works (Musto and Boyd 2014). Despite this, it is often claimed that technology has facilitated an explosion in sex trafficking (e.g., Hughes 2002; Farley et al. 2014). Paradoxically, technology is also portrayed as a panacea to sex trafficking, with some arguing that technology can even end sex trafficking (e.g., McKinley 2017; Petter et al. 2020). The assumption that we can eradicate sex trafficking with technological advances in policing is based on the notion that criminal networks operating online leave digital footprints, which, in turn, can be leveraged as OSINT. Often, as will become increasingly clear throughout the remainder of this book, research focused on analysing digital traces relating to the sex market tends to conflate the identified patterns with evidence of the presence of sex trafficking (Kjellgren 2022).

The empirical realities of sex trafficking, as has previously been argued, are often quite distinct from popular constructions of the issue (Albanese et al. 2022), and experiences of exploitation do not necessarily map well onto the legal definitions of sex trafficking (O'Connell Davidson 2013). This poses serious challenges for law enforcement in responding to, investigating and disrupting sex trafficking. Understanding how online technologies are used within the sex market—particularly how criminal networks use them to facilitate exploitation—is critical to identifying risks and harms within the sex market. Analysing digital traces is important to generate OSINT, but the precise role and utility of such intelligence are likely variable and context-specific. Furthermore, there are underlying questions of an epistemological nature that remain largely unanswered, namely what can we actually learn about sex trafficking from the analysis of digital traces within the sex market, and is it realistic to think that we can distinguish between sex workers vis-à-vis sex trafficking victims from online data? Much of the previous research has failed to answer these questions sufficiently, even though the questions are critical for policing and understanding internet-mediated exploitation. To effectively answer these questions, it is recognised that we need a more novel approach to social inquiry, one which incorporates critical theoretical perspectives from the social sciences and technologically sophisticated methods capable of identifying and interrogating patterns from unstructured digital traces. It is, at this intersection, that the current book is situated. Through a synthesis of criminological theory and concepts, and methods largely associated with the data sciences and social statistics, the current case study is an attempt at advancing computational criminology as a framework for understanding internet-mediated criminological phenomena, in this case, exploitation within contemporary sex markets.

In its essence, the case study presented in this book is a story about complexity. It is about the complexities associated with migration, sex work, exploitation and the use of digital traces and big data analytics to understand these complexities. It offers a critique against research which fails to appreciate these complexities, and it highlights the consequences this can have for the lives of migrants, sex workers and other populations subjected to intense surveillance and police scrutiny.

Scope and Research Questions

The current study seeks to address the complexities highlighted thus far. Before proceeding to outline the research questions, it is appropriate to briefly discuss the key definitions and parameters of this research. This book is focused on the policing of exploitation occurring in internet-mediated sex markets within Scotland, and more broadly, the UK. *Exploitation* is often a term which is more appropriate than *sex trafficking* because the latter implies a certain degree of knowledge of the three elements that make up sex trafficking—recruitment, transportation and exploitation. By referring more broadly to exploitation, it is also recognised that exploitation occurring within the sex market is not necessarily forced prostitution or sexual exploitation: sometimes victims may define their experiences as labour exploitation or economic exploitation, and other times, different forms of exploitation may form an overarching exploitative situation (O'Connell Davidson 2006). However, in some situations, which clearly are within the confines of the legal definitions of human trafficking, the term sex trafficking is used to specifically refer to instances where the process of victimisation corresponds to the three previously outlined elements.

The terms *sexual labour* or *sex work* are used rather than *prostitution*. The former two are broader and encapsulate a variety of behaviours associated with the provision of sexual services, and they also recognise that most people who provide sexual services are unlikely to be forced but do so of their own volition. It is recognised that in some situations, it is not appropriate to talk about choice; desperate circumstances and structurally constrained situations may render the term 'prostitution' more appropriate, since there may not be any other option to generate any form of income. Broadly speaking, however, the terms *exploitation* and *sex work* or *sexual labour*, rather than *sex trafficking*, *prostitution* or *sexual exploitation*, provide a more inclusive framework for examining all the complexities associated with the sex market.

Finally, the term *online technologies* is used throughout this book to refer more broadly to the internet and networked devices such as mobile phones and computers. Whilst online technologies encapsulate a wide spectrum of technologies, such as the dark web and advanced forms of encryption, it is primarily used in the basic sense of how commonly used networked technologies are used to perform everyday tasks, such as communication and browsing the web. Related to this, OSINT pertaining to the sex market could also encompass a variety of different data. In the context of this case study, it specifically refers to online escort adverts posted on ASWs on the open web.

With these definitions in mind, it is necessary to clarify the scope of the research. Whilst it is recognised that exploitation in the sex market may include individuals of all ages and genders, this case study specifically focuses on the experiences of adult women exploited in off-street sex markets, particularly in Scotland, but more widely, the UK, since there are no clearly defined borders when it comes to sex markets. Commercial exploitation, where one or more facilitators exploit one or more women to generate revenue, is the primary area of research. This is hypothesised as the scenario where technology potentially plays the most critical role, given the importance of online marketing. The book aims to contribute to our understanding of online technologies in the sex market, the process of policing exploitation, and the role and utility of OSINT in this context. The following research questions will be addressed:

1. How are online technologies used within the off-street sex market?
2. How do criminal networks and OCGs use online technologies to facilitate their operations, specifically with regard to advertising victims and connecting with sex buyers?
3. To what extent is it possible to identify networks operating within the off-street sex market, and patterns of vulnerability and exploitation, from online data?
4. To what extent could any identifiable patterns and network structures be useful for law enforcement and partner agencies?

To address these questions, a case study design was deemed appropriate. The study is diverse and original in its methodological approach, including a narrative literature review, semi-structured interviews, thematic qualitative analysis, web scraping, text mining, social network analysis and statistical modelling. It is important to bear in mind that the current study is not intended to be definitive; rather, it invites the reader to reflect upon the utility of using computational criminology, and the opportunities and challenges of conducting social science research in an era where many parts of our social lives generate digital traces. The book can also be perceived as a starting point for more thoughtful and comprehensive future research in this area of inquiry, since it reflects upon some of the core questions underpinning the complexities of internet-mediated exploitation.

Book Overview

Following this introductory chapter, the subsequent four chapters are based on a narrative literature review introducing the reader to critical perspectives on migration, exploitation, sexual labour, organised crime and big data analytics. These are intended to provide a solid foundation of the key complexities underpinning internet-mediated exploitation, and they serve as a useful primer for the empirical chapters which follow, some of which are more technical to read. Chapter "Journeys into the Precariat: Migration, Exploitation and Trafficking" explores the intricate and complex relationships among migration, exploitation and human trafficking. It elaborates upon these concepts in relation to the discourse of 'modern slavery', which is dominant in the UK context. An argument is made that the conceptualisation of 'modern slavery' and 'human trafficking' oversimplifies the complex realities faced by migrants—especially women—who often navigate systems of constrained choices in the context of global inequalities, restrictive immigration policies and socio-economic marginalisation. It is highlighted how migration is influenced by both macro-level factors, such as conflicts and poverty, and individual-level factors, including aspirations for upward social mobility, which, in this context, may be severely limited due to unequal access to different forms of capital and opportunity structures. The principal contribution of this chapter, however, is that it challenges dichotomous understandings of exploitation, and instead contends that exploitation falls along a continuum, as opposed to the binary of choice versus coercion, as is often implied in legal definitions of human trafficking and modern slavery. It concludes that reframing exploitation as a continuous phenomenon is critical to understanding contemporary internet-mediated exploitation and to improving criminal justice responses focused on identifying vulnerability and exploitation in sex markets.

In chapter "The Nature and Organisation of the Sex Market", the structure and dynamics of the UK's internet-mediated sex market are explored in more detail, and there is an emphasis on how online technologies have reshaped its organisation and, in turn, the implications for sex worker safety and vulnerability. The chapter begins by situating sex work within a historical and economic context, and it is argued that sexual labour is deeply embedded in global capitalism and shaped by local, cultural and legal structures. It connects this discussion to the male demand for sexual services, noting that motivations to purchase sex extend beyond biological urges to include emotional needs, fantasies and performances of masculinity. Indeed, it is highlighted how the commodification of sexual experiences, influenced by online pornography and consumer culture, has diversified client expectations and potentially creates an environment which pressures sex workers to offer increasingly extreme services. This chapter also elaborates upon how online technologies have expanded and diversified the sex market, enabling flexible working conditions and broader geographic reach, but also creating new risks. While many sex workers report increased safety and job satisfaction, others face harassment, stalking, or risk being 'outed' and having their identities revealed. There are also indications that organised crime groups have adapted to digital platforms, using them to recruit, control and market exploited individuals. The chapter concludes that online technologies have led to paradoxical developments in the sex market: they have increased sex worker autonomy and opportunity, whilst simultaneously being beneficial to facilitating exploitation.

Chapter "Criminal Networks, Opportunity Structures and the Process of Exploitation" critically examines the process of exploitation from a criminological perspective, drawing upon situational opportunity theory, and discusses the links between criminal networks, organised crime and exploitation. It begins by challenging traditional conceptions of organised crime as hierarchical and rigid structures. Instead, it emphasises how criminal networks tend to be fluid entities, and the chapter discusses how organised crime is embedded within the social world and fundamentally tied to, and driven by, opportunity structures. It draws upon crime script analysis (Cornish 1994) to break down the crime of sex trafficking into its three interlinked scenes - recruitment, transportation and exploitation - and considers how technology is mediating sex trafficking across the different scenes and facets. It is noted how recruitment strategies range from informal and deceptive arrangements to employment scams and emotionally manipulative tactics, sometimes facilitated through online platforms. Transportation, while often occurring legally and voluntarily, can involve debt bondage and isolation strategies, with technology playing a modest but enabling role. Exploitation is framed as a continuum, with control mechanisms ranging from soft (emotional manipulation, economic control) to hard (violence, confinement), and technology is increasingly used to monitor and advertise victims. The chapter highlights the strategic use of mobility and geographic dispersion to evade law enforcement and maintain victim dependency. It concludes by arguing that technology increases the available permutations in the sex trafficking crime script, or in other words, it has the potential to increase the flexibility in how criminal networks carry out the crime. However, it is also noted that the empirical evidence - particularly in the UK context - is very limited. Importantly, it is also noted that addressing exploitation requires not only disrupting criminal networks but also addressing the broader socio-economic conditions that sustain them and create vulnerability towards exploitation in the first place.

Chapter "Digital Traces, Big Data and Epistemological Shifts" explores the epistemological and ethical implications of using digital traces and big data analytics to study internet-mediated exploitation. It begins by outlining the emergence of the big data paradigm, characterised by algorithmic approaches to understanding the social world, favouring the identification of patterns inductively, as opposed to contextualisation and explanation using theory. It is argued that such approaches, when applied to the context of exploitation, risk reifying and revitalising flawed assumptions about trafficking and exploitation. It questions the assumptions underlying research associated with the so-called trafficking-technology nexus, where technology is simultaneously framed as both the cause of and solution to trafficking. It is argued that this duality, often driven by tech companies and anti-trafficking organisations, obscures the structural conditions underpinning exploitation and risks reducing complex social phenomena to technological problems, which can be resolved with technological solutions alone. A review of empirical studies reveals a troubling reliance on decontextualised escort adverts, 'indicators' of trafficking that are not empirically substantiated, biased training data and a conspicuous absence of 'ground truth'. Many studies reviewed conflate sex work with trafficking, fail to account for agency and lack theoretical grounding and a finer appreciation of the many nuances associated with migration, sexual labour and exploitation. It is argued that without a nuanced understanding of the sex market and the social contexts in which digital traces are produced, research risks misrepresenting sex workers as trafficking victims, and contributing to overpolicing and intensified police surveillance of potentially vulnerable populations. As such, it is concluded that theoretically informed approaches - which are aware of the limitations inherent to big data analytics - are required to advance knowledge on internet-mediated exploitation. Without this, research prioritising predictive accuracy and the inductive generation of patterns, as opposed to scientific, ethical and theoretical validity, may cause more harm than good to the very populations the research purports to protect.

Chapter "Methods in Practice: Designing an Effective Workflow in Computational Criminology" serves two distinct purposes. Firstly, it introduces the reader to computational criminology and the methods underpinning the empirical research of this book. Secondly, it also serves as a template for designing an efficient mixed methods workflow in computational criminology, which will be particularly beneficial to students and researchers considering mixed methods computational criminology research projects involving both online and offline data collection. In the chapter, it is argued that there is a need to integrate our sociological imagination (Mills 2000) with computational methods to address complex internet-mediated phenomena. It provides an introduction to the practical, ethical and epistemological challenges of using web scraping and open-source data, and by highlighting the research process of the current case study, it demonstrates how these were resolved. It presents methodological details, the development and assessment of automated algorithms for network identification, and a description of the datasets used as part of this case study. The chapter is largely structured around the 11 stages of the research process and provides a high-level overview of the methods used; some of the specific methodological details are provided in the subsequent empirical chapters (chapters "Exploitation and the Policing of Contemporary Sex Markets in Scotland", "Complexity, Similarity and Tie Formation in Advert Networks" and "Network Influences on Extreme Service Advertisement").

Chapter "Exploitation and the Policing of Contemporary Sex Markets in Scotland" presents the findings from a thematic analysis of the data gathered through semi-structured interviews. The interviews were conducted with human trafficking detectives and other stakeholders responding to harms related to the sex market and human trafficking. Its primary empirical contribution consists of a detailed analysis of how online technologies are used within the Scottish sex market—particularly in relation to criminal networks—and the principal role of OSINT in sex trafficking investigations. It also highlights several conceptually important themes relating to victim experiences of exploitation, and the process of policing the sex market. The chapter concludes with a discussion on the need for a highly targeted, ethically and epistemologically grounded approach, in which the limitations and potential harms of using OSINT in this context are recognised.

In chapter "Complexity, Similarity and Tie Formation in Advert Networks", the findings from a series of statistical analyses are presented. The first analysis critically examines the limitations of indicator-based approaches to identifying exploitation from online escort adverts. The analysis demonstrates how indicators provide a very limited and partial account of online advert networks, and fail to offer insight into the structure and organisation of the internet-mediated sex market, and thereby, how networks vary and compare to one another. This analysis highlights the limitations of focusing on online adverts themselves and, instead, shifts the focus to the relational qualities of online advert networks through the application of social network analysis. The focus of this analysis is to identify the marketing strategies that predict empirical tie formation and, moreover, the extent to which adverts within and between networks are similar. The findings from this chapter suggest strong differences between networks, which are chiefly attributable to a network's structural complexity.

Chapter "Network Influences on Extreme Service Advertisement" presents the findings from a multilevel statistical analysis of the adverts and networks identified throughout this research. In particular, it is focused on how a network's structure mediates the propensity to advertise what is commonly referred to as 'extreme services' (i.e., services that can be risky or otherwise deviate from more mainstream services). The findings suggest that more complex networks are significantly more likely to advertise extreme services, whilst controlling for other factors, including both advert and network-level variables. As such, the analysis finds support for the hypothesis that network structure is predictive of the advertising of extreme services, and in doing so, adds to our understanding of how sexual services are marketed online. The chapter concludes that whereas no analysis of online data alone can confirm the presence or absence of vulnerability and exploitation, any assessment is likely to provide a more nuanced result if the analysis is conducted on a network level, as opposed to an advert level, and furthermore, that it is perhaps more feasible to shift the focus from identifying vulnerability and exploitation, to consider the complexity of a network's digital footprints.

In chapter "Key Messages and Conclusions: Future Directions in the Computational Criminology of Internet-Mediated Exploitation", the final chapter of this book, the insights generated from the literature review, methodological development and empirical chapters, are synthesised through a socio-ecological framework. The chapter revisits the original research questions which guided the research process, highlights the key findings and discusses these in relation to the previous literature. Throughout these discussions, it elaborates upon how online technologies are used in contemporary internet-mediated sex markets, which improves the working conditions of sex workers but also leads to the configuration of 'dark spaces of precarity', which may be conducive to harms and exploitation. It discusses how criminal networks have been observed to utilise technologies to facilitate exploitation in Scotland and the UK, and the precise role of open-source intelligence in investigating and policing exploitation and sex trafficking. The chapter also outlines methodological and practitioner-oriented implications and offers suggestions on how future research may build upon the insights generated from this book to conduct even more rigorous (and desperately needed) research into internet-mediated exploitation.

This book makes no claim of being a definitive authority on migration, sex work, exploitation or sex trafficking; on the contrary, it serves as a starting point for more methodologically and epistemologically rigorous investigations into the intersection of technology and exploitation, and through the practical application of computational criminology. As such, the aim of this book is to inspire future students and scholars in these areas to think more critically about how online data can be utilised in this context, and I sincerely hope to see future contributions - both qualitative and quantitative - to further illuminate this complex area of inquiry.

References

Agustín LM (2007) Sex at the Margins: Migration, Labour Markets and the Rescue Industry, 1st edn. Zed Books Ltd., London

Albanese J, Broad R, Gadd D (2022) Consent, Coercion, and Fraud in Human Trafficking Relationships. J Hum Traff 8(1):13–32. https://doi.org/10.1080/23322705.2021.2019529

APPG (2018) Behind Closed Doors: Organised Sexual Exploitation in England and Wales. All-Party Parliamentary Group on Prostitution and the Global Sex Trade, London

Atkinson C, Hamilton-Smith N (2022) Still an 'Invisible Crime'? Exploring Developments in the Awareness and Control of Human Trafficking in Scotland. Eur J Criminol 19(5):911–931. https://doi.org/10.1177/1477370820931868

Castells M (2010) The Rise of the Network Society, 2nd edn. John Wiley & Sons, Ltd., Chichester

Cockbain E, Brayley-Morris H (2018) Human Trafficking and Labour Exploitation in the Casual Construction Industry: An Analysis of Three

Major Investigations in the UK Involving Irish Traveller Offending Groups. Policing 12(2):129–149. https://doi.org/10.1093/police/pax032
Cockbain E, Bowers K, Hutt O (2022) Examining the Geographies of Human Trafficking: Methodological Challenges in Mapping Trafficking's Complexities and Connectivities. Appl Geogr 139:102643. https://doi.org/10.1016/j.apgeog.2022.102643
Cornish DB (1994) The Procedural Analysis of Offending and Its Relevance for Situational Prevention. In: Clarke RV (ed) Crime Prevention Studies, 2nd edn. Criminal Justice Press, New York, pp 151–196
Crocker R, Webb S, Garner S, Skidmore M (2017) The Impact of Organised Crime in Local Communities. The Police Foundation, London
Farley M, Franzblau K, Kennedy MA (2014) Online Prostitution and Trafficking. Albany Law Rev 77(3):1039–1094
Hughes DM (2002) The Use of New Communications and Information Technologies for Sexual Exploitation of Women and Children. Hastings Women's L J 13(1):127–146
Kjellgren R (2022) Good Tech, Bad Tech: Policing Sex Trafficking with Big Data. Int J Crime Justice Soc Democr 11(1):149–166. https://doi.org/10.3316/agispt.20220412065553
Leukfeldt ER, Kleemans ER, Kruisbergen EW, Roks RA (2019) Criminal Networks in a Digitised World: On the Nexus of Borderless Opportunities and Local Embeddedness. Trends Organ Crime 22(3):324–345. https://doi.org/10.1007/s12117-019-09366-7
Malloch M, Rigby P (2016) Contexts and Complexities. In: Malloch M, Rigby P (eds) Human Trafficking: The Complexities of Exploitation. Edinburgh University Press, Edinburgh, pp 1–17
McKinley N (2017) Our Generation and the Fight Against Slavery. Huffpost, 6 December. https://www.huffpost.com/entry/our-generation-and-the-fi_b_9996634
Milivojevic S, Segrave M (2017) Gendered Exploitation in the Digital Border Crossing? An Analysis of the Human Trafficking and Information Technology Nexus. In: Gender, Technology and Violence. Routledge, pp 28–44
Mills CW (2000) The Sociological Imagination. Oxford University Press
Musto JL, Boyd D (2014) The Trafficking-Technology Nexus. Soc Polit Int Stud Gend State Soc 21(3):461–483. https://doi.org/10.1093/sp/jxu018
O'Connell Davidson J (2013) Troubling Freedom: Migration, Debt, and Modern Slavery. Migr Stud 1(2):176–195. https://doi.org/10.1093/migration/mns002

O'Connell Davidson J (2006) Will the Real Sex Slave Please Stand Up? Fem Rev 83(1):4–22

Pajón L, Walsh D (2018) Proposing a Theoretical Framework for the Criminal Investigation of Human Trafficking Crimes. Policing 14(2):493–511. https://doi.org/10.1093/police/pay031

Petter S, Giddens L, Fullilove M (2020) The Challenges of Using of Information Technology to Counter Human Trafficking. Association for Information Systems, pp 1–10

Sanders T, Scoular J, Campbell R, Pitcher J, Cunningham S (2018) Internet Sex Work: Beyond the Gaze, 1st edn. Springer Nature, Cham

Sanders T, Vajzovic D, Brooks-Gordon B, Mulvihill N (2021) Policing Vulnerability in Sex Work: The Harm Reduction Compass Model. Polic Soc 31(9):1100–1116. https://doi.org/10.1080/10439463.2020.1837825

Scoular J, Pitcher J, Sanders T, Cunningham S, Campbell R (2019) Beyond the Gaze and Well Beyond Wolfenden: The Practices and Rationalities of Regulating and Policing Sex Work in the Digital Age. J L Soc 46(2):211–239

Stratton G, Powell A, Cameron R (2017) Crime and Justice in Digital Society: Towards a 'Digital Criminology'? International Journal for Crime, Justice and Social. Democracy 6(2):17–33. https://doi.org/10.5204/ijcjsd.v6i2.355

Vajzovic D (2019) National Policing Sex Work and Prostitution Guidance. National Police Chiefs' Council, London

Verhoeven M, van Gestel B, de Jong D, Kleemans E (2013) Relationships Between Suspects and Victims of Sex Trafficking. Exploitation of Prostitutes and Domestic Violence Parallels in Dutch Trafficking Cases. Eur J Crim Policy Res 21(1):49–64. https://doi.org/10.1007/s10610-013-9226-2

Journeys into the Precariat: Migration, Exploitation and Trafficking

Migration and Precarious Journeys

The terms 'modern slavery' and 'human trafficking' do little to illuminate the plethora of complexities associated with them (Malloch and Rigby 2016). Within the contemporary UK, the debate on exploitation is dominated by a discourse of modern slavery. Whilst encapsulating forced labour, slavery, servitude, forced marriage, human trafficking, and other forms of exploitation, sex trafficking has been most prominent in public discourse (Lammasniemi 2017; Birks and Gardner 2019). Whilst the exploitation of British nationals certainly does occur in the UK, this chapter is focused on the experiences of migrants since this tends to be the focus of contemporary discussions on sex trafficking and exploitation. The complexities associated with migration, particularly for sexual labour, are often ignored in the current political landscape. There is a longstanding association between migration and the provision of sexual services (Castles et al. 2014), and in the context of globalisation, migrants tend to make up the majority of those who sell sex (Mai 2013). To fully understand contemporary exploitation in the UK, it is crucial to explore

R. Kjellgren, *Internet-Mediated Exploitation in the Scottish Online Sex Market*,
Transnational Crime, Crime Control and Security,
https://doi.org/10.1007/978-3-032-09275-5_2

the mechanisms underpinning migration, and consequently, what conditions make migrants vulnerable to exploitation.

Migration is affected by a variety of interlinked processes. Macro-level structures are commonly outlined as important for instigating migration. War, disaster, political instability, poverty and oppression increase the flow of migrants and refugees (Castles et al. 2014). Often, migration is theorised as the intersection of different 'push' and 'pull' factors (Bauer and Zimmermann 1999). High levels of unemployment may serve as a factor pushing individuals to migrate, whereas labour demand in a neighbouring country may attract individuals. After all, employment opportunities and upward mobility are not evenly distributed worldwide. A limited opportunity structure in the home country and possible opportunities in other countries can thus act as powerful instigators of migration (de Haas 2010; Koser 2011; Windzio et al. 2019). Macro-level changes, such as globalisation, inevitably affect levels of migration. According to Petras and Veltmeyer (2007, p. 33), globalisation has previously been referred to as:

> the upsurge in direct investment and liberalisation and deregulation in cross-border flows of capital, technology and services, as well as the creation of a global production system – a new global economy.

Amongst other things, one of the outcomes of globalisation is the deterioration of economies in the Global South, with increasingly concentrated ownership of capital in the Global North (Petras and Veltmeyer 2007).

Besides large-scale structural processes, migration is often fuelled by a desire for upward mobility, which for some is severely limited by the lack of opportunities in their home countries (Mai 2013). Nevertheless, individual aspiration alone is not enough to enable migration; a specific combination of various forms of capital is required to realise these aspirations (van Meeteren et al. 2018). Human capital, such as skills, education and location-specific knowledge, has previously been outlined as central to migrant decision-making processes (Chiswick 2008). Besides human capital, migration is a costly endeavour, usually requiring no small amount of economic capital, which is why it is often a decision made within families (Koser 2011). The role of social capital in this context cannot be understated. A starting point in this discussion is Bourdieu's (1985, p. 248) conceptualisation of capital, in which social capital is defined as:

> the aggregate of the actual or potential resources which are linked to possession of a durable network of more or less institutionalized relationships of mutual acquaintance or recognition.

As such, it is important to point out that the networks themselves are distinct from the resources which can be mobilised through them (de Haas 2010). The number of connections within a network is essential, but so is the amount of capital individuals within the network possess. Social capital is thus important precisely because it can be converted into other forms of capital, be it economic, human or cultural (de Haas 2010). Social networks spanning the borders of countries act as location-specific social capital that reduces the cost of migration (Massey 1990). This affects the decision-making processes of prospective migrants in selecting their destination.

Patriarchal gender orders are found worldwide, and whilst manifested differently depending on the local contexts, they share the commonalities that power and status tend to be disproportionately distributed amongst men and the masculine (Turner 2016). Structural adjustment programs, used by organisations such as the International Monetary Fund, require measures of austerity, which most heavily affects sectors predominantly occupied by women (Castles et al. 2014; Turner 2016). This, coupled with a shift to service-based economies in the minority world, and industrialisation in the majority world, creates a global demand for feminised, cheap, flexible, low-skilled positions, leading to what has been termed the 'feminisation of migration' (Sassen 2002; Castles et al. 2014). However, whereas this implies feminised migration as a new phenomenon—which it certainly is not (Agustín 2007)—it is a useful concept in describing migratory routes predominantly undertaken by women (Russell 2014). The concepts of 'feminisation of poverty' and 'feminisation of survival' are also central in this context. The structural configurations present in our globalised world place an uneven economic burden upon the back of women; they may be the sole breadwinners for their families and thus at an increased pressure to provide, whilst not having access to the same opportunities as men (Sassen 2002; Russell 2014). This burden might increase the propensity of women to migrate, as both the sending states and the women's families rely on vital remittances, often earned from precarious labour in the informal markets within the Global North (Russell 2014).

Those migrating to engage in sex work, like other migrants, have incredibly diverse trajectories. A common denominator is negotiating structural constraints to realise aspirations of social mobility (Chimienti 2009; Mai 2009). Evidence from qualitative studies suggests that migrating for sexual labour is often an informed choice; however, these choices are usually made in a context where women have little to no knowledge concerning the circumstances in which they will be working (Kempadoo 2004; Agustín 2006a; Chimienti 2009; Plambech 2017). Under these circumstances, the notion of 'choice' becomes deeply problematic (Agustín 2006b; Mai 2013). Women who made an informed choice to migrate for sex work can be faced with appalling conditions and highly exploitative working arrangements, violence, threats and other forms of abuse; yet, they might also accept these conditions due to commitments to family members back home, whose survival might depend upon their remittances (Oso Casas 2009). The pathways into exploitation are complicated, and the processes and mechanisms in place to regulate migration further exacerbate vulnerability towards exploitation.

Criminal law and immigration law are different legal entities, yet, they are both part of broader systems of exclusion and inclusion (Stumpf 2006). Whilst immigration law is civil law, it has been merged with criminal law throughout the past decades, resulting in what Stumpf (2006) termed 'crimmigration'. Often, this is a racialised process with certain migrant groups being ascribed to particular criminogenic behaviour—such as Nigerian sex traffickers or violent Eastern Europeans—with the consequence of increasing the surveillance, marginalisation, imprisonment or deportation of the targeted groups (Menjívar et al. 2018). The state operates by subjecting groups of undesirable 'Others' to these measures, drawing a firm line of who should be included within the social contract, often based on citizenship and ethnicity (Stumpf 2006).

As Bosworth et al. (2017b, p. 44) point out, "to be tough on crime is to be tough on immigration and crime". With a political desire to punish and control alien populations, crimmigration is intrinsically linked to securitisation processes. With regard to migration, this refers to constructing particular groups of migrants as security threats (Léonard 2010; Bourbeau 2015). The implications of securitising migration are the militarisation of national borders (e.g., military technology and strategies) and increased control measures, including surveillance and policing (Williams 2016). When migration is constructed as a security threat, these exceptional measures employed are often at the expense of the human rights of migrants (Bosworth et al. 2017b).

With increasingly restrictive immigration policies, the opportunities for legal migration become severely limited. As a result, there is a greater demand for irregular migration channels, and the services of human smugglers (O'Connell Davidson 2013; Augustova and Suber 2023). Ironically, the illegitimate side of the migration industry—human smugglers and traffickers—has flourished due to restrictive migration policies (Castles et al. 2014). The principal function of these organisations is to overcome the obstacles put in place by securitisation measures (Koser 2011). The illegitimate migration industry offers migrants an opportunity to exchange economic capital for social capital: the contacts and resources necessary to facilitate the journey to the destination country (Collyer 2005; McCollum and Findlay 2017), and this is particularly important for those lacking social networks to facilitate their migration (Fitzgerald 2015). In other words, smuggling organisations operate on the meso-level, allowing migrants to overcome the structural constraints limiting their mobility and are thus vital in structuring migration patterns (McCollum and Findlay 2017). In contemporary politicised discourses, smugglers are often framed as violent exploiters (if they are not directly conflated with traffickers), and whereas that certainly can be the case, they can also be honest, fair and offer a valued service to their clients (Modood and Salt 2011; O'Connell Davidson 2013).

Notwithstanding the important role of smugglers, their services can be exorbitantly expensive, and far from all prospective migrants can afford them (Agustín 2006a). Using the services of smugglers often requires the pooling of financial resources, and potentially involves many decision-makers, such as other family members (Koser 2011; Bryceson 2019). Alternatively, the prospective migrant might fund their migration project through loans, take on huge debts or agree to bonded labour (Agustín 2006a; Mai 2009). For instance, in Plambech's (2017) research with Nigerian sex workers, it was reported that the fees ranged from $6500 to $12,000 (USD), and the debt sometimes increased upon reaching their destination. In the most extreme cases, migrants owed up to $50,000. It is precisely under these circumstances that the risk of exploitation is exacerbated (Koser 2011).

It is important to consider the role of agency in this context. To understand *why* migrants consent to potentially exploitative situations through the accumulation of substantial debts, it must be recognised that decisions are often made under severely constrained circumstances. With limited opportunities, clandestine migration is risky but potentially offers high rewards, which can be the only realistic opportunity to achieve upward mobility (Koser 2011; O'Connell Davidson 2013). As Mai (2016) argues, it is impossible to separate agency from exploitation because, in certain situations, agency is constructed and achieved by consenting to exploitative arrangements. The agency of migrants, particularly migrant sex workers, is always subject to change and can be considered liminal (Chimienti 2009; Andrijasevic 2010). Given the complex reasons underpinning transnational sex work, self-coercion becomes a prominent feature: in the absence of third parties or organised crime groups forcing women to sell sex to repay their debts, women may force themselves to remain in exploitative situations simply because their families are dependent upon their remittances (Russell 2014; Igbinomwanhia 2021).

Taken together, the restrictive border regimes currently operating throughout Europe make migrants, particularly women, more vulnerable to different exploitation forms. Laws and policies often force women to rely upon third-parties to facilitate their travelling, and in some instances, these arrangements can be severely exploitative. It has previously been reported that women are subjected to rape, sexual abuse and violence through their clandestine migratory journeys and that sex is used for bartering necessities or protection (Bosworth et al. 2017a; Tyszler 2019). In addition, Andrijasevic's (2010) study also showed that there is an increased risk of exploitation and violence the longer the clandestine journey is. Similarly, women may owe significant sums of money which cannot be repaid through conventional forms of employment, due to their irregular migrant status and the structural marginalisation occurring in the destination country. Even if the purpose of migration was not to engage in sex work, many might find it the only realistic option to repay their debts (Turner 2016; Plambech 2017). The question, then, is to consider the extent to which conceptualisations of human trafficking can adequately capture the complexities associated with migration for sexual labour. The following section will examine this in more depth.

Defining Human Trafficking and Modern Slavery

The crimes of modern slavery and sex trafficking are regulated under the Human Trafficking and Exploitation (Scotland) Bill 2015, and in the Modern Slavery Act 2015. The legal definitions of human trafficking and modern slavery can be traced back to the United Nations (2000) *Protocol to Prevent, Suppress and Punish Trafficking in Persons, Especially Women and Children* (henceforth the 'Palermo Protocol'). In Article 3a, human trafficking is defined as:

> the recruitment, transportation, transfer, harbouring or receipt of persons, by means of the threat or use of force or other forms of coercion, of abduction, of fraud, of deception, of the abuse of power or of a position of vulnerability or of the giving or receiving of payments or benefits to achieve the consent of a person having control over another person, for the purpose of exploitation. Exploitation shall include, at a minimum, the exploitation of the prostitution of others or other forms of sexual exploitation, forced labour or services, slavery or practices similar to slavery, servitude or the removal of organs. (United Nations Office of the High Commissioner 2019)

Since its adoption, the Palermo Protocol has been subject to widespread criticism. Indeed, as Wijkman and Kleemans (2019) point out, its definition is by no means neutral and imbued with ideology. More specifically, it is underpinned by a liberal framework of paradoxical dualisms (O'Connell Davidson 2010, 2013). Freedom is constructed as opposed to slavery, and social actors are imagined as having free will and being in control of their labour-power, unless in a condition of slavery; consent is thus what distinguishes these two conditions (Doezema 2005). This binary proposes that we agree voluntarily to contractual obligations or are coerced into them and, in doing so, cross the threshold into slavery, reduced to mere objects (O'Connell Davidson 2013). However, these liberal assumptions fit poorly with the lived experience of marginalised populations; the extent to which choice truly can be considered 'free', or that we act out of our own volition, is highly questionable in this context (Doezema 2005). In comparison, if we perceive exploitation through a Marxist lens, we might be more inclined to recognise that the power differentials and relations between classes, under the capitalist mode of production, contribute to an *intrinsically exploitative* relationship (Marx 1976). This is where the Palermo Protocol falters: it offers no convincing definitions of either 'exploitation' or 'coercion' that are sensitive to the experiences of individuals in precarious conditions (O'Connell Davidson 2013).

Notwithstanding its lack of preciseness, trafficking is also defined as a process crime (e.g., recruitment, transportation, exploitation) and thus involves a series of interlinked actions (O'Connell Davidson 2006). There is little consensus on exactly which actions should be encompassed by the term 'trafficking'. Besides, 'transportation' often implies the crossing of borders, however, a significant portion of identified sex trafficking victims in the UK are British nationals (NCA 2019), and transportation might not be an important feature. In addition, it does not capture exploitation within the formal economy given its focus on 'recruitment' and 'transportation': migrants enter states through legal channels and find legal employment, yet end up severely exploited (O'Connell Davidson 2006). As Malloch (2016) points out, trafficking is constructed as a phenomenon believed to be distinguished from other forms of injustice and exploitation that are part of the experience of many migrants. Similarly, distinguishing between smuggling and trafficking is challenging. Smuggling is legally constructed around the consent of the migrant, and trafficking is distinguished by involving force, fraud, deception or coercion. However, regarding clandestine movement, there is always a risk that what began as a voluntary arrangement can turn exploitative (O'Connell Davidson 2013).

The conceptual difficulties inherent to the legal definition of trafficking pose serious issues around the extent to which we can appreciate the scale of the issue. Despite this, organisations, states and moral entrepreneurs keenly produce statistics on its prevalence. For instance, the Global Slavery Index estimated that 40.3 million people were 'modern slaves' in 2016 (GSI 2018). Arriving at such a precise number raises a series of questions. Different jurisdictions interpret and construct trafficking and modern slavery according to their local and institutional contexts, meaning that numbers are not necessarily comparable between states (Jahnsen and Skilbrei 2015; Lott 2018). Furthermore, it revitalises liberal ideas that the experiences of millions of people can be neatly classified into a binary variable of 'free' and 'slave' (O'Connell Davidson 2016b). Given the clandestine nature of the crime, there is likely to be a significant dark figure, obscured not only by imprecise conceptualisations but also by victims' reluctance to report their victimisation (Malloch and Rigby 2016; Munro 2016). There is a dearth of empirical data on human trafficking; the lack of representative samples means that we can never grasp the true extent of it (Weitzer 2007), and when there is empirical data, it tends to be qualitative and context-specific (Cockbain and Kleemans 2019). Nevertheless, the brittle foundations of our knowledge are of little concern to those promulgating the modern slavery discourse. Indeed, there is a firm belief that we can, in the words of former prime minister Theresa May (May 2016), "rid our world of this barbaric evil" without necessarily understanding or addressing its root causes.

Ideal Victims, Evil Traffickers, and the Politics of Choice and Coercion

Attempts to regulate female sexuality are nothing new, and between the mid-nineteenth and mid-twentieth century, panic arose in Western states concerning the supposed traffic of European women. The moral panic of 'white slavery' was built upon narratives about the abduction of white women to be sexually exploited in the Global South (Doezema 2005). Intertwined with the fear of increasing autonomy for women was a generalised fear of foreigners, migrants and natives of contemporary colonies (Doezema 1999). Victims of white slavery were portrayed as naïve young women, deceived and exploited by racialised 'Others' (Doezema 1999; Lammasniemi 2017). As such, Doezema (1999, p. 26) has previously argued that white slavery is a cultural myth; not necessarily false, but "a collective belief that simplifies reality". We can now observe a remarkably similar perpetuation of a novel myth, that of the 'modern slave' (Lammasniemi 2017).

As Cohen (2011) has previously acknowledged, societies do, under certain conditions, experience episodes of 'moral panic'; a group of individuals defined as a threat to society and its values, presented in a highly simplistic manner by popular media, and 'experts' keen to offer universal solutions to resolve the problems. In contemporary times, the 'pimp', 'trafficker', 'smuggler' or 'slaver' emerge as threats against vulnerable victims worthy of protection, the societal values that since long outlawed slavery, and the very security of the nation-state (Weitzer 2007; Broad 2015; Gadd and Broad 2018). The personification of evil in this context—the trafficker—is one of our contemporary folk devils (Weitzer 2007; Musto 2009; Gadd and Broad 2018). There is little room for diversity within this discourse; the offender is typically male, from a racialised minority, and uses abundant force to subjugate his victims. Anti-trafficking efforts have been tremendously successful in using this particular imagery of victimhood:

> one of the most powerful symbols in the pantheon of Western imagery, the innocent, young, girl dragged off against her will to distant lands to satisfy the insatiable sexual cravings of wanton men. (McDonald 2004, p. 158)

According to Christie (1986), certain individuals or groups are more readily than others given the status of 'legitimate' victims and thus represent what he termed 'ideal victims'. This certainly applies to the victim of trafficking, and in comparison to previous concerns about 'white slavery', our contemporary ideal victim is a woman from the Global South, trafficked for sexual exploitation (Sharma 2005). These ideal victims are often said to be abducted from their homes or coerced into leaving, physically imprisoned in brothels, and continuously exploited for profit (Hoyle et al. 2011). However, the problem is that neither victims nor offenders fit these stereotypes well.

Media imagery continues to reinforce this narrative and has been remarkably successful in doing so (Sharapov and Mendel 2018). Causation is often attributed to poverty; however, it fails to recognise that poverty is produced and reproduced through current economic systems (Lott 2018). Victimisation is viewed through the binary lens of choice and coercion, which neglects the social context in which exploitation occurs and deprives victims of their agency (O'Connell Davidson 2016b). A firm distinction is drawn between victim and non-victim, and shocking and horrible narratives exemplifying this are used to perpetuate the trafficking discourse (O'Connell Davidson 2016b). Here, sexual labour is unequivocally defined as a form of gendered violence and a social ill, and since no woman would willingly enter prostitution, she is therefore a victim (e.g., APPG 2018). This also assumes that we can easily distinguish between labour exploitation and sexual exploitation. In certain circumstances, these are combined into an overarching situation of exploitation (O'Connell Davidson 2006). In other words, it is important how an individual perceives their situation, and the extent to which they do, or do not, consider themselves to have been victimised.

Given the lack of empirical, reliable data on trafficking, moral ideology and anecdotal evidence replace the role of rigorous research (Musto 2009). At this stage of the moral panic, the horror stories of slavery and trafficking often provide a rationale, and indeed a timely opportunity, to push agendas of anti-prostitution and national security through draconian measures of punishment and control (Weitzer 2007; Musto 2009; O'Connell Davidson 2016b; Gadd and Broad 2018). The result is increased border control measures at the expense of all migrants (Sharma 2005) and legislation that makes sex workers more vulnerable to exploitation (Chapman-Schmidt 2019). According to Cohen (2011), such changes are expected within the final stages of a moral panic, and the tragic irony is that an increasingly hostile immigration system is likely to make people more vulnerable to exploitation.

Considering how the modern slavery frame is constructed and portrays exploitation, the question is, what is it obscuring for us to better understand exploitation? First, it neglects the complexities surrounding migration by focusing on trafficking victims rather than everyday exploitative situations faced by migrants (Gadd and Broad 2018). Indeed, political turmoil, conflicts, and other social ills mean that irregular migration might be the only option to migrate (Munro 2016). Migrants often lack rights and legal protections, and clandestine movement in combination with acquiring debts for travelling means that exploitation is always a risk (Sharma 2005; Lammasniemi 2017; Gadd and Broad 2018). By focusing on trafficking, we divert our attention away from the securitisation and strict border regimes that drive vulnerability and reliance on facilitators in the first place (Broad 2015). In addition, migrants are also deprived of their agency—particularly those migrating for sexual labour (Doezema 2010). The modern slavery frame does not recognise that migrants do in fact exercise agency, albeit sometimes in very constrained situations (Broad 2015). What the modern slavery discourse describes as 'slavery' is often the best option for many (Okyere 2017; Lott 2018).

Similarly, sex workers—not only migrant sex workers—are perceived as unwilling victims of the sex trade (Weitzer 2007). However, there is considerable variation in how sex workers perceive their trade as exploitative (Weitzer 2015). Performing sexual labour is a livelihood strategy employed by migrants and nationals within their countries; there may or may not be alternative strategies available, but it remains clear that many do sex work out of their own volition (Doezema 1999). There is a tendency to describe migrant sex workers as trafficking victims within the modern slavery discourse, regardless of their own decision to migrate for sexual labour; as such, the complexities surrounding migration and sex work are reduced to a simple dichotomy of absolute choice or absolute coercion (Doezema 1999).

What further complicates criminal justice responses to exploitation is that the line between offender and victim is not always clear-cut. In the context of exploitation in the sex market, it is not uncommon that women are part of trafficking networks (Broad 2015) and that those previously victimised go on to exploit others (Wijkman and Kleemans 2019). There are many reasons that this might occur, including being forced to or out of compulsion, especially if there is a romantic relationship between victim and offender. According to Malloch (2016), there are primarily two factors that contribute to the criminalisation of trafficking victims: irregular migration and survival offences (for instance, crimes committed after escaping from an exploiter) or crimes committed while being exploited (i.e., having been forced to commit a crime). Indeed, conceptualisations of modern slavery and trafficking that assume the victim-offender dichotomy fail to account for the severely constrained contexts in which decision-making occurs (Broad 2015).

Finally, the modern slavery frame obscures the interrelation between the state, social structures, legal context and power, producing inequalities in the first place (O'Connell Davidson 2017). Focusing on individual actors exploiting victims results in a failure to account for the structural context that nourishes exploitation. With the rollback of welfare systems, deindustrialisation in the minority world, and industrialisation in the majority world, workers' social protections have been weakened, even more so in weaker economies (O'Connell Davidson 2016a,b). Those without social protection and marginalised by structural inequalities may have little choice but to become part of the informal economy and the precariat: the marginalised class of people with unpredictable futures, and without the employment security characterising more privileged populations (Munro 2016). The result is a global working class that, even though situated within the informal economy, is very much part of our contemporary free labour market (Munro 2016). An uncomfortable fact for anti-traffickers is that our global economy depends on an increasingly precarious, exploited labour force to maintain growth (Munro 2016; Gadd and Broad 2018). By focusing on the choice-coercion dichotomy, organisations and political actors need not question the underlying machinery producing inequality nor recognise their complicity in maintaining it (Chuang 2015; Ras and Gregoriou 2019).

Reframing Trafficking: A Continuum of Experiences

Whilst there is no doubt that severe exploitation occurs, the extent to which victims' experiences map onto stereotypical binaries is questionable (Doezema 1999; Weitzer 2007; O'Connell Davidson 2014). Liberal ideas of the individual as autonomous are problematic in the context of vulnerable populations, particularly regarding the constrained environments associated with migration (Doezema 2010). The complexities surrounding notions of 'deception', 'choice', 'coercion' and 'consent' become exacerbated in the context of sex trafficking. In relation to deception, many labelled victims knew beforehand that they would be working in the sex industry, and if they are deceived, it is usually about the working conditions rather than that they will be doing sex work (Doezema 2010). 'Choice' is only meaningful in the context of viable alternatives; the intersectionality of gender, ethnicity, citizenship and class means that many women, at best, have very limited options (Turner 2016; Lott 2018). In the context of these inequalities, 'choices' may include consenting to acquire large debts to finance migration or even consenting to exploitation simply because it is preferable to more dire conditions elsewhere (Bjelland 2016; Turner 2016). Coercion is far from the only mechanism by which victims become exploited; we should instead examine the conditions that produce and constrain liminal agency.

To adequately understand trafficking, we need to situate it in a frame that recognises a continuum of exploitation (O'Connell Davidson 2015; Malloch and Rigby 2016). The realities of marginalised populations are more complex than binary constructions of victim-offender, slave-free or choice-coercion. Whilst it is rare to be physically abducted, it is considerably more common to transgress a continuum of exploitation in the context of limited opportunities, labour market segmentation and immigration laws (Gadd and Broad 2018). With absolute volition at one end of the spectrum and absolute coercion at the other, the experiences of those labelled trafficking victims will likely fall along the continuum rather than the extreme ends, as the current modern slavery discourse would have us believe. These flawed perceptions obscure the structures and processes that create vulnerabilities towards exploitation and affect criminal justice responses and victim identification (Broad 2015; Lott 2018; Cruz et al. 2019). A responsible framework must recognise how inequalities and exploitation are reproduced by the structures of globalisation and deregulated markets (Munro 2016), how clandestine movement is a result of restrictive immigration laws (Sharapov et al. 2019), and seek to illuminate the socio-economic conditions that push women into sex work (Weitzer 2007), and subsequently, make them vulnerable to exploitation (Chapman-Schmidt 2019). Narrow conceptualisations of exploitation inevitably hinder law enforcement's ability to identify victims (Broad 2015; Farrell et al. 2019) or criminalise them in the worst case (Malloch 2016).

These considerations may seem far detached from the very specific issue of internet-mediated exploitation in contemporary sex markets; however, I would encourage the reader to ponder the extent to which the complex processes and mechanisms discussed above can be captured in online data, such as escort adverts. A key point to take away from this chapter is that there are many shades and nuances of exploitation, and what is inevitably the most important consideration is, of course, how an individual understands their situation, and whether or not they consider it exploitative. In later chapters, as we delve deeper into the uncertainties associated with online spaces facilitating exploitation, it is paramount to remember how exploitation and trafficking can be considered 'complex' crimes for the reasons discussed in this chapter, and that we need to account for this when we attempt to interpret patterns in online data.

To conclude, this chapter has examined how sex trafficking is currently framed within the modern slavery discourse and relates to the complexities associated with migration for sexual labour. It has been demonstrated how the construction of a dichotomy of 'ideal victims' and 'evil traffickers', underpinned by dubious statistics and limited empirical research, perpetuates a myth that we can 'end slavery' without acknowledging (and changing) the structural conditions which contribute to processes of exploitation in the first place. It has, furthermore, been argued that we need to reframe trafficking as a continuum of exploitation that recognises the complexities of sexual labour and migration. Without an adequate framework to understand trafficking, criminal justice responses and policing will inevitably struggle to locate vulnerability and exploitation. These considerations are also of utmost importance in relation to how we interpret and understand internet-mediated exploitation. Precisely as migration, exploitation and trafficking are multifaceted phenomena, there are many complexities surrounding sexual labour and sex markets, and this will be the focus of the next chapter.

References

Agustín LM (2006a) The Disappearing of a Migration Category: Migrants Who Sell Sex. J Ethn Migr Stud 32(1):29–47. https://doi.org/10.1080/13691830500335325

Agustín LM (2006b) The Conundrum of Women's Agency: Migrations and the Sex Industry. In: O'Neill M, Campbell R (eds) Sex Work Now, 1st edn. Willan Publishing, Cullompton, pp 116–140

Agustín LM (2007) Sex at the Margins: Migration, Labour Markets and the Rescue Industry, 1st edn. Zed Books Ltd., London

Andrijasevic R (2010) Migration, Agency and Citizenship in Sex Trafficking, 1st edn. Palgrave Macmillan, Basingstoke

APPG (2018) Behind Closed Doors: Organised Sexual Exploitation in England and Wales. All-Party Parliamentary Group on Prostitution and the Global Sex Trade, London

Augustova K, Suber DL (2023) The Kurdish kaçakçı on the Iran-Turkey Border: Corruption and Survival as EU Sponsored Counter-Smuggling Effects. Trends Organ Crim 26(1):48–63. https://doi.org/10.1007/s12117-023-09484-3

Bauer TK, Zimmermann KF (1999) Assessment of Possible Migration Pressure and its Labour Market Impact Following EU Enlargement to Central and Eastern Europe. IZA Institute of Labor Economics, London

Birks J, Gardner A (2019) Introducing the Slave Next Door. Anti-Traffick Rev 13:66–81. https://doi.org/10.14197/atr.201219135

Bjelland HF (2016) Identifying Human Trafficking in Norway: A Register-Based Study Of Cases, Outcomes and Police Practices. Eur J Criminol 14(5):522–542. https://doi.org/10.1177/1477370816677619

Bosworth M, Fili A, Pickering S (2017a) Women and Border Policing at the Edges of Europe. J Ethn Migr Stud 44(13):2182–2196. https://doi.org/10.1080/1369183x.2017.1408459

Bosworth M, Franko K, Pickering S (2017b) Punishment, Globalization and Migration Control: 'Get Them the Hell Out of Here. Punishment Soc 20(1):34–53. https://doi.org/10.1177/1462474517738984

Bourbeau P (2015) Migration, Resilience and Security: Responses to New Inflows of Asylum Seekers and Migrants. J Ethn Migr Stud 41(12):1958–1977. https://doi.org/10.1080/1369183x.2015.1047331

Bourdieu P (1985) The Forms of Capital. In: Richardson JG (ed) Handbook of Theory and Research for the Sociology of Education, 1st edn. Greenwood, New York, pp 241–258

Broad R (2015) 'A Vile and Violent Thing': Female Traffickers and the Criminal Justice Response. Brit J Criminol 55(6):1058–1075. https://doi.org/10.1093/bjc/azv072

Bryceson DF (2019) Transnational Families Negotiating Migration and Care Life Cycles Across Nation-State Borders. J Ethn Migr Stud 45(16):3042–3064. https://doi.org/10.1080/1369183x.2018.1547017

Castles S, de Haas H, Miller MJ (2014) The Age of Migration: International Population Movements in the Modern World, 5th edn. Palgrave Macmillan, Basingstoke

Chapman-Schmidt B (2019) 'Sex Trafficking' as Epistemic Violence. Anti-Traffick Rev 12(1):172–187

Chimienti M (2009) Selling Sex in Order to Migrate: The End of the Migratory Dream? J Ethn Migr Stud 36(1):27–45. https://doi.org/10.1080/13691830903266101

Chiswick B (2008) Are Immigrants Favorably Self-Selected? In: Brettell CB, Hollifield JF (eds) Migration Theory: Talking Across Disciplines, 2nd edn. Routledge, New York, pp 63–82

Christie N (1986) The Ideal Victim. In: Fattah EA (ed) From Crime Policy to Victim Policy. Macmillan, London

Chuang J (2015) The Challenges and Perils of Reframing Trafficking as 'Modern-Day Slavery'. Anti-Traffick Rev 5:146–149. https://doi.org/10.14197/atr.20121559

Cockbain E, Kleemans ER (2019) Innovations in Empirical Research into Human Trafficking: Introduction to the Special Edition. Crime Law Soc Chang 72(1):1–7. https://doi.org/10.1007/s10611-019-09852-7

Cohen S (2011) Folk Devils and Moral Panics: The Creation of the Mods and Rockers. Routledge, Oxon

Collyer M (2005) When Do Social Networks Fail to Explain Migration? Accounting for the Movement of Algerian Asylum-Seekers to the UK. J Ethn Migr Stud 31(4):699–718. https://doi.org/10.1080/13691830500109852

Cruz K, O'Connell Davidson J, Sanchez Taylor J (2019) Tourism and Sexual Violence and Exploitation in Jamaica: Contesting the 'Trafficking and Modern Slavery' Frame. J Br Acad 7(1):189–214. https://doi.org/10.5871/jba/007s1.189

Doezema J (1999) Loose Women or Lost Women? The Re-emergence of the Myth of White Slavery in Contemporary Discourses of Trafficking in Women. Gend Issues 18(1):23–50

Doezema J (2005) Now You See Her, Now You Don't: Sex Workers at the UN Trafficking Protocol Negotiation. Soc Leg Stud 14(1):61–89. https://doi.org/10.1177/0964663905049526

Doezema J (2010) Sex Slaves and Discourse Masters: The Construction of Trafficking, 1st edn. Zed Books Ltd., London

Farrell A, Dank M, Vries I, Kafafian M, Hughes A, Lockwood S (2019) Failing Victims? Challenges of the Police Response to Human Trafficking. Criminol Public Policy 18(3):649–673. https://doi.org/10.1111/1745-9133.12456

Fitzgerald DS (2015) The Sociology of International Migration. In: Brettell CB, Hollifield JF (eds) Migration Theory: Talking Across Disciplines, 3rd edn. Routledge, New York, pp 115–137

Gadd D, Broad R (2018) Troubling Recognitions in British Responses to Modern Slavery. Brit J Criminol 58(6):1440–1461. https://doi.org/10.1093/bjc/azx082

GSI (2018) The Global Slavery Index 2018

de Haas H (2010) The Internal Dynamics of Migration Processes: A Theoretical Inquiry. J Ethn Migr Stud 36(10):1587–1617. https://doi.org/10.1080/1369183x.2010.489361

Hoyle C, Bosworth M, Dempsey M (2011) Labelling the Victims of Sex Trafficking: Exploring the Borderland between Rhetoric and Reality. Soc Leg Stud 20(3):313–329. https://doi.org/10.1177/0964663911405394

Igbinomwanhia OG (2021) Human Trafficking and Poverty in South-south Nigeria. PhD Thesis, University of Stirling.

Jahnsen S, Skilbrei M-L (2015) From Palermo to the Streets of Oslo: Pros and cons of the trafficking framework. Anti-Traffick Rev 4(4):156–160. https://doi.org/10.14197/atr.201215410

Kempadoo K (2004) Sexing the Caribbean: Gender, Race and Sexual Labor, 1st edn. Routledge, Oxon

Koser K (2011) Why Take the Risk? Explaining Migrant Smuggling. In: Modood T, Salt J (eds) Global Migration, Ethnicity and Britishness, 1st edn. Palgrave Macmillan, Basingstoke, pp 65–83

Lammasniemi L (2017) Anti-White Slavery Legislation and its Legacies in England. Anti-Traffick Rev 9(1):64–76

Léonard S (2010) EU Border Security and Migration into the European Union: FRONTEX and Securitisation Through Practices. Eur Sec 19(2):231–254. https://doi.org/10.1080/09662839.2010.526937

Lott T (2018) Contextualizing Slavery's Wrongness. In: Brace L, O'Connell Davidson J (eds) Revisiting Slavery and Antislavery: Towards a Critical Analysis. Palgrave Macmillan, London, pp 35–64

Mai N (2009) Migrant Workers in the UK Sex Industry: Full Research Report. Economic Social and Research Council, Swindon

Mai N (2013) Embodied Cosmopolitanisms: The Subjective Mobility of Migrants Working in the Global Sex Industry. Gend Place Cult 20(1):107–124. https://doi.org/10.1080/0966369x.2011.649350

Mai N (2016) Too Much Suffering': Understanding the Interplay between Migration, Bounded Exploitation and Trafficking through Nigerian Sex Workers' Experiences. Sociol Res Online 21(4):1–14. https://doi.org/10.5153/sro.4158

Malloch M (2016) Criminalising Victims of Human Trafficking: State Responses and Punitive Practices. In: Malloch M, Rigby P (eds) Human Trafficking: The Complexities of Exploitation. Edinburgh University Press, Edinburgh, pp 175–193

Malloch M, Rigby P (2016) Contexts and Complexities. In: Malloch M, Rigby P (eds) Human Trafficking: The Complexities of Exploitation. Edinburgh University Press, Edinburgh, pp 1–17

Marx K (1976) Capital: A Critique of Political Economy. Pelican Books, London

Massey DS (1990) Social Structure, Household Strategies, and the Cumulative Causation of Migration. Popul Index 56(1):3–26

May T (2016) My Government Will Lead the Way in Defeating Modern Slavery. The Telegraph, 30 July. https://www.telegraph.co.uk/news/2016/07/30/we-will-lead-the-way-in-defeating-modern-slavery/

McCollum D, Findlay A (2017) Oiling the Wheels? Flexible Labour Markets and the Migration Industry. J Ethn Migr Stud 44(4):558–574. https://doi.org/10.1080/1369183x.2017.1315505

McDonald WF (2004) Traffic Counts, Symbols & Agendas: A Critique of the Campaign Against Trafficking of Human Beings. Int Rev Vict 11(1):143–176 van Meeteren M, Engbersen G, van San M (2018) Striving for a Better Position: Aspirations and the Role of Cultural, Economic, and Social Capital for Irregular Migrants in Belgium. Int Migr Rev 43(4):881–907. https://doi.org/10.1111/j.1747-7379.2009.00788.x

Menjívar C, Gómez Cervantes A, Alvord D (2018) The Expansion of "Crimmigration," Mass Detention, and Deportation. Sociol Compass 12(4):1–15. https://doi.org/10.1111/soc4.12573

Modood T, Salt J (2011) Global Migration, Ethnicity and Britishness. In: Modood T, Salt J (eds) Global Migration, Ethnicity and Britishness, 1st edn. Palgrave Macmillan, Basingstoke, pp 248–268

Munro W (2016) Human Trafficking: Capital Exploitation and the Accursed Share. In: Malloch M, Rigby P (eds) Human Trafficking: The Complexities of Exploitation. Edinburgh University Press, Edinburgh, pp 224–245

Musto JL (2009) What's in a Name? Women's Stud Int Forum 32(4):281–287. https://doi.org/10.1016/j.wsif.2009.05.016

NCA (2019) National Referral Mechanism Statistics – End of Year Summary 2018. National Crime Agency, London

O'Connell Davidson J (2006) Will the Real Sex Slave Please Stand Up? Fem Rev 83(1):4–22

O'Connell Davidson J (2010) New Slavery, Old Binaries: Human Trafficking and the Borders of 'Freedom'. Global Netw 10(2):244–261

O'Connell Davidson J (2013) Troubling Freedom: Migration, Debt, and Modern Slavery. Migrat Stud 1(2):176–195. https://doi.org/10.1093/migration/mns002

O'Connell Davidson J (2014) Let's Go Outside: Bodies, Prostitutes, Slaves and Worker Citizens. Citizsh Stud 18(5):516–532. https://doi.org/10.1080/13621025.2014.923703

O'Connell Davidson J (2015) Modern Slavery: The Margins of Freedom. Palgrave Macmillan, New York

O'Connell Davidson J (2016a) Treble Troubles? Marketization, Social Protection and Emancipation Considered Through the Lens of Slavery. In: Karner C, Weicht B (eds) The Commonalities of Global Crises: Markets, Communities and Nostalgia. Palgrave Macmillan, London, pp 87–114

O'Connell Davidson J (2016b) 'Things' Are Not What They Seem: On Persons, Things, Slaves, and the New Abolitionist Movement. Curr Leg Probl 69(1):227–257. https://doi.org/10.1093/clp/cuw008

O'Connell Davidson J (2017) Editorial: The Presence of the Past: Lessons of History for Anti-Trafficking Work. Anti-Traffick Rev 9(1):1–12

Okyere S (2017) 'Shock and Awe': A Critique of the Ghana-Centric Child Trafficking Discourse. Anti-Traffick Rev 9(1):92–105

Oso Casas L (2009) Money, Sex, Love and the Family: Economic and Affective Strategies of Latin American Sex Workers in Spain. J Ethn Migr Stud 36(1):47–65. https://doi.org/10.1080/13691830903250899

Petras J, Veltmeyer H (2007) Globalisation or Imperialism? Camb Rev Int Aff 14(1):32–48. https://doi.org/10.1080/09557570008400327

Plambech S (2017) Sex, Deportation and Rescue: Economies of Migration among Nigerian Sex Workers. Fem Econ 23(3):134–159. https://doi.org/10.1080/13545701.2016.1181272

Ras I, Gregoriou C (2019) The Quest to End Modern Slavery: Metaphors in Corporate Modern Slavery Statements. Anti-Traffick Rev 13:100–118. https://doi.org/10.14197/atr.201219137

Russell A (2014) "Victims of Trafficking": The Feminisation of Poverty and Migration in the Gendered Narratives of Human Trafficking. Societies 4(4):532–548. https://doi.org/10.3390/soc4040532

Sassen S (2002) Women's Burden: Counter-Geographies of Globalization and the Feminization of Survival. Nord J Int Law 71(2):255–274. https://doi.org/10.1163/157181002761931378

Sharapov K, Mendel J (2018) Trafficking in Human Beings: Made and Cut to Measure? Anti-trafficking Docufictions and the Production of Anti- trafficking Truths. Cult Soc 12(4):540–560. https://doi.org/10.1177/1749975518788657

Sharapov K, Hoff S, Gerasimov B (2019) Editorial: Knowledge is Power, Ignorance is Bliss: Public perceptions and responses to human trafficking. Anti-Traffick Rev 13:1–11. https://doi.org/10.14197/atr.201219131

Sharma N (2005) Anti-Trafficking Rhetoric and the Making of a Global Apartheid. NWSA J 17(3):88–111. https://doi.org/10.2979/nws.2005.17.3.88

Stumpf J (2006) The Crimmigration Crisis: Immigrants, Crime, and Sovereign Power. Am Univ Law Rev 56(2):367–419

Turner J (2016) Root Causes, Transnational Mobility and Formations of Patriarchy in the Sex Trafficking of Women. In: Malloch M, Rigby P (eds) Human Trafficking: The Complexities of Exploitation, 1st edn. Edinburgh University Press, Edinburgh, pp 194–209

Tyszler E (2019) The Performative Effects of the European War on Migrants. Masculinities and Femininities at the Moroccan-Spanish Border. Gend výzk/Gend Res 2(1):40–66. https://doi.org/10.13060/25706578.2019.20.1.462

United Nations Office of the High Commissioner (2019) Protocol to Prevent, Suppress and Punish Trafficking in Persons Especially Women and Children

Weitzer R (2007) The Social Construction of Sex Trafficking: Ideology and Institutionalization of a Moral Crusade. Polit Soc 35(3):447–475. https://doi.org/10.1177/0032329207304319

Weitzer R (2015) Human Trafficking and Contemporary Slavery. Annu Rev Sociol 41(1):223–242. https://doi.org/10.1146/annurev-soc-073014-112506

Wijkman M, Kleemans E (2019) Female Offenders of Human Trafficking and Sexual Exploitation. Crime Law Soc Chang 72(1):53–72. https://doi.org/10.1007/s10611-019-09840-x

Williams JM (2016) The Safety/Security Nexus and the Humanitarianisation of Border Enforcement. Geogr J 182(1):27–37. https://doi.org/10.1111/geoj.12119

Windzio M, Teney C, Lenkewitz S (2019) A Network Analysis of Intra-EU Migration Flows: How Regulatory Policies, Economic Inequalities and the Network-Topology Shape the Intra-EU Migration Space. J Ethn Migr Stud 47:1–19. https://doi.org/10.1080/1369183x.2019.1643229

The Nature and Organisation of the Sex Market

Theorising the Sex Market

From the Mesopotamian temples in ancient times (Ringdal 2004) to the 'dollymops' in the Victorian era, supplementing their meagre incomes from the factories by sex work (Walkowitz 1980), and to the internet-mediated sex worker performing digital sexual labour in the period of late capitalism (Sanders et al. 2018b), sex work has been present in all societies, and continues to be so (Jenness 1990). However, whilst sex work is not a novel phenomenon, structural changes throughout society shape and reshape its character. As a result, sexual markets are dynamic and constantly evolving, as are the politics surrounding them, the laws regulating them and the nature and organisation of sexual labour.

Studies on sex workers and clients tend to individualise the commercial transactions related to sexual labour, often at the expense of examining the socio-economic contexts in which the forces of supply and demand take place (Malloch et al. 2017). Indeed, the sex industry is deeply intertwined with the broader structures of the global economy, political and social institutions, localised cultures and practices, and situated within the context of late capitalism, in which the commodification

R. Kjellgren, *Internet-Mediated Exploitation in the Scottish Online Sex Market*, Transnational Crime, Crime Control and Security,
https://doi.org/10.1007/978-3-032-09275-5_3

of experiences—including sexual ones—has become intensified (O'Neill 2010; Phipps 2013). Whilst sexual labour predates capitalism, contemporary market forces have been central in facilitating the growth of the sex industry (Agustín 2007). It is, however, important to note that there is a plurality of markets within the sex industry; pornography, the sale of sex toys, exotic dancing and prostitution, to name but a few. Whereas this section focuses on the latter, it must still be recognised that there are considerable overlaps, with the possibility that many performing sexual labour do so in various capacities (Anderson and O'Connell Davidson 2002; Sanders et al. 2018b).

Sexual labour, as other forms of labour, is tied to the global economy and localised socio-political contexts, resulting in variable employment relations within this sector (Anderson and O'Connell Davidson 2002; Malloch et al. 2017). At one end of the spectrum, independent, self-employed sex workers may enjoy a high degree of control of their working environment. At the other extreme, however, the term 'sex worker' ceases to be appropriate as there are individuals forced, either by desperate circumstances or the control of a third-party, to perform sexual labour under appalling conditions (Anderson and O'Connell Davidson 2002). The stratification and differentiation of sexual labour are affected by processes related to supply and demand, and the following analysis will shed more light on these complexities.

Earlier biological accounts of the male demand for sexual services link the propensity to buy sex with the need for a sexual outlet. In other words, sex buyers are predicted to be men who cannot satisfy their urges through conventional outlets, whereas sexually active men would be less inclined to pay for sexual services. However, the predictions fall short in light of more contemporary empirical research (Sanders 2008). Indeed, sex buyers are likely to be married (Phipps 2013) and also report a higher number of unpaid partners than non-sex buyers (Groom and Nandwani 2006; Jones et al. 2015).

Consumption, not only in regard to sexual services, allows consumers to confirm their social status and identity; essentially, it is a form of display, performance or manifestation of norms and values (Anderson and O'Connell Davidson 2002). When masculinity is constructed upon notions of sexual voraciousness and promiscuity, the rewards of using sexual services reach far beyond the satisfaction of biological urges; it offers males an opportunity to reaffirm their masculinity, and partake in a gendered performance, by conforming to gendered norms and engaging in behaviours reinforcing their masculinity (Anderson and O'Connell Davidson 2002, 2003). Males who feel that their masculinity is threatened may be more inclined to consume sexual services. Similarly, in a society that devalues femininity, the greater the need is for males to distance themselves from the feminine by reaffirming their masculinity (Anderson and O'Connell Davidson 2002).

Assessing the scale of demand for sex work is perhaps impossible. Available empirical evidence suggests it is not uncommon to pay for sex, though sex buyers remain a minority (Jones et al. 2015). According to the most recent version of *The National Surveys of Sexual Attitudes and Lifestyles* (Natsal-3, 2012), a large-scale survey (n = 15,162) using probability sampling, 11% of male respondents in the UK reported ever paying for sex, and 3.6% of men had paid for sex in the last year (Jones et al. 2015). Previous research on male demand also suggests that the motivations for purchasing sex are varied, and clients are not a homogeneous group. First, it is essential to point out that men do not solely engage in commercial sex to satisfy their sexual needs (Soothill and Sanders 2005). The need for companionship, or what Lever and Dolnick (2010, p. 188) termed the "illusion of intimacy", appears to be central to many clients (Soothill and Sanders 2005). In addition, Xantidis and McCabe (2000) highlight how novelty and the potential variety of encounters motivate sex buyers. This reverberates with a study of 143 male sex buyers in Scotland, in which McKeganey and Barnard (1996) identified five key motivations for purchasing sex: (1) the opportunity to pay for specific sexual acts; (2) access to a variety of women; (3) the possibility to buy sex from women with particular characteristics; (4) the possibility of temporary relationships; and (5) the thrill associated with the activity.

According to Sanders (2008), particular push and pull factors can also be linked to the male desire to buy sexual services. Indeed, among the factors that push men to buy sex, emotional needs, unsatisfactory sexual relationships and ambivalence toward conventional dating are important. Pull factors, on the other hand, are linked to the attraction of the sex industry; in the context of late capitalism, the expansion of services and market specialisation increasingly provides individualised and touristic experiences catering to a wide variety of demands. The allurement of particular fantasies might thus make men more prone to pay for pleasure (Sanders 2008).

Aside from the underlying motivations to buy sex, clients within the UK are, on average, 30 years old, married, have no previous convictions and are in full-time employment (Soothill and Sanders 2005; Phipps 2013). In addition, available evidence suggests that buying sex is not a sporadic or temporary activity; men usually have a long trajectory of buying sex (Soothill and Sanders 2005). It remains clear that sex buyers are by no means 'extraordinary' or associated with peculiar characteristics; on the contrary, they often seem to differ little from men who do not purchase sexual services (Soothill and Sanders 2005). Considering the mundane realities of sex buyers, it is perhaps unsurprising that the majority of clients are not violent (Phipps 2013). However, of more concern is that there is a subgroup of sex buyers that are engaging in predatory behaviour and are disproportionately responsible for the amount of violence directed towards sex workers (Phipps 2013). It is of particular concern when the demands for novelty and variety in sexual encounters intersect with misogynist and racist attitudes; an extremely toxic combination with potentially dire consequences. Bearing testimony to this is the fact that sex workers are at the highest risk of occupational homicide in the UK, and furthermore, an increasing trend of migrant sex workers being targeted (Cunningham et al. 2018).

To fully understand exploitation and violence within the sex market, it is essential to examine how wider structures of racism and misogyny shape demand and, in turn, the role of pornography in promoting the hypersexualisation of women and reinforcing these structures. Pornography promotes particular notions of masculinity and femininity (DeKeseredy and Corsianos 2016). Men are usually portrayed as domineering and hypermasculine, displaying certain levels of aggression or violence towards women, who are objectified and often represented without agency (Corsianos 2007), or in the words of DeKeseredy and Corsianos (2016, p. 11):

> always orgasmic, willing to do anything, often reacting by doing what they're told, or by being physically moved into position to perform in particular ways, always accepting of what is being done to them regardless of the level of humiliation or level of violence, and always wanting more. The fact that these images have become so mainstream with the audience wanting more tells us a lot about the fantasies of many straight males and/or the acceptance of these images.

The link between sex work and pornography is increasingly becoming entwined. Many porn sites link to escort advertisements; conversely, it can also be observed how 'porn star experiences' are marketed by sex workers in their adverts (Bindel et al. 2013). Indeed, the promulgation of online pornography may have resulted in diversifying sexual demands and normalising acts previously considered deviant (DeKeseredy and Corsianos 2016). Some have previously argued that sex workers are increasingly becoming pushed towards more extreme services (e.g., porn star experience, unprotected intercourse, anal sex), commonly associated with pornography and beyond traditional conceptions of sexual activity, such as the 'girlfriend experience' (Monto 2010; Bindel et al. 2013). In the context of late capitalism, sex workers may feel inclined to agree to more extreme forms of sexual services to gain a competitive advantage (Adriaenssens and Hendrickx 2012). It is not inconceivable that the most vulnerable sex workers have fewer options to refuse extreme services, or at the extreme end, trafficked or exploited women may be forced to do services other women can negotiate.

Whilst the demand for sexual services has been considered, it is also essential to examine the nature of performing sexual labour. It has previously been pointed out that sex work is a form of emotional labour, and according to Sanders (2008, p. 46):

> consuming sexual services, whether direct or indirect, is constructed through fantasy. The sex industry is predicated on meeting the desired fantasy of the paying client. Sex workers … work hard to exploit their femininity, sexuality, bodily capital and emotional labour to provide the customer with his ultimate fantasy, albeit for a few hours.

Sex work is more than sexual intercourse—it commodifies emotional and sexual experiences (Rodríguez García 2016). Sex workers need not only to recognise the emotional needs of their clients but to satisfy them (Agustín 2007). Considering the potential variety of clients, and appetite for particular sexual services, as discussed in the preceding paragraphs, sex work encapsulates a plethora of experiences, including both negatives and positives and variations in risks and rewards (Sanders and Campbell 2007).

At one end of the spectrum, sexual labour can be a survival strategy for those in the most desperate circumstances. It has previously been reported that women in the UK trade sexual services for food, shelter, transportation, rent, or to fuel substance or alcohol use (Seebohm and Smiles 2008; Croxford et al. 2015; Hester et al. 2019). Limited opportunity structures, commonly associated with deregulated market economies, also affect the propensity to engage in sex work (Mai 2009). In particular, periods of austerity within the UK are believed to leave women with little choice but to engage in sex work to get by financially (Hester et al. 2019). It has previously been noted how women in Dundee that had reduced their involvement or left sex work were returning to street prostitution due to stringent benefit sanctions (Malloch 2017).

Sex workers do exercise agency; however, it is essential to acknowledge that some do it under severely constrained circumstances. For some, sex work might be preferable to other forms of labour, even if they have a choice to do something completely different. Indeed, some are highly qualified, but are motivated by the prospect of significant earnings and flexible working hours (Pitcher 2015a; Sagar et al. 2016). A survey of 240 internet-mediated sex workers suggests high levels of job satisfaction, with many highlighting the positive aspects, such as financial rewards, flexibility and high decision-making power in their work (Sanders et al. 2016). It is nonetheless important to note that the respondents within this particular survey are likely to be a subset of more privileged sex workers. What remains clear is that some sex workers perceive their occupation as not only a financially viable option but also as an enjoyable profession (Hester et al. 2019; Sanders et al. 2016) or alternatively, as a means to upward social mobility (Mai 2009).

The Changing Geographies of Sex Work: Streets, Brothels and Virtual Markets

The mechanisms linked to supply and demand, and the characteristics and behaviours associated with sex workers and buyers, are central to structuring the sex market. Erotic capital—the physical characteristics and gendered presentation deemed preferable in localised contexts (Jones 2015a)—is differentially distributed within the sex worker population. Sex workers are therefore subjected to processes of stratification based on social divisions such as ethnicity, nationality and age, and in accordance with particular local demands. Amongst other outcomes, this results in women working in different segments of the sex market (Mai 2009; Jones 2015a; Pitcher 2015b; Turner 2016; Hester et al. 2019). The components that make up the sex market are not only tied to economic factors but are also affected by legal structures, policing strategies and moral codes within neighbourhoods; as a result, sex workers are clustered in different geographical areas (Hubbard 2016). In turn, the geographical spaces where sex work occurs affect their experiences (Karandikar and Prospero 2010; Sanders 2016). The most important distinction can be made between street-based markets and off-street markets (also referred to as 'indoor' markets); however, as will become increasingly clear throughout this chapter, the emergence of online technologies alters the relationship between the different components.

Women involved in street-based sex work are significantly more vulnerable than off-street sex workers (Phipps 2013). Some women in this segment have complex support needs, including homelessness, substance or alcohol use, mental health issues and backgrounds characterised by abuse and deprivation (Malloch 2017; Hester et al. 2019). Poor working conditions and low wages signify street-based sex work and make it a significantly more dangerous activity than the off-street market (Phipps 2013). Violence, including sexual and economic violence, is much more prevalent within street-based work (Church et al. 2001; Sanders 2016), and sex workers also need to manage other risks, such as harassment from the community, and criminalisation from the police (Sanders 2004). Even more concerning, street-based sex workers are at an increased risk of homicide (Cunningham et al. 2018). They are at an increased risk because their working environment can be considered criminogenic: interactions usually occur in the dark, out-of-sight and usually during nocturnal hours (Sanders 2016). Besides this, there are links between street-based sex markets and drug markets, and the latter tends to promulgate violence (Phipps 2013).

In contrast to street-based sex work, more favourable working conditions tend to be found within the off-street sex market. Traditionally, brothels primarily targeted a higher-class clientele, were more rigorous in their operations and offered a more protected environment than street-based sex work. Whilst indoor sex workers experience violence, theft, robbery and other crimes, they are less susceptible to serious violence (Hubbard and Prior 2012). Partly, this can be attributed to the fact that indoor workers are more protected from the criminogenic conditions associated with the streets, but also because it is easier for sex workers to control the interaction with clients within their own premises (Sanders 2016). This also applies to those working in other controlled premises—such as brothels—where staff is usually present to facilitate client interaction (Phipps 2013). In terms of geography, and though there are overlaps, off-street sex workers tend to fall into the following categories: (1) independent sex workers operating from their own premises or doing out-calls to a client's locale; (2) commercial (licensed) brothels and massage parlours; (3) residential brothels across local communities and (4) 'pop-up brothels', usually based in rented flats or short-term accommodation, and signified by mobility, operating in one space temporarily before relocating (Crocker et al. 2017; Hester et al. 2019). Off-street sex workers used to advertise their services in magazines or by distributing cards in public spaces; however, what radically changed their marketing strategies was the advent of the internet (Hester et al. 2019).

New technologies have continuously reshaped the landscape of commercial sex (Jones 2015b). With the availability of pagers and phones, sex workers had increased opportunities to engage in off-street sex work, and the occupation itself allowed for more autonomous working conditions (Jones 2015b). The introduction of online technologies has further advanced this process. Indeed, the majority of sex work is now either mediated or provided through the internet (Sanders et al. 2016, 2018a), and it is not simply that street-based sex work has been displaced to a more virtual environment; instead, there has been an overall expansion of the entire sex market (Finn and Stalans 2016). Brothels and massage parlours tend to have an online presence, allowing clients to browse sex workers online (Hester et al. 2019). Additionally, the internet allows for a more favourable working environment (e.g., flexibility and increased safety) for independent sex workers, making it more attractive to individuals from various social backgrounds, contributing to a diversification of the overall market (Jones 2015b).

The adaptation of online technologies has also reconfigured the significance of geographical space; red light districts are in decline, and sex workers can work more widely throughout the community (Malloch 2017). Online technologies have reshaped the off-street sex market by making it more fluid and providing more flexibility and autonomy for sex workers (Sanders et al. 2018b). Whilst the services provided are delivered offline, the internet primarily mediates all the communication and marketing; in effect, sex work has been augmented with an online dimension, effectively renegotiating the importance of geographical boundaries (Mendel and Sharapov 2014; Hubbard et al. 2016; Sanders et al. 2018b). The behaviour of clients, sex workers, organised crime groups and criminal networks has changed accordingly (Sanders et al. 2018b; Skidmore et al. 2018).

Technology and Paradoxical Changes in Safety and Vulnerability

Online technologies can be considered a recent innovation in the context of sexual labour. It has, nevertheless, fundamentally reconfigured how clients source for sexual services (Soothill and Sanders 2005) and, additionally, how sex workers market their services to appeal to the demands of the market (Döring 2009; Cunningham et al. 2017). The intersection of commercial sex and online technologies has also led to paradoxical developments regarding the safety and vulnerability within the sex market. Online technologies tend to improve the working conditions and offer greater autonomy for the majority of sex workers (Cunningham et al. 2017; Sanders et al. 2018b); however, they have also left a minority of individuals vulnerable to exploitation as organised crime groups and criminal networks can operate in an increasingly clandestine atmosphere (Crocker et al. 2017; Skidmore et al. 2018).

For sex buyers, the emergence of networked technologies has transformed the experience of commercial sex; indeed, sex buyers are presented with a virtual smorgasbord of sexual services, and it has previously been argued that the widespread availability of sexual services means that clients can be more particular in their demands (Bindel et al. 2013). The prevalence of online reviews puts them in a position of advantage over sex workers, who depend on positive reviews to increase marketability (Cunningham et al. 2017). Indeed, increased connectivity and exposure allow clients to exercise power over sex workers by rating their performance, and often writing detailed descriptions of their encounters to encourage or discourage other buyers from using the services of particular sex workers. As a result, communities of sex buyers have been flourishing within online forums, and transformed what was previously an isolated and independent activity (Soothill and Sanders 2005).

There is a continuum within internet-mediated sex work regarding levels of autonomy. Some sex workers perceive themselves as entrepreneurs, whereas others work long hours to make ends meet in the context of an increasingly competitive market and the 'gig economy', driven mainly by customer reviews (Scoular et al. 2019). One of the key features of online mediated sex work is that it offers greater fluidity and transitions between different kinds of sexual labour, such as webcamming or escorting (Sanders et al. 2018b). As in other sectors, there are different forms of employment within the off-street sex market. Whilst there are overlaps, and not uncommon that sex workers may engage in a variety of employment forms, four main categories can be identified: (1) independent escorts; (2) sex worker collectives or informal co-operatives; (3) brothels and massage parlours and (4) online agencies. Independent escorting is associated with a high level of autonomy and flexibility, and the financial uncertainties associated with self-employment (Pitcher 2015b). Collectives of sex workers may form for various reasons, including offering services together, increasing safety or sharing costs associated with renting a space to work from (Pitcher 2015b).

Employment relations, and the associated experiences of working, are somewhat different for those working for a third-party. These include individuals working in brothels and massage parlours, and an employee-employer relationship signifies this category of sex workers. In this regard, there are not the same levels of flexibility compared to independent escorts, but on the other hand, it may offer more financial security in having a steady amount of hours of work each week. Additionally, working from a location with others also decreases potential violent encounters (Scoular et al. 2019). There is also, nevertheless, the possibility of an employee-employer relationship becoming exploitative, whether it is economic exploitation or individuals coerced into remaining in exploitative arrangements.

Online escort agencies have elements similar to independent escorting and brothel work, and it offers a certain degree of flexibility for sex workers, such as specifying their rates and services offered. However, marketing and client connection is often outsourced to the agency. Agencies tend to focus on providing out-call services at a location of the client's choosing. As such, there is always a possibility for violence to occur. As Pitcher (2015b) points out, modes of employment within the off-street sex market affect the safety of sex workers, and these are mediated by the legal context in which the transactions occur. For instance, current laws in the UK against brothel-keeping—the criminalisation of two or more sex workers working on the same premises without a license—is counter-productive to sex worker safety. Even though sex workers are direct beneficiaries of working in collectives, it is criminalised and pushes individuals to work alone in low-visibility environments (Scoular et al. 2019).

While evidence suggests that online-mediated sex workers, to a lesser extent, experience serious crimes such as rape and assault (Hubbard and Prior 2012; Sanders 2016), the internet has also enabled other forms of crime. For instance, sex workers may be 'outed' by vengeful clients and have their identities revealed. Similarly, sex workers are frequently experiencing harassment and stalking (Sanders et al. 2018b). In addition to this, online technologies serve to make sexual labour more visible, and sex buyers can sometimes leverage this: it has previously been reported that the detrimental effects of unregulated competition result in wage penalties for sex workers that do not offer more extreme forms of services, such as unprotected sex (Adriaenssens and Hendrickx 2012; Sanders et al. 2016).

There have indeed been paradoxical developments regarding safety and vulnerability following the widespread adoption of online technologies. Working off-street means sex workers are not exposed to some of the threats associated with street-based sex work. New safety mechanisms such as screening clients or communicating with other sex workers promote safety. Campbell et al. (2019) highlight the importance of 'blended safety repertoires' as central in contemporary online-mediated sex work. This, for instance, involves using traditional safety mechanisms such as a 'buddy system'—letting a trusted other know the details of the interaction, including client information—and coupling them with strategies evolved as part of an increasingly networked society (Campbell et al. 2019). An example would be services such as the 'National Ugly Mugs' scheme (NUM 2020)—a report and alert system enabling sex workers to identify violent and threatening clients (Campbell et al. 2019). Whilst the internet offers new tools to improve the safety of sex workers, there are also emerging concerns—not only in the form of victimisation from clients—but becoming increasingly vulnerable to organised exploitation (Scoular et al. 2019).

Though systematic and comprehensive research is limited, there are indications that organised crime groups and criminal networks are adopting online technologies to facilitate their operations (Europol 2011; Latonero 2011, 2012; Turner 2016; Walby et al. 2016). The low visibility offered by online technologies means that sex workers, in particular market segments, can be increasingly vulnerable to exploitation (Scoular et al. 2019). Paradoxically, whilst online and networked technologies equip sex workers with tools that increase their safety, technological innovation also benefits those seeking to exploit others. Indeed, organised crime groups and criminal networks can utilise new methods to recruit and market exploited individuals but also use technology to increase their surveillance of victims, communicate with sex buyers and transmit information internally through encrypted channels (Sykiotou 2007). As such, organised crime groups in the UK are well-equipped—and have been found to utilise online technologies—to facilitate their operations within the off-street sex market (Skidmore et al. 2016, 2018; Crocker et al. 2017). Whereas these groups and individuals used to be bound by geographical constraints, online technologies afford these groups greater mobility and flexibility in their *modus operandi*, as well as the means to more successfully operate outwith the periphery of law enforcement (Walby et al. 2016; Skidmore et al. 2018).

To conclude, this chapter has demonstrated how various factors influence the contemporary sex market. Demand can be tied to the socially constructed nature of masculinity and the allure of commodified sexual fantasies, whereas the propensity to provide sexual services is connected to differentiated opportunity structures. These transactions do not appear in a social vacuum; they are part of broader developments in the commodification of experiences in the context of late capitalism. As such, societal structures, the global economy, localised contexts and individual circumstances all contribute to the propensity to either buy or sell sex. With advancements in online technologies and a changing virtual landscape, sex work will likely be increasingly intertwined with online pornography, resulting in women being portrayed beyond traditional conceptions of sexuality. In addition, these technologies also renegotiate the significance of geographical space; street work tends to be associated with the most vulnerable individuals, whereas off-street sex work offers better working conditions. The internet has not only diversified sexual commerce, but it has also increased the safety of sex workers, whilst paradoxically contributing to an ideal environment for exploitation to flourish. Given the complex organisation of the sex market, encompassing individuals with high levels of autonomy and those subjected to exploitation, policing becomes increasingly difficult. This is the primary focus of the following chapter: the logistics of criminal networks and the online hybridisation of sex trafficking.

References

Adriaenssens S, Hendrickx J (2012) Sex, Price and Preferences: Accounting for Unsafe Sexual Practices in Prostitution Markets. Sociol Health Illn 34(5):665–680

Agustín LM (2007) Sex at the Margins: Migration, Labour Markets and the Rescue Industry, 1st edn. Zed Books Ltd., London

Anderson B, O'Connell Davidson J (2002) Trafficking – A Demand Led Problem? Part I: Review of Evidence and Debates. Stockholm

Anderson B, O'Connell Davidson J (2003) Is Trafficking in Human Beings Demand Driven? A Multi-Country Pilot Study. International Organization for Migration, Geneva

Bindel J, Breslin R, Brown L (2013) Capital Exploits: A Study of Prostitution and Trafficking in London. Eaves, London

Campbell R, Teela S, Scoular J, Pitcher J, Cunningham S (2019) Risking Safety and Rights: Online Sex Work, Crimes and 'Blended Safety Repertoires'. Br J Sociol 70(4):1539–1560. https://doi.org/10.1111/1468-4446.12493

Church S, Henderson M, Barnard M, Hart G (2001) Violence by Clients Towards Female Prostitutes in Different Work Setting: Questionnaire Survey. Br Med J 322(1):524–525

Corsianos M (2007) Mainstream Pornography And "Women": Questioning Sexual Agency. Crit Socio 33(5):863–885

Crocker R, Webb S, Garner S, Skidmore M (2017) The Impact of Organised Crime in Local Communities. The Police Foundation, London

Croxford S, Platt L, Hope VD, Cullen KJ, Parry JV, Ncube F (2015) Sex Work Amongst People Who Inject Drugs in England, Wales and Northern Ireland: Findings from a National Survey of Health Harms and Behaviours. Int J Drug Policy 26(4):429–433. https://doi.org/10.1016/j.drugpo.2014.09.014

Cunningham S, Sanders T, Scoular J, Campbell R, Pitcher J, Hill K, Valentine-Chase M, Melissa C, Aydin Y, Hamer R (2017) Behind the Screen: Commercial Sex, Digital Spaces and Working Online. Technol Soc 53(1):47–54. https://doi.org/10.1016/j.techsoc.2017.11.004

Cunningham S, Sanders T, Platt L, Grenfell P, Macioti PG (2018) Sex Work and Occupational Homicide: Analysis of a U.K. Murder Database. Homicide Stud 22(3):321–338. https://doi.org/10.1177/1088767918754306

DeKeseredy WS, Corsianos M (2016) Violence Against Women in Pornography, 1st edn. Routledge, Oxon

Döring NM (2009) The Internet's Impact on Sexuality: A Critical Review of 15 Years of Research. Comput Hum Behav 25(5):1089–1101. https://doi.org/10.1016/j.chb.2009.04.003

Europol (2011) Trafficking in Human Beings in the European Union. Europol, Hague

Finn MA, Stalans LJ (2016) How Targeted Enforcement Shapes Marketing Decisions of Pimps: Evidence of Displacement and Innovation. Vict Offenders 11(4):578–599. https://doi.org/10.1080/15564886.2016.1187694

Groom TM, Nandwani R (2006) Characteristics of Men Who Pay for Sex: a UK Sexual Health Clinic Survey. Sex Transm Infect 82(5):364–367. https://doi.org/10.1136/sti.2006.020537

Hester M, Mulvihill N, Matolcsi A, Sanches AL, Walker S (2019) The Nature and Prevalence of Prostitution and Sex Work in England and Wales Today. University of Bristol, London

Hubbard P (2016) Sex Work, Urban Governance and the Gendering of Cities. In: Brown G, Browne K (eds) The Routledge Research Companion to Geographies of Sex and Sexualities, 1st edn. Routledge, London, pp 313–320

Hubbard P, Prior J (2012) Out of Sight, Out of Mind? Prostitution Policy and the Health, Well-Being and Safety of Home-Based Sex Workers. Crit Soc Policy 33(1):140–159. https://doi.org/10.1177/0261018312449807

Hubbard P, Collins A, Gorman-Murray A (2016) Introduction: Sex, Consumption and Commerce in the Contemporary City. Urban Stud 54(3):567–581. https://doi.org/10.1177/0042098016682685

Jenness V (1990) From Sex as Sin to Sex as Work: COYOTE and the Reorganization of Prostitution as a Social Problem. Soc Probl 37(3):403–420

Jones A (2015a) For Black Models Scroll Down: Webcam Modeling and the Racialization of Erotic Labor. Sex Cult 19(4):776–799. https://doi.org/10.1007/s12119-015-9291-4

Jones A (2015b) Sex Work in a Digital Era. Sociol Compass 9(7):558–570. https://doi.org/10.1111/soc4.12282

Jones KG, Johnson AM, Wellings K, Sonnenberg P, Field N, Tanton C, Erens B, Clifton S, Datta J, Mitchell KR, Prah P, Mercer CH (2015) The Prevalence of, and Factors Associated with, Paying for Sex among Men Resident in Britain: Findings from the Third National Survey of Sexual Attitudes and Lifestyles (Natsal-3). Sex Transm Infect 91(1):116–123. https://doi.org/10.1136/sextrans-2014-051683

Karandikar S, Prospero M (2010) From Client to Pimp: Male Violence Against Female Sex Workers. J Interpers Violence 25(2):257–273. https://doi.org/10.1177/0886260509334393

Latonero M (2011) Human Trafficking Online: The Role of Social Networking Sites and Online Classifieds. University of Southern California, Los Angeles

Latonero M (2012) The Rise of Mobile and the Diffusion of Technology-Facilitated Trafficking. University of Southern California, Los Angeles

Lever J, Dolnick D (2010) Call Girls and Street Prostitutes: Selling Sex and Intimacy. In: Weitzer R (ed) Sex for Sale: Prostitution, Pornography, and the Sex Industry, 2nd edn. Routledge, London, pp 187–205

Mai N (2009) Migrant Workers in the UK Sex Industry: Full Research Report. Economic Social and Research Council, Swindon

Malloch M (2017) Exploring Available Knowledge and Evidence on Prostitution in Scotland via Practitioner-based Interviews. Edinburgh, Scottish Government

Malloch M, Robertson L, Forbes E (2017) Evidence Assessment of the Impact of the Criminalisation of the Purchase of Sex: A Review. Edinburgh, Scottish Government

McKeganey NP, Barnard M (1996) Sex Work on the Streets: Prostitutes and Their Clients. Open University Press, Buckingham

Mendel J, Sharapov K (2014) Human Trafficking and Online Networks: Policy Briefing (Updated Version, October 2014). Centre for Policy Studies, Central European University, Budapest

Monto MA (2010) Prostitutes' Customers: Motives and Misconceptions. In: Weitzer R (ed) Sex for Sale: Prostitution, Pornography, and the Sex Industry, 2nd edn. Routledge, London, pp 233–254

NUM (2020) National Ugly Mugs: Fighting Stigma and Saving Lives

O'Neill M (2010) Cultural Criminology and Sex Work: Resisting Regulation Through Radical Democracy and Participatory Action Research (PAR). J Law Soc 37(1):210–232

Phipps A (2013) Violence Against Sex Workers. In: McMillan L, Lombard N (eds) Violence Against Women. Jessica Kingsley Publishers, London, pp 87–102

Pitcher J (2015a) Direct Sex Work in Great Britain: Reflecting Diversity. Grad J Soc Sci 11(2):76–100

Pitcher J (2015b) Sex Work and Modes of Self-employment in the Informal Economy: Diverse Business Practices and Constraints to Effective Working. Soc Policy Soc 14(1):113–123. https://doi.org/10.1017/S1474746414000426

Ringdal NJ (2004) Love for Sale: A World History of Prostitution, 2nd edn. Grove/Atlantic, Inc., New York

Rodríguez García M (2016) Defining Commercial Sexualities, Past and Present. In: Brown G, Browne K (eds) The Routledge Research Companion to Geographies of Sex and Sexualities, 1st edn. Routledge, Oxon, pp 321–330

Sagar T, Jones D, Symons K, Tyrie J, Roberts R (2016) Student Involvement in the UK Sex Industry: Motivations and Experiences. Br J Sociol 67(4):697–718. https://doi.org/10.1111/1468-4446.12216

Sanders T (2004) The Risks of Street Prostitution: Punters, Police and Protesters. Urban Stud 41(9):1703–1717. https://doi.org/10.1080/0042098042000243110

Sanders T (2008) Paying for Pleasure: Men who Buy Sex, 1st edn. Willan Publishing, Devon

Sanders T (2016) Inevitably Violent? Dynamics of Space, Governance, and Stigma in Understanding Violence against Sex Workers. Stud Law Politics Soc 71(1):93–114. https://doi.org/10.1108/S1059-433720160000071005

Sanders T, Campbell R (2007) Designing Out Vulnerability, Building in Respect: Violence, Safety and Sex Work Policy. Br J Sociol 58(1):1–19. https://doi.org/10.1111/j.1468-4446.2007.00136.x

Sanders T, Connelly L, King LJ (2016) On Our Own Terms: The Working Conditions of Internet-Based Sex Workers in the UK. Sociol Res Online 21(4):1–14. https://doi.org/10.5153/sro.4152

Sanders T, Campbell R, Cunningham S, Pitcher J, Scoular J (2018a) The Point of Counting: Mapping the Internet Based Sex Industry. Soc Sci 7(5):233–241. https://doi.org/10.11648/j.ss.20180705.15

Sanders T, Scoular J, Campbell R, Pitcher J, Cunningham S (2018b) Internet Sex Work: Beyond the Gaze, 1st edn. Springer Nature, Cham

Scoular J, Pitcher J, Sanders T, Cunningham S, Campbell R (2019) Beyond the Gaze and Well Beyond Wolfenden: The Practices and Rationalities of Regulating and Policing Sex Work in the Digital Age. J Law Soc 46(2):211–239

Seebohm L, Smiles S (2008) Hidden for Survival: Peer Research into the Lives of Sex Workers Within Newcastle, Gateshead, Sunderland, South Tyneside and North Tyneside. Tyneside Cyrenians

Skidmore M, Garner S, Crocker R, Webb S, Graham J, Gill M (2016) The Role and Impact of Organised Crime in the Local Off-Street Sex Market. The Police Foundation, London

Skidmore M, Garner S, Desroches C, Saggu N (2018) The Threat of Exploitation in the Adult Sex Market: A Pilot Study of Online Sex Worker Advertisements. Policing 12(2):210–218. https://doi.org/10.1093/police/pax007

Soothill K, Sanders T (2005) The Geographical Mobility, Preferences and Pleasures of Prolific Punters: a Demonstration Study of the Activities of Prostitutes' Clients. Sociol Res Online 10(1):1–14

Sykiotou A (2007) Trafficking in Human Beings: Internet Recruitment. Strasbourgh, Council of Europe, Directorate General of Human Rights and Legal Affairs

Turner J (2016) Root Causes, Transnational Mobility and Formations of Patriarchy in the Sex Trafficking of Women. In: Malloch M, Rigby P (eds) Human Trafficking: The Complexities of Exploitation, 1st edn. Edinburgh University Press, Edinburgh, pp 194–209

Walby S, Apitzsch B, Armstrong J, Balderston S, Follis K, Francis B, Kelly L, May-Chahal C, Rashid A, Shire K, Towers J, Tunte M (2016) Study on the Gender Dimension of Trafficking in Human Beings: Final Report. European Commission, Luxembourg

Walkowitz JR (1980) Prostitution and Victorian Society: Women, Class, and the State, 1st edn. Cambridge University Press, Cambridge

Xantidis L, McCabe M (2000) Personality Characteristics of Male Clients of Female Commercial Sex Workers in Australia. Arch Sex Behav 29(2):165–176. https://doi.org/10.1023/a:1001907806062

Criminal Networks, Opportunity Structures and the Process of Exploitation

Organised Crime or Crime That Is Organised?

In Scotland, organised crime groups involved in various forms of exploitation can be noticed throughout our communities (Fraser et al. 2018). Sex trafficking is often framed as a manifestation of organised crime, with traffickers depicted as highly successful, and capable of generating a near-infinite amount of revenue through continuously exploiting their victims (Campana 2016). The trafficking of human beings can certainly be profitable; however, the illegality of their operations presents unique organisational challenges for criminal networks (Morselli 2009; Campana 2016). There is, nevertheless, a paucity of robust empirical evidence and research on criminal networks in the sex market, and it is questionable whether what research has been conducted on the issue is transferable to a UK context.

There is generally a lack of consensus regarding how 'organised crime' should be defined, and definitions vary between authorities and jurisdictions (Cavanagh et al. 2016). The National Crime Agency (NCA 2014, p. 7) defines organised crime as:

R. Kjellgren, *Internet-Mediated Exploitation in the Scottish Online Sex Market*, Transnational Crime, Crime Control and Security,
https://doi.org/10.1007/978-3-032-09275-5_4

> serious crime planned, co-ordinated and conducted by people working together on a continuing basis. Their motivation is often, but not always, financial gain.

Defining organised crime in broad terms can be useful from an operational point of view (Campana and Varese 2018) since it allows flexibility in targeting organised crime groups (OCGs); however, it does little to illuminate the plethora of activities and the variation in offender constellations associated with opportunistic criminal networks. OCGs are often opportunistic entities (Bouchard and Morselli 2014), filling the role of producers and suppliers of goods and services in different markets (Campana and Varese 2018). Opportunities for criminal profits are embedded within the networks of offenders (Morselli 2009). There is often a symbiotic relationship between legitimate and illegitimate markets and actors; the commission of certain acts can depend upon mobilising resources (e.g., transportation companies to traffic drugs) from legitimate organisations (Morselli and Siguère 2006).

There is merit in perceiving organised crime as a result of intricate webs of relations interwoven with opportunity. Indeed, criminal networks vary along a continuum of organisation, from co-offending for a particular criminal opportunity to large-scale operations determined to monopolise a criminal market (Morselli 2009). By shifting our focus to networks and connectivity rather than organised crime per se, we are better positioned to describe patterns of criminal co-operation (Kleemans 2007). The longstanding idea of organised crime groups as hierarchical organisations with a strict division of labour is more well-suited to describe the traditional mafia, rather than the ephemeral, fluid and flexible networks common in the contemporary context of organised crime (Kleemans 2007; Bouchard and Morselli 2014).

The sex market is attractive for OCGs, given the potential profits it can generate, and also because of the relatively low risk of detection associated with off-street locations (Crocker et al. 2017). In a Scottish context, there is evidence of organised crime groups involved in facilitating prostitution and sex trafficking, though the structure of these groups remains unclear (Malloch 2017). Like other forms of serious organised crime, and whilst there is limited empirical evidence on the issue, trafficking is also likely to be underpinned by networks, connectivity and opportunities. Cockbain's (2018) research on internal sex trafficking networks, though focused on minors, showed that peer networks for both offenders and victims were central in the recruitment process, and offenders were opportunistic in targeting victims. Similarly, also in the context of internal child sex trafficking within the UK, Cockbain and Wortley (2015, p. 1) demonstrate how the routine activities of victims and perpetrators are central in facilitating abuse and that "the people, places and processes involved are shown to be far from exceptional". However, the extent to which child sex trafficking networks are similar to networks facilitating the exploitation of adults is questionable.

The structure of criminal networks is linked to the opportunities available. Sex trafficking networks have been found to differ in scale, ranging from small-scale networks engaging in exploitation on a sporadic basis, medium-scale groups operating during a slightly longer timeframe and involving more victims, and large-scale networks with a more pronounced division of labour, involving transnational intermediaries (Englund et al. 2008). However, there is little research which is specific to the UK context, and we currently do not know the extent and structure of criminal networks in the UK's sex markets. The timeframe of exploitation can be incredibly varied: in Zimmerman and colleagues' (2006) study of 207 sex trafficking victims, 89% had been exploited for more than a month, and 10% for over two years. Small networks have been found to operate locally, whereas medium-sized networks can operate across borders through links to similar groups, and larger networks can control the entire trafficking process (McRedmond 2010). For instance, Mancuso's (2013) research demonstrates how Nigerian sex trafficking networks are primarily structured around ethnicity and family, with contacts available throughout the transportation phase and within the destination country.

Campana's (2016) analysis of a dismantled Nigerian trafficking operation suggests that the network studied could facilitate the transportation and exploitation of approximately 200 victims annually. At the other end of the spectrum, smaller networks have also been observed, sometimes with only one known perpetrator, often romantically involved with one or more victims (Verhoeven et al. 2013). Under certain conditions, it may be appropriate to consider criminal networks in the sex market as

OCGs; however, if they are too hastily labelled as organised crime, there is a risk of obscuring the less organised aspects of it. In its essence, trafficking is a relational crime; social ties are important in explaining patterns of victimisation and opportunities for offending (Verhoeven et al. 2013). What is often conspicuously absent in research on the networks underpinning exploitation and trafficking are accounts by sex workers, or those labelled victims, themselves, and how they perceive their labour and position within the network. In other words, there is a tendency in the literature to describe networks as 'criminal' or as facilitating 'trafficking', without input from those suggested to be exploited.

Social Embeddedness, Connectivity and Opportunity Structures

To disrupt and reduce organised crime, it is vital to acknowledge that crime is embedded within the social world (Englund et al. 2008). Societies are made up of connections between individuals, groups and organisations, and as such, offenders differ little from non-offenders; indeed, they seldom operate in a vacuum consisting only of ties to other offenders (Van De Bunt et al. 2014). On the contrary, ties often span the legitimate and illegitimate spheres of society and are conducive to the success of criminal networks (Morselli and Giguère 2006; Kleemans 2014). Two distinctions can be made at this point: first, relational embeddedness refers to ties between different individuals; second, structural embeddedness refers to the relations between businesses, organisations and similar entities operating on a meso-level (van de Bunt et al. 2014). Macro relations are also prevalent, such as those between neighbourhoods, communities and ethnic groups, or geographical places of significance related to particular criminal markets (van de Bunt et al. 2014), and there is some evidence to suggest sex trafficking to be embedded within the off-street sex market (Crocker et al. 2017). However, there is also a local element to it, for instance, women exploited in Amsterdam's window prostitution (Verhoeven 2017) or the exploitation of migrants throughout closed ethnic communities within the UK (Easton and Matthews 2012).

Social ties between individuals, organisations or institutions are the channels through which we can mobilise resources and become aware of various opportunities—criminal or not (Cockbain 2018). Connections become increasingly important given the hostile and unpredictable environment in which criminal networks operate (Kleemans 2014). Trafficking and exploitation can be considered more logistically complex than volume crime (e.g., assault, burglary), which partly explains why co-offenders may be required for the successful execution of certain acts (Kleemans and de Poot 2008). Whilst the potential rewards can be high, there are also considerable risks, whether financial, physical, or being arrested, and therefore, trust plays a pivotal role in criminal networks (Morselli et al. 2007; Campana and Varese 2013).

In an environment conducive to suspicion, distrust and the potential for deception and betrayal, offenders in organised crime tend to favour working with family or friends (Kleemans 2007; Calderoni et al. 2020). The principle of homophily appears central to structuring these relationships; living in proximity to one another, education, employment, ethnicity and similarly shared attributes are often present within criminal networks (Kleemans 2014). However, clustered social relations also reduce the diversity of resources within the network and, by extension, criminal opportunities (Bijlenga and Kleemans 2017). It might therefore be necessary to establish ties between other individuals or criminal groups to expand the network and commit complex crimes successfully. In the terms of Burt (1992), individuals spanning these structural holes are in powerful brokerage positions and can control the flow of information and resources between otherwise disconnected networks (Kleemans 2007). As such, brokers, though not necessarily part of criminal organisations, are potentially vital to adding flexibility to criminal networks—a core component of sustainability in this hostile environment (Morselli and Roy 2008; Bouchard and Morselli 2014).

To operate within a covert and risky setting, the structure of the criminal network is essential (Morselli 2009). Unsurprisingly, larger networks are more susceptible to risk, as more members can be targeted by law enforcement and infiltration, and trust between members tends to be lower (Bouchard and Morselli 2014). Whilst large criminal networks certainly exist, empirical evidence suggests that smaller, opportunistic criminal networks comprise the bulk of organised crime (Bouchard and Morselli 2014; Bright et al. 2015). Indeed, fluidity and flexibility are crucial to adapting to law enforcement targeting and market constraints, and smaller networks can quickly form and dissolve depending on the need to execute actions related to the commission of crimes. Similarly, mobility has previously been suggested to be tied to criminal earnings (Morselli and Royer 2008), and flexible networks, drawing on social capital spanning borders, are better positioned to expand to new markets (Morselli et al. 2011). Traditional conceptions of hierarchical OCGs with easily identifiable 'kingpins' are largely outdated (Cavanagh et al. 2016), as partnership and criminal collaboration between smaller networks are more beneficial operational units in responding to criminal opportunities (Morselli and Petit 2007). Flexibility renders criminal networks resilient to law enforcement activities; central actors can usually be replaced, and intense enforcement tactics tend to decentralise networks and thus actively shape the structure of criminal networks (Morselli and Petit 2007; Morselli and Roy 2008).

Another reason networks and connectivity are essential in organised crime is that they increase criminal opportunities. Crime, like other behaviours, can be perceived as a result of the interaction between situation and disposition (Cockbain and Wortley 2015). Drawing on so-called situational theories of crime (Clarke and Cornish 1985) allows us to examine the immediate contexts in which specific crimes occur (Cockbain 2018). As such, the focus lies within the constraints and opportunities structured within the network (Kleemans 2014). To increase opportunities, groups potentially need to establish ties with individuals outwith their immediate network, and some research suggests that brokers are usually the most successful actors within criminal networks (Leukfeldt et al. 2017). The routine activities of offenders lead to offender convergence settings, the milieu in which interaction with similar others is likely (Felson 2003).

Offender convergence settings generate the potential for criminal opportunities and co-offending, resulting from the conjunction of time and space (Morselli 2009; Kleemans et al. 2012; Kleemans 2014). The underlying assumptions of offenders as quasi-rational decision-makers would thus suggest that, in the context of market-oriented crime, mechanisms of supply and demand are central in structuring offending, as offenders try to minimise risk and maximise rewards (Cockbain and Bowers 2019). It has previously been reported that labour traffickers in the UK tended towards generalist offending patterns, that is, responding and seizing available opportunities, be they part of their regular offending repertoire or not (Cockbain and Brayley-Morris 2018). According to this situational framework, offending is goal-oriented and based on purposive action, and the availability or lack of opportunities guides decision-making processes (Morselli 2005). It should be noted, however, that the processes relating to labour exploitation, or other forms of organised criminal activity, are not necessarily transferable to the context of exploitation within sex markets—and particularly in the UK context. The research reviewed is useful to theorise how criminal networks and organised crime groups may operate in the sex market, but it needs to be noted that the current evidence base—with regards to the structure of criminal networks more broadly, but for exploitation and trafficking specifically—is very limited.

Unpacking the Sex Trafficking Crime Script

In light of how criminal networks are structured and organised, it is essential to examine the evidence for how criminal networks facilitate sex trafficking. A suitable framework for understanding the acts involved in sex trafficking is crime script analysis (Cornish 1994). Each crime consists of a number of 'scenes', that is, logistical steps in the crime-committing process (Morselli and Roy 2008; Brayley et al. 2011), and recruitment, transportation and exploitation make up the scenes of the trafficking crime script. Within these scenes, several facets, or actions, may be available for various ways to commit the crime successfully. The combination of scenes and actions determines the available permutations required to execute the crime script (Morselli and Roy 2008). In other words, for crime scripts with a high degree of permutations, the criminal network has more flexibility in successfully committing the crime since there will be different opportunities to achieve their ends. In the following paragraphs, evidence on the modus operandi of criminal groups involved in sex trafficking and exploitation within the sex market will be reviewed and considered in the light of Cornish's (1994) crime script analysis. The crime script in Fig. 1 represents an attempt to visualise the processes involved in exploitation and sex trafficking, and the different actions, scenes and facets will be explored in more detail below.

Recruitment

Previous literature suggests that recruitment can take several forms, depending on whether international travel is required. First, three key recruitment strategies can be identified, most likely related to the size and overall structure of the criminal network: (1) informal recruitment, (2) formal recruitment and (3) mutual arrangements. Previous research suggests that a potentially common approach for international trafficking is to rely on informal recruitment strategies (Englund et al. 2008). This primarily involves two distinct scenarios: (a) women actively seek out facilitators to migrate for sexual labour (and subsequently become exploited) or (b) facilitators or traffickers actively target women. Deception plays a role in both scenarios. If women knew that they would be doing sex work, they might be deceived about the conditions in which they would be working (Englund et al. 2008). Personal networks and venues associated with sex work are conduits for recruitment, and the tendency of homophily appears to mediate this process, as victims and exploiters usually come from the same region, share the same ethnicity and are of similar socio-economic status (Zimmermann et al. 2006; Englund et al. 2008; Wijkman and Kleemans 2019). A relatively recent innovation in informal recruitment is online technologies; Di Nicola et al. (2017) suggest that initial contact tends to be made on public social media sites, followed by more extensive communication through mobile phones, Skype or similar applications.

Formal recruitment methods are also used to recruit women into the sex industry, whether exploitation is present or not (Di Nicola et al. 2017). The first action for offenders in this part of the script is to broadcast employment opportunities, possibly involving different degrees of deception. Whilst employment adverts historically were placed in

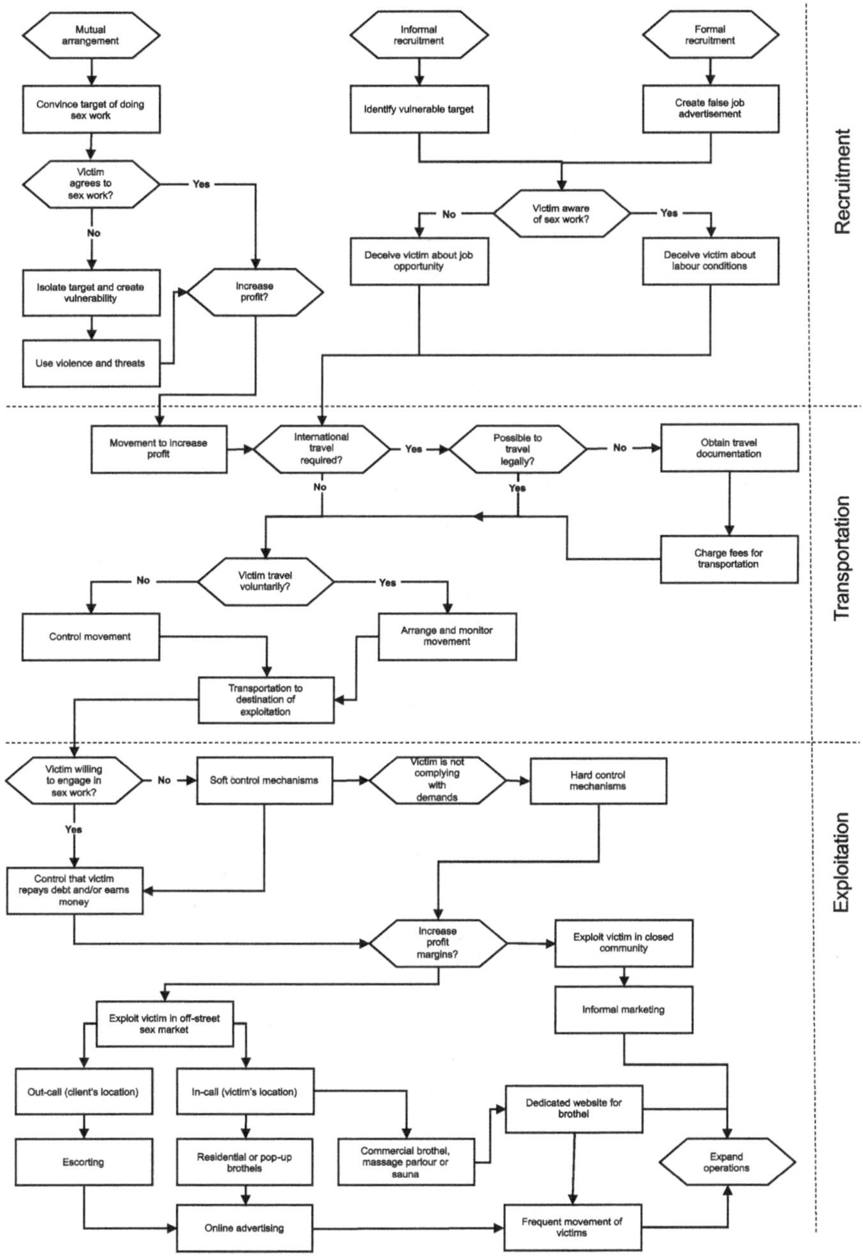

Fig. 1 Crime script derived from literature review

newspapers or magazines (Englund et al. 2008), contemporary recruiting tends to involve online adverts (Sarkar 2015; Di Nicola et al. 2017). Again, employment opportunities might indicate that the candidate will engage in sex work, in which deception usually involves the working conditions or remuneration (Di Nicola et al. 2017). It also appears to be common to advertise non-existent jobs and (at a later stage in the crime script) coerce women into exploitation (Diba et al. 2018).

Mutual arrangements on the sex market are not inherently exploitative; however, pre-existing power differentials mean this is an omnipresent threat (Morselli et al. 2014). This encapsulates scenarios in which, usually, one individual exploits their partner or initiates contact with a woman with the intention to exploit her. The offender aims to convince their target to do sex work; depending on the victim's willingness, different control strategies may be applied (Morselli et al. 2014). Victims have also been reported to be emotionally manipulated into engaging in sex work. The so-called loverboy method has been highlighted, especially in the American and Dutch literature, in which an exploiter actively initiates contact with a target:

> by feigning romantic interest and the intention to form a relationship and then gradually to coerce or threaten her into prostitution. (Kleemans and Smit 2014, p. 387)

If the victim does not agree to engage in sex work, the offender may use strategies to create vulnerabilities conducive to coercion control, which can quickly transcend into exploitation, threats and violence (Karandikar and Prospero 2010; Morselli et al. 2014).

Victims themselves may also be involved in recruiting other victims (Kleemans and Smit 2014; Rigby et al. 2017), and whilst motivations to do so may vary, one plausible explanation is that recruiting other victims might please their exploiters (Cockbain et al. 2011), or that they receive more favourable working conditions upon doing so (Kleemans and Smit 2014). In this context, it is not uncommon that recruiters are female, with the underlying assumption being that it is easier to establish trust with victims when the recruiter is also a woman (Wijkman and Kleemans 2019).

What little evidence there is suggests that recruitment strategies may be mediated by the size and structure of the criminal network. Identifying vulnerable victims or creating vulnerability appears key. In general, online technologies may allow for increased flexibility in executing the crime script; for instance, the scale of recruitment can be increased by online advertising, and various social media platforms can allow for targeting specific victims (Diba et al. 2018). However, it is important to remember that online technologies are by no means essential for recruitment, nor is it known the extent to which they are used in this context.

Transportation

Given this case study's focus on migrant exploitation, transportation refers to the initial itinerary between the country of origin and destination. The frequent mobility associated with exploitation is more aptly covered in the next section. The size of the criminal network and the citizenship of victims and offenders are important in this context. It is essential to note that transportation often occurs legally, and victims usually cooperate and move willingly (Di Nicola et al. 2017). If victims are moving voluntarily and can enter the country legally, there is no need to control the movement. When irregular migration is the only option, fake documentation, including study and tourism visas, has been used (Mancuso 2013). Campana (2018) previously demonstrated how small, localised networks facilitate smuggling at different stages throughout the smuggling route. If it is not possible to enter the destination country legally, victims usually have to pay substantial fees for transportation. Debts exacerbate vulnerability, as traffickers can use debt to coerce their victims into exploitation (Agustín 2006; Plambech 2017). Transportation can also be used as a strategy to isolate victims from important support structures in their home countries, rendering victims easier to control in the destination country (Sarkar 2014).

Whilst there is limited evidence on this issue, online technologies may only play a modest role in the transportation phase, and what limited evidence there is suggests they may be used to obtain counterfeit travel documentation and advertise smuggling services on social media sites (Di

Nicola et al. 2017; Diba et al. 2019). In addition, networked technologies, such as mobile phones, are used during transportation for maintaining contact with victims, as a less resource-intensive means of monitoring and coordination (Di Nicola et al. 2017). In the absence of more robust evidence, it is challenging to suggest online technology to be central to this phase of trafficking crime script. As with the recruitment phase, technology arguably enhances the crime script by providing novel opportunities to monitor and facilitate transportation, but it does not appear critical. Even so, most research is not specific to the UK, and it is highly uncertain how transportation may occur in this context.

Exploitation

Whilst trafficking requires exploitation, 'exploitation' itself, as was discussed earlier, is not easily defined. Assuming that an individual has been recruited and transported, a starting point is to consider whether that person willingly engages in sex work. An individual may already agree to do so before departure; in that case, exploitation tends to become present later (Campana and Varese 2015). If a victim has acquired debt as part of the transportation costs, the individual might voluntarily engage in sex work to more quickly repay their debts (Plambech 2017) or to send remittances back home (Oso Casas 2009). If that is the situation, control is exercised over the person to ensure that the debt is paid, and at this stage, the two parties might part ways after fulfilling their contractual obligations. However, it has previously been reported that debts are increased, often for arbitrary reasons, and to increase the exploiters' profit margins (Englund et al. 2008; Kleemans and Smit 2014). For instance, Verhoeven et al. (2013) noted that several women in their research had to pay off significant amounts of money if they wanted to cease working, ranging from €6000 to €50,000, and clearly, both economic and sexual exploitation can thus be intertwined into an overall experience of exploitation.

Previous research suggests that control mechanisms are variable, especially when an individual does not wish to engage in sex work; such situations can perhaps more easily be identified as sex trafficking. A first step is often to use so-called soft control mechanisms, where control can be exercised without violence (Kleemans and Smit 2014). An example of this includes debt bondage, in which an individual might be able to move freely and have a certain degree of autonomy, but nevertheless forced to work by circumstance or the subtle influence of the exploiters (Englund et al. 2008). Economic control is potentially effective in this situation, particularly if the individual lacks adequate support structures in the destination country; it has previously been reported that traffickers directly control the economic transactions with clients (Englund et al. 2008).

Emotional manipulation has also been outlined as a control strategy, mainly in the context of intimate relationships between exploiters and victims (Kleemans and Smit 2014; Morselli et al. 2014). Establishing trust is outlined as an important feature of indirect forms of control; victims may become increasingly dependent upon their traffickers, especially if they have a limited social network outwith their immediate working environment (Englund et al. 2008). As Cockbain (2018) notes, in the context of internal child trafficking, violence is often used as a last resort; threats, insults and emotional abuse appear to be more common control strategies. Whereas this appears to be the case in relation to child trafficking, it is nevertheless uncertain if this indeed also is the case in the exploitation of adults. However, it has also been suggested that online technologies play an increasingly important part in monitoring victims during the exploitation phase, for instance, demanding victims to be in constant communication with their controllers (Englund et al. 2008) or directly monitoring their usage of communication technology to cut off their interaction with friends and families (Di Nicola et al. 2017). Even if that is the case, the extent to which this occurs is currently unknown.

There are reports of traffickers using 'hard control mechanisms', which usually involve limiting victims' movement and using physical means of control (Easton and Matthews 2012). There is evidence of traffickers withholding travel documentation (e.g., passports) from victims, both in Scotland (Lebov 2010; Easton and Matthews 2012) and more widely throughout Europe (Walby et al. 2016), and precarious migrants being threatened with deportation (Kleemans and Smit 2014). Even more concerning, however, is that physical confinement has also been reported in some cases (Easton and Matthews 2012; Verhoeven et al. 2013;

Zimmermann et al. 2006). Alcohol and drugs have also reportedly been used to increase the victims' dependency upon the exploiters and as a means of control to ensure compliance (Easton and Matthews 2012; Walby et al. 2016). According to qualitative research, involving interviews with 207 victims of sex trafficking, the vast majority reported threats of violence (89%), and some reported threats directed at their families (36%). In addition, close to all (95%) had experienced physical or sexual violence (Zimmermann et al. 2006). Threats appear to be a common strategy to ensure obedience, and in some instances, these threats are followed up by actual violence or rape (Englund et al. 2008; Easton and Matthews 2012; Mancuso 2013; Verhoeven et al. 2013; Morselli et al. 2014). What is often overlooked in popular discourses of trafficking, as Campana (2016, 2017) points out, is that controlling a victim for the purpose of exploitation is a resource-intensive process with high monitoring costs. It is in the interest of offenders to ensure that their operations run smoothly, and resorting to violence and hard control measures is not a viable, long-term strategy, given their risks and costs (Morselli et al. 2014).

An integral part of increasing revenue within the sex market is mobility (Englund et al. 2008; Sanders et al. 2018). In other words, novelty may be key to meeting local demands, and a regular rotation of women has been noted in a variety of settings, including independent sex workers 'touring' (Scoular et al. 2019), migrant sex workers moving within ethnic communities (Silverstone 2011), and sex trafficking victims moving within a country or across borders (Kleemans and Smit 2014). Turner (2016) notes how European women are circulated throughout the UK to satisfy the demand for the 'exotic other'. However, constant relocation and operating through loosely structured, geographically dispersed networks also attract less attention from law enforcement (Englund et al. 2008). Besides, it also has a vital control function: victims cannot establish local ties, develop location-specific knowledge, and become increasingly dependent upon their exploiters (Sarkar 2014).

The location of exploitation is an important consideration for criminal networks, as it is inevitably linked to profit (Kleemans and Smit 2014). The network size influences the loci of exploitation, as larger groups can operate across larger geographical areas, whereas smaller networks may be confined to fewer locations (Englund et al. 2008). If adult women are exploited to maximise profits, they are likely to be exploited within the off-street sex market (Lebov 2010; Easton and Matthews 2012; Crocker et al. 2017; Malloch 2017). There are several reasons for this, including that it is easier to remain outwith the periphery of law enforcement (Lebov 2010) and that the earnings are higher than the street market (Phipps 2013). Victims have been found to be exploited within brothels around the UK (Jackson et al. 2010; Lebov 2010), including: commercial brothels; saunas and massage parlours; residential brothels, located throughout neighbourhoods; and 'pop-up' brothels, usually based in rented short-term accommodation and operated during limited periods before relocating (Crocker et al. 2017). Commercial brothels, disguised as legitimate enterprises, require a certain degree of stability, given the importance of brand-building and high set-up costs (Jackson et al. 2010), whereas residential brothels and pop-up brothels allow for more flexible forms of operations (Crocker et al. 2017).

If women are exploited within the off-street sex market, marketing and attracting clients are essential. As was discussed in chapter "The Nature and Organisation of the Sex Market", online advertisement plays a pivotal role in off-street sex markets. There is evidence to suggest that traffickers are increasingly using legitimate platforms to advertise their victims (Englund et al. 2008). In 27% of closed sex trafficking cases (n = 140) reviewed by Farrell and Pfeffer (2014), the advertisement of victims occurred online. Similarly, Bouché (2015) interviewed former victims of sex trafficking (n = 115), and 63% reported being advertised online. These findings reverberate with Sarkar's (2015) study of victims (n = 97) and traffickers (n = 64), in which 68% of the former used online platforms to attract clients, and 92% of the latter posted online adverts to recruit victims. Others have also emphasised how internet-mediated marketing plays an increasingly prominent role in marketing trafficking victims (Europol 2011, 2020; Latonero 2011, 2012; Walby et al. 2016; Crocker et al. 2017). However, there is a lack of rigorous research in the context of the UK, and a significant portion of research on this issue appears anecdotal, and also signified by an absence of perspectives from individuals with lived experience.

It should be noted that there is an absence of extensive empirical evidence on the role of online technologies in advertising victims, particularly within the UK. Beyond small sample sizes, convenience or purposive sampling methods and anecdotal data, we do not know the extent to which traffickers use online technologies for this purpose. Nevertheless, what little evidence there is would suggest that using online technologies can be advantageous for traffickers: it makes it easier to attract clients, they can limit the information they provide (Di Nicola et al. 2017), it conceals the organisation of the criminal network, and it offers greater flexibility in terms of where they can exploit their victims, whilst also remaining largely invisible to law enforcement (Englund et al. 2008). In relation to the crime script, it is clear that technology potentially has the most critical role in the exploitation phase of sex trafficking. It is advantageous because it has the potential to add flexibility to the crime script and is arguably necessary to penetrate the off-street sex market and maximise profits.

To conclude this chapter, it has been argued that traditional conceptions of organised crime as hierarchical organisations can be inappropriate in capturing the nuances related to exploitation. By shifting our theoretical lens to recognise exploitation and trafficking as relational phenomena, we can better understand how the commission of crimes depends on the opportunity structures and networks in which offenders are embedded. However, generally speaking, there is a lack of robust and thoughtful research on exploitation and sex trafficking, particularly with regard to the UK, and the extent to which previous research on organised crime and criminal networks can be generalisable to this context is questionable.

If the commercial exploitation of adult women occurs on a larger scale, previous empirical and theoretical research would suggest that a pool of offenders is required to commit the crime successfully. The introduction of online technologies potentially adds a new dimension to sex trafficking. More specifically, novel opportunities possibly become more available in the three trafficking scenes, and technology appears particularly prominent in the exploitation phase. Technology can arguably increase the number of available permutations in executing the crime script, though further empirical research is required to examine this supposition. Given what has been discussed in previous chapters regarding the structural drivers of sexual labour and precarious migration, measures to tackle these issues will require substantial policy changes at a global level (Gallagher and Holmes 2008; Kleemans and Smit 2014). If organised crime and criminal networks indeed are operating in the UK's sex markets, achieving long-term impact and a harm reduction would require these to be tackled in parallel with addressing the structural determinants of vulnerability to exploitation; by focusing policing efforts on disrupting the activities of criminal groups, their potential to grow and their capability of exploiting individuals and local communities is significantly reduced (Fraser et al. 2018). To this end, the following chapter considers how digital data can be utilised to identify and disrupt sex trafficking.

References

Agustín LM (2006) The Conundrum of Women's Agency: Migrations and the Sex Industry. In: O'Neill M, Campbell R (eds) Sex Work Now, 1st edn. Willan Publishing, Cullompton, pp 116–140

Bijlenga N, Kleemans ER (2017) Criminals Seeking ICT-Expertise: An Exploratory Study of Dutch Cases. Eur J Crim Policy Res 24(3):253–268. https://doi.org/10.1007/s10610-017-9356-z

Bouchard M, Morselli C (2014) Opportunistic Structures of Organized Crime. In: Paoli L (ed) The Oxford Handbook of Organized Crime, 1st edn. Oxford University Press, Oxford, pp 288–302

Bouché V (2015) A Report on the Use of Technology to Recruit, Groom and Sell Domestic Minor Sex Trafficking Victims. Thorn Foundation, Fort Worth

Brayley H, Cockbain E, Laycock G (2011) The Value of Crime Scripting: Deconstructing Internal Child Sex Trafficking. Policing 5(2):132–143. https://doi.org/10.1093/police/par024

Bright DA, Greenhill C, Ritter A, Morselli C (2015) Networks within Networks: Using Multiple Link Types to Examine Network Structure and Identify Key Actors in a Drug Trafficking Operation. Glob Crime 16(3):219–237. https://doi.org/10.1080/17440572.2015.1039164

Burt RS (1992) Structural Holes: The Social Structure of Competition, 1st edn. Harvard University Press, Boston

Calderoni F, Campedelli GM, Comunale T, Marchesi ME, Savona EU (2020) Recruitment into Organised Criminal Groups: A Systematic Review. Trends Issues Crime Crim Justice 583(1):1–28

Campana P (2016) The Structure of Human Trafficking: Lifting the Bonnet on a Nigerian Transnational Network. Brit J Criminol 56(1):68–86. https://doi.org/10.1093/bjc/azv027

Campana P (2017) The Market for Human Smuggling into Europe: A Macro Perspective. Policing 11(4):448–456. https://doi.org/10.1093/police/paw058

Campana P (2018) Out of Africa: The Organization of Migrant Smuggling Across the Mediterranean. Eur J Criminol 15(4):481–502. https://doi.org/10.1177/1477370817749179

Campana P, Varese F (2013) Cooperation in Criminal Organizations: Kinship and Violence as Credible Commitments. Ration Soc 25(3):263–289. https://doi.org/10.1177/1043463113481202

Campana P, Varese F (2015) Exploitation in Human Trafficking and Smuggling. Eur J Crim Policy Res 22(1):89–105. https://doi.org/10.1007/s10610-015-9286-6

Campana P, Varese F (2018) Organized Crime in the United Kingdom: Illegal Governance of Markets and Communities. Brit J Criminol 58(6):1381–1400. https://doi.org/10.1093/bjc/azx078

Cavanagh B, Hamilton-Smith N, Mackenzie S (2016) Organised Crime in Scotland and the Criminal Justice Response. In: Croall H, Mooney G, Munro M (eds) Crime, Justice and Society in Scotland, 1st edn. Routledge, Oxon, pp 115–130

Clarke RV, Cornish DB (1985) Modeling Offenders' Decisions: A Framework for Research and Policy. Crime Justice 6(1):147–185

Cockbain E (2018) Offender and Victim Networks in Human Trafficking, 1st edn. Routledge, Oxon

Cockbain E, Bowers K (2019) Human Trafficking for Sex, Labour and Domestic Servitude: How Do Key Trafficking Types Compare and What Are Their Predictors? Crime Law Soc Chang 72(1):9–34. https://doi.org/10.1007/s10611-019-09836-7

Cockbain E, Brayley-Morris H (2018) Human Trafficking and Labour Exploitation in the Casual Construction Industry: An Analysis of Three Major Investigations in the UK Involving Irish Traveller Offending Groups. Policing 12(2):129–149. https://doi.org/10.1093/police/pax032

Cockbain E, Wortley R (2015) Everyday Atrocities: Does Internal (Domestic) Sex Trafficking of British Children Satisfy the Expectations of Opportunity

Theories of Crime? Crime Sci 4(1):35. https://doi.org/10.1186/s40163-015-0047-0

Cockbain E, Brayley H, Laycock G (2011) Exploring Internal Child Sex Trafficking Networks Using Social Network Analysis. Policing 5(2):144–157. https://doi.org/10.1093/police/par025

Cornish DB (1994) The Procedural Analysis of Offending and Its Relevance for Situational Prevention. In: Clarke RV (ed) Crime Prevention Studies, 2nd edn. Criminal Justice Press, New York, pp 151–196

Crocker R, Webb S, Garner S, Skidmore M (2017) The Impact of Organised Crime in Local Communities. The Police Foundation, London

Di Nicola A, Baratto G, Martini E (2017) The Role of the Internet in People Smuggling and Human Trafficking. Directorate-General Migration and Home Affairs, European Commission, Trento

Diba P, Antonopoulos GA, Papanicolaou G (2018) The Role of the Internet in the Process of Trafficking Humans in the UK. In: Van Duyne P, Strémy T, Harvey J, Antonopoulos GA, Von Lampe K (eds) The Janus-Faces of Cross-border Crime in Europe, 1st edn. Eleven International Publishing, The Hague, pp 97–124

Diba P, Papanicolaou G, Antonopoulos GA (2019) The Digital Routes of Human Smuggling? Evidence from the UK. Crime Prev Community Saf 21(2):159–175. https://doi.org/10.1057/s41300-019-00060-y

Easton H, Matthews R (2012) Investigating the Experiences of People Trafficked into Commercial Sexual Exploitation in Scotland. Glasgow, Equalities and Human Rights Commission

Englund C, Viuhko M, Jokinen A, Aromaa K, Resetnikova A, Markina A, Söderström U, Nilsen M (2008) The Organisation of Human Trafficking: A Study of Criminal Involvement in Sexual Exploitation in Sweden, Finland and Estonia. Stockholm, Swedish National Council for Crime Prevention

Europol (2011) Trafficking in Human Beings in the European Union. Europol, Hague

Europol (2020) The Challenges of Countering Human Trafficking in the Digital Era. Europol Operations Directorate, Hague

Farrell A, Pfeffer R (2014) Policing Human Trafficking: Cultural Blinders and Organizational Barriers. Ann Am Acad Pol Soc Sci 653(1):46–64. https://doi.org/10.1177/0002716213515835

Felson M (2003) The Process of Co-offending. In: Smith MJ, Cornish DB (eds) Crime Prevention Studies. Criminal Justice Press, Monsey, pp 149–167

Fraser A, Hamilton-Smith N, Clark A, Atkinson C, Graham W, McBride M, Doyle M, Hobbs D (2018) Community Experiences of Serious Organised Crime in Scotland. Scottish Government, Edinburgh

Gallagher A, Holmes P (2008) Developing an Effective Criminal Justice Response to Human Trafficking. Int Crim Justice Rev 18(3):318–343. https://doi.org/10.1177/1057567708320746

Jackson K, Jeffery J, Adamson G (2010) Setting the Record: The Trafficking of Migrant Women in the England and Wales off-Street Prostitution Sector. ACPO and Regional Intelligence Unit for the South West, London

Karandikar S, Prospero M (2010) From Client to Pimp: Male Violence Against Female Sex Workers. J Interpers Violence 25(2):257–273. https://doi.org/10.1177/0886260509334393

Kleemans ER (2007) Organized Crime, Transit Crime, and Racketeering. Crime Justice 35(1):163–215. https://doi.org/10.1086/501509

Kleemans ER (2014) Theoretical Perspectives on Organized Crime. In: Paoli L (ed) The Oxford Handbook of Organized Crime, 1st edn. Oxford University Press, Oxford, pp 32–52

Kleemans ER, de Poot CJ (2008) Criminal Careers in Organized Crime and Social Opportunity Structure. Eur J Criminol 5(1):69–98. https://doi.org/10.1177/1477370807084225

Kleemans ER, Smit M (2014) Human Smuggling, Human Trafficking, and Exploitation in the Sex Industry. In: Paoli L (ed) The Oxford Handbook of Organized Crime, 1st edn. Oxford University Press, Oxford, pp 381–401

Kleemans ER, Soudijn MRJ, Weenink AW (2012) Organized Crime, Situational Crime Prevention and Routine Activity Theory. Trends Organ Crime 15(2–3):87–92. https://doi.org/10.1007/s12117-012-9173-1

Latonero M (2011) Human Trafficking Online: The Role of Social Networking Sites and Online Classifieds. University of Southern California, Los Angeles

Latonero M (2012) The Rise of Mobile and the Diffusion of Technology-Facilitated Trafficking. University of Southern California, Los Angeles

Lebov K (2010) Human Trafficking in Scotland. Eur J Criminol 7(1):77–93. https://doi.org/10.1177/1477370809347944

Leukfeldt ER, Kleemans ER, Stol WP (2017) A Typology of Cybercriminal Networks: From Low-tech All-rounders to High-tech Specialists. Crime Law Soc Chang 67(1):21–37. https://doi.org/10.1007/s10611-016-9662-2

Malloch M (2017) Exploring Available Knowledge and Evidence on Prostitution in Scotland via Practitioner-based Interviews. Edinburgh, Scottish Government

Mancuso M (2013) Not All Madams have a Central Role: Analysis of a Nigerian Sex Trafficking Network. Trends Organ Crime 17(1–2):66–88. https://doi.org/10.1007/s12117-013-9199-z

McRedmond P (2010) Defining Organized Crime in the Context of Human Trafficking. In: Wylie G, McRedmond P (eds) Human Trafficking in Europe: Character, Causes and Consequences, 1st edn. Palgrave Macmillan, Basingstoke, pp 181–197

Morselli C (2005) Contacts, Opportunities, and Criminal Enterprise, 1st edn. University of Toronto Press, Toronto

Morselli C (2009) Inside Criminal Networks, 1st edn. Springer, New York

Morselli C, Giguère C (2006) Legitimate Strengths in Criminal Networks. Crime Law Soc Chang 45(3):185–200. https://doi.org/10.1007/s10611-006-9034-4

Morselli C, Petit K (2007) Law-Enforcement Disruption of a Drug Importation Network. Glob Crime 8(2):109–130. https://doi.org/10.1080/17440570701362208

Morselli C, Roy J (2008) Brokerage Qualifications in Ringing Operations. Criminology 46(1):71–98. https://doi.org/10.1111/j.1745-9125.2008.00103.x

Morselli C, Royer M-N (2008) Criminal Mobility and Criminal Achievement. J Res Crime Delinq 45(1):4–21. https://doi.org/10.1177/0022427807309630

Morselli C, Giguère C, Petit K (2007) The Efficiency/Security Trade-off in Criminal Networks. Soc Netw 29(1):143–153. https://doi.org/10.1016/j.socnet.2006.05.001

Morselli C, Turcotte M, Tenti V (2011) The Mobility of Criminal Groups. Glob Crime 12(3):165–188. https://doi.org/10.1080/17440572.2011.589593

Morselli C, Weitzer R, Zhang SX, Savoie-Gargiso I (2014) Coercion, Control, and Cooperation in a Prostitution Ring. Ann Am Acad Pol Soc Sci 653(1):247–265. https://doi.org/10.1177/0002716214521995

NCA (2014) National Strategic Assessment of Serious and Organised Crime 2014. National Crime Agency, London

Oso Casas L (2009) Money, Sex, Love and the Family: Economic and Affective Strategies of Latin American Sex Workers in Spain. J Ethn Migr Stud 36(1):47–65. https://doi.org/10.1080/13691830903250899

Phipps A (2013) Violence Against Sex Workers. In: McMillan L, Lombard N (eds) Violence Against Women. Jessica Kingsley Publishers, London, pp 87–102

Plambech S (2017) Sex, Deportation and Rescue: Economies of Migration among Nigerian Sex Workers. Fem Econ 23(3):134–159. https://doi.org/10.1080/13545701.2016.1181272

Rigby P, Owens L, Shapira M (2017) Child Sexual Exploitation: A Multi-Agency Case Study. Child Protection Committee Glasgow, University of Stirling, Stirling

Sanders T, Scoular J, Campbell R, Pitcher J, Cunningham S (2018) Internet Sex Work: Beyond the Gaze, 1st edn. Springer Nature, Cham

Sarkar S (2014) Trans-Border Sex Trafficking: Identifying Cases and Victims in the UK. Migrat Dev 3(1):95–107. https://doi.org/10.1080/21632324.2013.869958

Sarkar S (2015) Use of Technology in Human Trafficking Networks and Sexual exploitation: A Cross-sectional Multi-country Study. Transnational Soc Rev 5(1):55–68. https://doi.org/10.1080/21931674.2014.991184

Scoular J, Pitcher J, Sanders T, Cunningham S, Campbell R (2019) Beyond the Gaze and Well Beyond Wolfenden: The Practices and Rationalities of Regulating and Policing Sex Work in the Digital Age. J Law Soc 46(2):211–239

Silverstone D (2011) From Triads to Snakeheads: Organised Crime and Illegal Migration Within Britain's Chinese Community. Glob Crime 12(2):93–111. https://doi.org/10.1080/17440572.2011.567831

Turner J (2016) Root Causes, Transnational Mobility and Formations of Patriarchy in the Sex Trafficking of Women. In: Malloch M, Rigby P (eds) Human Trafficking: The Complexities of Exploitation, 1st edn. Edinburgh University Press, Edinburgh, pp 194–209

Van De Bunt H, Siegel D, Zaitch D (2014) The Social Embeddedness of Organized Crime. In: Paoli L (ed) The Oxford Handbook of Organized Crime, 1st edn. Oxford University Press, Oxford, pp 321–342

Verhoeven M (2017) Government Policies and Sex Work Realities: Human Trafficking in the Regulated Sex Industry. In: Government Policies and Sex Work Realities: Human Trafficking in the Regulated Sex Industry. Vrije Universiteit, Amsterdam

Verhoeven M, van Gestel B, de Jong D, Kleemans E (2013) Relationships Between Suspects and Victims of Sex Trafficking. Exploitation of Prostitutes and Domestic Violence Parallels in Dutch Trafficking Cases. Eur J Crim Policy Res 21(1):49–64. https://doi.org/10.1007/s10610-013-9226-2

Walby S, Apitzsch B, Armstrong J, Balderston S, Follis K, Francis B, Kelly L, May-Chahal C, Rashid A, Shire K, Towers J, Tunte M (2016) Study on the

Gender Dimension of Trafficking in Human Beings: Final Report. European Commission, Luxembourg

Wijkman M, Kleemans E (2019) Female Offenders of Human Trafficking and Sexual Exploitation. Crime Law Soc Chang 72(1):53–72. https://doi.org/10.1007/s10611-019-09840-x

Zimmermann C, Hossain M, Yun K, Roche B, Morison L, Watts C (2006) Stolen Smiles: A Summary Report on the Physical and Psychological Health Consequences of Women and Adolescents Trafficked in Europe. The London School of Hygiene & Tropical Medicine, London

Digital Traces, Big Data and Epistemological Shifts

The Big Data Paradigm

In the later stages of our networked society (Castells 2010), data are constantly produced in myriad ways. Plurality is key in this context, as data can involve everything from images, voice recordings, sensor readings or unstructured text gleaned from social media. Emerging forms of data are often ill-suited for traditional forms of statistical analysis; 'found' data are often relational and dynamic (Törnberg and Törnberg 2018). This necessitates novel analytical techniques to derive structure from vast, noisy and sometimes unconnected datasets (Kitchin 2014). It was noted in earlier chapters that sexual labour is increasingly augmented with a digital dimension. Because technology is used extensively, predominantly to advertise sexual services, all types of networks leave publicly available digital traces, including criminal networks facilitating exploitation. UK police forces are already monitoring adult services websites (ASWs) to gather intelligence on sex trafficking (Scoular et al. 2019), and the interest within and beyond academia to produce 'actionable intelligence' in this context has risen sharply. However, analysing digital traces is difficult, predominantly because of the epistemological challenges associated

R. Kjellgren, *Internet-Mediated Exploitation in the Scottish Online Sex Market*,
Transnational Crime, Crime Control and Security,
https://doi.org/10.1007/978-3-032-09275-5_5

with this type of data (Kjellgren 2022). Much of the current research is preoccupied with identifying patterns indicative of sex trafficking, implicitly assuming that those can be distinguished from the data and patterns generated by independent sex workers. However, in doing so, many neglect the social context in which exploitation occurs and even fail to consider the precise role and utility of open-source intelligence (OSINT) in policing sex trafficking.

Big data usually involves huge datasets, although this is not necessarily its defining feature. According to Boyd and Crawford (2012, p. 663), what characterises big data is "the capacity to search, aggregate and cross-reference" large, heterogeneous, granular and noisy datasets (Resnyansky 2019). Big data analytics, in turn, usually involve new forms of primarily inductive statistical approaches (Resnyansky 2019). Often, big data analytics are framed as a powerful tool capable of addressing fundamentally social problems (Boyd and Crawford 2012; Bunnik et al. 2016). Nevertheless, the promises of big data rest on epistemological assumptions quite far detached from the social sciences. In fact, the emergence and widespread adoption of big data analytics resemble a paradigm shift (Kitchin 2014).

Indeed, there is an emphasis on descriptive patterns and their utility at the expense of reflecting more critically upon issues of validity and causality (DiMaggio 2015). Contrary to epistemological approaches associated with the social sciences, big data are often preoccupied with gaining insights from the data itself, thus rejecting the value of theory and knowledge *a priori* (Kitchin 2014). To process huge quantities of data, and to do so inductively, requires new forms of analysis. Algorithms form the basis of this paradigm and are suggested by big data evangelists to make decision-making more informed and objective (Christin 2017). In its essence, algorithms are computational procedures, consisting of sequences of instructions, designed to solve particular problems or perform specific tasks (Dourish 2016). Algorithms, as mathematical constructs, traditionally require their designer to specify the rules to achieve the designated task; however, what has dramatically changed the algorithmic landscape is the development of machine learning (Mittelstadt et al. 2016). The principal strength of machine learning lies in its capacity to redefine or modify decision-making rules autonomously by responding to input data fed to the algorithms (Mittelstadt et al. 2016).

Various models are employed depending on the nature of the data and the desired outcome, for instance, logistic regression, neural networks and Naïve Bayes (Burrell 2016). In turn, the model offering the best fit can be applied to the 'unseen data' to derive structure based on what the model previously learned. There are different approaches to machine learning, and a crucial distinction can be made between supervised and unsupervised learning. In the former, the model seeks to identify the variables that best improve model fitness in predicting a predefined outcome variable (Bechmann and Bowker 2019). In contrast, in unsupervised learning, input data are used in attempts to build the best model by inductively classifying the data into different categories.

Machine learning is part of a wider spectrum of artificial intelligence, and often, these methods are focused on extracting some form of 'actionable knowledge' from vast quantities of data (Reid 2016). Consequently, big data is often framed as superior at decision-making simply because algorithms can process more data than humans (Christin 2017). An extension of this argument also pertains that algorithms are more objective than humans, and thus capable of making value-neutral decisions (Christin 2017). In combination with the widespread adoption of social media, big data analytics is increasingly important to security agencies and law enforcement. The processing of vast amounts of data is an alluring prospect for organisations tasked with producing intelligence to inform decision-making (Smith 2018), and the policing of sex trafficking and exploitation has not been exempted from this. However, as shall become increasingly clear as we progress throughout this chapter, there are numerous pitfalls in atheoretical analyses, which an abundance of data and sophisticated algorithms seldom can remedy.

The Trafficking-Technology Nexus: Paradigmatic Shifts in Anti-Trafficking?

Concerns about the role of online technologies in facilitating exploitation are nothing new. For instance, Hughes (2002, p. 146) noted:

> The use of new communication and information technologies for the sexual exploitation of women and children is creating a crisis for women and children's status, rights, and dignity all over the world … [sexual exploitation] continues to grow with the increased number of users on the internet.

Close to 20 years later, there are still uncertainties in regard to precisely how this 'trafficking-technology nexus' works (Musto and Boyd 2014; Milivojevic and Segrave 2017; Volodko et al. 2019), and as was noted in chapter "Criminal Networks, Opportunity Structures and the Process of Exploitation", there is a lack of robust empirical evidence on how exploiters use technology to facilitate exploitation. Within the narrative surrounding this nexus, the distinction between prostitution and trafficking is often neglected. Moreover, technology is paradoxically constructed both as a dangerous threat to the wellbeing of women and children and as a powerful disrupting force of exploitation and trafficking (Musto and Boyd 2014). Promulgating this narrative is a coalition of data scientists, anti-trafficking advocates, tech companies and non-governmental organisations (NGOs), who perceive the emergence of new technologies as the driving force behind trafficking, and technological innovation as the means to end human trafficking. The founder of DeliverFund, a non-profit organisation devoted to eradicating modern slavery by technological means, exemplifies this atheoretical, paradigmatic shift in anti-trafficking:

> Our generation is the first to leverage internet technology as a scalable solution to social injustice … we understand the technology being used to exploit these slaves, therefore our generation is uniquely positioned to end this scourge. (McKinley 2017)

It becomes obvious that the paradigmatic shift resulting from the widespread adoption of big data analytics also has spread its influence on the debate surrounding exploitation and trafficking. However, flawed understandings of these phenomena, in combination with epistemological assumptions and methods associated with big data, can have serious consequences for sex workers and migrants if applied uncritically to the issue of trafficking (Musto and Boyd 2014). Perhaps the most pressing concern is that a deeply complex social problem is reconfigured into a technological issue, which effectively diverts attention from social structures and processes contributing to the emergence and expansion of exploitation in the first place (Kjellgren 2022). In addition, such flawed beliefs also produce a type of knowledge that is neither valuable for policy nor reflective of the lived experiences of exploitation. In other words, there is a danger when actors with limited understandings of exploitation are involved in producing knowledge for policy-makers and developing software solutions for law enforcement. To date, various anti-trafficking software has been adopted by several jurisdictions within the US (Deeb-Swihart et al. 2019), and within the UK, some forces have already begun to experiment with these 'solutions' (Kearns and Muir 2019). Even though the often-assumed trafficking-technology nexus is poorly understood, it has nevertheless risen to prominence within the big data community. As a result, several studies have been published throughout the last decade, which further exacerbates the misconceptions and uncertainties associated with this nexus.

The following paragraphs will unpack some of the research aimed at generating actionable intelligence from digital traces. Research on sex trafficking and exploitation utilising digital traces tends to fall within two distinct categories: social scientific studies, primarily qualitative, relying on relatively small samples and computationally limited methods, manual harvesting of data, visual examinations and little to no statistical methods; and research situated within the computer sciences, lacking in theory and empirical rigour, and using big data analytics and vast sample sizes.

In an exploratory study from the UK, Skidmore et al. (2018) sought to identify sex workers potentially vulnerable to exploitation and trafficking by analysing online sex worker profiles at AdultWork. The researchers used a case-study approach and extracted the profiles and phone numbers of active sex workers within the South West of England (n = 795). In total, they identified 18 discrete groups from their sample; some groups were argued to be at an increased risk due to offering risky services and involving movement. The approach used by Skidmore et al. (2018) certainly demonstrates that interesting patterns can be derived from analysing online profiles from a policing perspective; though, as the authors do point out, it is currently unclear precisely what indicators are reliable in this context, and we must be cautious in how we interpret this type of data.

Volodko et al. (2019) approached exploitation from a more critical lens and used quantitative methods to substantiate their argument. Though focused on labour trafficking, it still offers valuable methodological contributions. Also relying on a case study approach, the researchers focused on online job advertisements (n = 430) from a Lithuanian website dedicated to people seeking employment abroad. The authors sought to examine the prevalence of indicators commonly outlined as central to labour trafficking (see Volodko et al. 2019, p. 8). A quantitative content analysis was performed in which the presence or absence of ten different indicators was dichotomously coded. A median of three indicators was identified across the sample, and virtually all adverts contained at least one indicator. Perhaps the most valuable indicator used—violations of working hour regulations and national minimum wage—was present in a fifth of all advertisements. Whilst Volodko et al. (2019) effectively demonstrate how difficult it is to assess the possibility of exploitation through the application of typically 'offline' indicators to an online context, they also show how the prevalence of multiple indicators, when analysed in relation to each other, can help to narrow down suspected instances of labour trafficking. Volodko et al. (2019) provided a valuable case study, underpinned by the well-grounded assumption that exploitation must be tackled on a continuum, which effectively utilises online data to explore a phenomenon difficult to study due to its clandestine nature.

Antonopoulos et al. (2020) examined the role of technology in human smuggling and trafficking, taking a case study approach and utilising a mixture of data sources from Italy and the UK. Relevant to this section is the virtual ethnography of the surface and dark web, in which the researchers set out to "gather primary data on the role played by the Internet in the recruitment, transportation/entry … and exploitation stages of the process of human trafficking" (Antonopoulos et al. 2020, p. 5). Immediately, it becomes quite clear that the researchers could benefit from a more critical approach: assuming that online data can be considered 'primary data' on human trafficking is only a valid assumption in circumstances when this can be ascertained by more reliable forms of evidence (e.g., police intelligence; closed cases). Using an exploratory approach, keywords were identified and used within searches on social networking sites and search engines; however, the keywords themselves are very dubious (e.g., brothel, prostitute, sex worker, model), and it is unclear how these would be capable of distinguishing between exploitation and sex work. In regard to the Italian case study, the authors go on to argue that elements such as advertisements involving third parties, shared phone numbers and inconsistent details are "indicating the presence of sex forced activities [*sic*]" (Antonopoulos et al. 2020, p. 28). The UK case study appears to have involved a spasmodic analysis of online escort adverts, and amongst other findings, the authors report thus:

> In one striking example, we found the presence of a potentially widespread trafficking ring operating in several areas of London, in which several Eastern European women were listed as being "hot new girls", "sexy girls", "new VIP party girls", or "new girls in London" under the same set of mobile phone numbers, and with all profiles exhibiting the same writing style. (Antonopoulos et al. 2020, p. 58)

> [T]he poor use of the language of the country in the profile text – in our case English – regarding spelling, grammatical and punctuation errors can point to *two robust indications of trafficking*. (Antonopoulos et al. 2020, p. 63, emphasis added)

These sentiments are unconvincing and could be equally indicative of migrant sex worker collectives. Similarly, the authors fail to grasp the complex (and unknown) relationship between the poster(s) of the adverts and the data themselves: the data are by no means (necessarily) reflective of reality but are, after all, digital traces of online marketing strategies, of which we currently possess very limited knowledge. Put differently, the online marketing strategies within escort adverts do not allow for the contextual understandings required to differentiate exploitation from other forms of sexual labour (Kjellgren 2022). It is very bold of Antonopoulos and colleagues (2020) to equate anecdotal, decontextualised online data as equivalent to "robust indications" of actual instances of human trafficking, and then go on to conclude that:

> An important implication of our findings, which is specific to the UK context, regards a possible reappraisal of the prevalence of smuggling and human trafficking. (Antonopoulos et al. 2020, p. 66)

This is a particularly problematic and empirically unsubstantiated claim; relying on an unsystematic and by no means quantitative approach to analysing escort adverts does very little to illuminate the extent of trafficking.

Whereas the three studies discussed are based within the social sciences, the vast majority of studies produced are within the data sciences, and associated with the earlier discussed big data paradigm. Kennedy (2012, p. 9), the co-founder of the anti-trafficking tech company Marinus Analytics,[1] argues that "sex advertisement data can help understand patterns of sex trafficking". Drawing on adverts from Backpage,[2] Kennedy (2012) attempted to identify three different kinds of adverts: those potentially representing underage victims; posts indicative of movement; and adverts suggesting a 'shared management' situation. However, a deeply problematic assumption of the latter two categories is that they are equated with trafficking, thus failing to recognise that sex workers can be organised without being the result of trafficking. Moreover, independent sex workers also travel to generate more revenue. Earlier studies exploring digital traces focused on constructing large-scale databases without conducting any form of meaningful analysis and instead presented the proposed methodologies and practical demonstrations as equivalent to

[1] https://www.marinusanalytics.com/.

[2] Backpage was an online classified website popular for the advertising of sexual services. It was subsequently shut down by the FBI in 2018 for facilitating the advertisement of child sexual exploitation.

empirical evidence. For instance, Wang et al. (2012, p. 249) compiled online escort adverts (n = 483,000), including images (n = 1,800,000), and used posts "believed to be those of minors" as a training set to inform machine learning algorithms, without any meaningful elaboration on the features *believed* to be indicative of trafficking.

Hovy et al. (2014) designed a system to identify underage victims of sex trafficking from online adverts, focusing in particular on extracting metadata to track the possible movement of individuals. A similarity matching algorithm was used to compute near neighbours from the textual component of the adverts, and adverts sharing facial images were also treated as related. The authors claim to filter out irrelevant adverts (i.e., those not indicative of underage victims), but they fail to describe this process. Whilst they develop a convincing querying system, capable of identifying clusters of adverts and mobility patterns, there is a lack of critical discussion regarding false-positives. In other words, when using measures of similarity, and a threshold is used to determine when two adverts are related, there is always a risk that the relationships identified are spurious. After all, adverts are produced to appeal to the market, and we would expect phrases to be similar, even if there is no meaningful offline connection.

Lopez and Truesdale-Moore (2020) also show a concerning lack of understanding of trafficking in their research on the spatial characteristics of human trafficking. Whilst they are right in pointing out that the geographical distribution of sex trafficking is important in informing policy and intervention, their analysis is less convincing since it is based on prostitution arrests rather than any data actually involving sex trafficking. In this case, it is not that their choice of methods is inappropriate, only their interpretation of what their data represents. As a point of comparison, Voloshin et al. (2016) sought to understand the spatial characteristics of the off-street sex market within St. Petersburg. With one dataset consisting of the locations of various venues and facilities, and sociologically meaningful variables (e.g., health and socioeconomic inequalities) and another dataset of geocoded sex worker profiles (n = 1796), the authors used various machine learning algorithms to build models capable of predicting the location of the profiles. The more successful models were demonstrated to produce hot spots similar to the actual distribution of sex worker profiles. Whilst this study uses similar methods and data as other studies reviewed, the authors are indeed careful not to generalise the patterns identified outwith their immediate context, that is, the spatial distribution of adverts and associated predictors.

Shahrokh Esfahani et al. (2019) attempted to move away from using keywords in mining escort adverts by using topic modelling. This is a form of unsupervised machine learning aimed at uncovering topics prevalent within a corpus, and the authors used it "to engineer features that allowed for understanding the context of sexual ads" (Shahrokh Esfahani et al. 2019, p. 1183). The authors claimed to use "a database consisting of phone numbers associated with trafficking victims, constructed in conjunction with human trafficking domain experts" (Shahrokh Esfahani et al. 2019, p. 1181). Unfortunately, they provide no other information regarding this database, how they obtained the data, nor how the victim status has been confirmed. Nevertheless, what is clear is that they do not offer any convincing evidence to suggest that they have achieved a contextual understanding of the adverts; instead, they only present the prediction rates of their models. As Mützel (2015) points out, topic modelling still requires substantive interpretation, albeit later in the analysis (i.e., the machine uncovers the topics, and the reader interprets them). These data, digital traces taken out of context, can only be made meaningful if the interpreter is aware of the contexts in which they are produced (Boyd and Crawford 2012; Bornakke and Due 2018).

In a similar vein, Dubrawski et al. (2015) analysed 37,000 online escort adverts, of which 40% were claimed to contain phone numbers of 'known' traffickers, obtained by a victim advocacy group. The authors do not elaborate on any distinguishing features between adverts labelled as trafficking versus those that are not. In addition to this, they also demonstrate how entity resolution, a machine learning function aimed at identifying plausible links utilising 'weak' features (e.g., age, ethnicity and physical characteristics) in the absence of strong features (e.g., shared phone numbers), can be used to identify links between adverts. This approach seems particularly promising in linking adverts across large datasets, and tracking movement over time, in which phone numbers may change.

Drawing on the work of Dubrawski et al. (2015), Nagpal et al. (2017) applied a similar methodology to a substantially larger dataset of approximately five million online adverts. Entity resolution was used to predict if two adverts originated from the same source, using phone numbers as a strong feature. Once clusters of adverts had been identified, those deemed indicative of sex trafficking were isolated and subject to a random forest classification algorithm to predict adverts linked to trafficking. While this approach has merit, particularly in its capability to process huge amounts of textual data and identify structures, it is less certain that they capture adverts indicative of trafficking. Indeed, there is no discussion of what the patterns are actually indicative of; without a valid 'ground-truth' dataset, it is difficult to claim that the approach is effective at identifying sex trafficking. Hundman et al. (2018) offer a more promising approach and claim to have a repository of over a hundred million online adverts. Whilst their models assume trafficking to be a binary, part of their training data consists of adverts provided by law enforcement, either historical, recent or suspected cases of trafficking. Nevertheless, they do not contribute with any details as to exactly how these cases differ from adverts deemed unrelated to trafficking, nor how many adverts they analyse, which are actual cases of trafficking. Such knowledge, rather than model accuracy scores, could potentially make a meaningful contribution to our understanding of internet-mediated exploitation.

Epistemological Conundrums and Confusion

A number of questionable epistemological assumptions seem to underpin much of the big data-oriented research reviewed. Most concerning appears to be a lack of understanding of what escort adverts—as a form of data—are actually representing. Escort adverts cannot be understood outwith their immediate context, and any patterns found within them will only become meaningful to the extent that we have adequate conceptual frames for interpreting them (Dourish and Gómez Cruz 2018). For example, much of the examined literature seeks to identify the movement patterns of trafficking victims. Whilst there is merit in doing so, if done uncritically—and without a theoretically informed frame—efforts are likely to conflate victims of exploitation with sex workers 'on tour' (Scoular et al. 2019); after all, both the criminal networks moving victims and those working out of their own volition appeal to localised demand and seek to maximise their profit margins by relocating to new markets. If we continue to ignore the pivotal and complex role that agency plays in delineating sex trafficking vis-à-vis sex work, we will undoubtedly fail at achieving this through big data analytics.

An important lesson from these studies is that biased training data can further entrench inequalities and contribute to ill-informed policing (Benbouzid 2019). In other words, most training data used are based on speculations and imaginations of how patterns of criminal networks are manifested online. Without an adequate theoretical understanding of exploitation, these speculations will be biased towards more simplistic assumptions of trafficking. Gradecki and Curry (2017, p. 4) highlight an important point related to this: "Automated classification does not make erroneous data more accurate, it only automates the same errors across a larger dataset". Suppose we perceive trafficking as a dichotomous phenomenon and continue to label adverts as indicative or not indicative of trafficking. In that case, machine learning will only reinforce (and exacerbate) this binary and take us further from a more nuanced understanding, recognising exploitation within a continuum of experiences (Kjellgren 2022).

It has previously been reported that characteristics such as age, ethnicity and nationality are used in this context to appeal to clients seeking novelty and other characteristics possessed by sex workers (e.g., Antonopoulos et al. 2020). Kitchin (2014, pp. 4–5), though referring more broadly to big data, perfectly captures the point that online data are produced and situated in particular contexts:

> data are not simply natural and essential elements that are abstracted from the world in neutral and objective ways and can be accepted at face value; data are created within a complex assemblage that actively shapes its constitution.

The patterns identified from escort adverts cannot be divorced from the wider context in which they are produced; they allow us to observe patterns indicative of certain marketing strategies, and the extent to which patterns differ between sex workers and criminal networks is still unclear. Unless we understand sex trafficking, the sex market and the wider theoretical landscape dedicated to explaining these phenomena, we are unlikely to produce any meaningful insights. The literature reviewed did include several methodologically impressive contributions, and amongst them, advanced forms of machine learning capable of clustering adverts together into elaborate networks and patterns. Certainly, social behaviour mediated by online technologies offers an exciting new avenue for social scientists to explore, though fruitful analyses can only be conducted if we account for the limitations inherent to the data (Breiger 2015; Lewis 2015), and most important of all, never assume that data can speak for themselves (Kitchin 2014).

Whilst classification is an important cornerstone of scientific investigation and reasoning, the very act of classifying items will inevitably favour some categories at the expense of others (Bechmann and Bowker 2019). How are we, conceptually and algorithmically, to draw a firm line between sex workers and trafficking victims, when experiences of exploitation fall along a continuous variable rather than, as is often assumed, a discrete one? There is no easy answer to this question. It is important to remember that algorithms used in machine learning often rely on fairly novel variables in predictive efforts (e.g., emoticons, semantics, keywords); whatever categories are derived from these will need to be translated back into fundamentally sociological categories (Bolin and Andersson Schwarz 2015), for instance, victim, non-victim, independent worker and so forth. When we collapse noisy and unstructured data into categorical variables, we inevitably reduce much of its complexities, and often, this occurs at the expense of not adequately examining the features associated with each category. This has been evident in many of the studies reviewed, in which only the accuracy scores from models are presented (and often disguised as empirical evidence). What could have contributed to meaningful insights would have been an examination of which features distinguish, say, independent sex workers, from sex workers organised within collectives, or those deemed at greatest risk of exploitation. The theoretical validity of such features could thence be examined by comparing them to the rich body of theory and empirical research that has previously been highlighted throughout this literature review.

In the quest for actionable intelligence, the ethics of big data-oriented and predictive policing are often ignored. Kaufmann et al. (2019) argue that the patterns derived from big data analytics seldom encourage critical reflection on how they were produced but rather appeal to a policing culture of metrification and efficiency. However, without delving into the details of these patterns and without appropriate reflection, contextualisation and narration, we are unlikely to understand the significance of patterns of criminality (Kaufmann et al. 2019). Few studies consider the extent to which OSINT is useful, and under the precise circumstances, this type of intelligence is valuable; there appears to be an implicit assumption that because data are available, it must be important to police sex trafficking. More concerning, there is no consideration of the collateral consequences and intrusion of sex workers' privacy that stems from this type of surveillance.

The process of collecting and analysing data on *everyone*, as opposed to individuals under suspicion, has previously been referred to as *dragnet surveillance* (Brayne 2020). *All* escort adverts are collected and scrutinised in this research context, including those posted by independent sex workers. The application of dubious and unsubstantiated indicators of human trafficking, as argued by De Vries and Cockbain (2023, p. 1), "can give an undue illusion of objectivity and reliability when they are neither neutral nor unskewed". The labelling of escort adverts as suspicious of trafficking is often justified due to this supposed objectivity in decision-making, and independent sex workers risk intense police scrutiny. Eusebi et al. (2022) have pointed out that algorithmic decision-making can severely impact individuals' life trajectories. In this context, being algorithmically labelled as a trafficking victim can trigger a police response, which, in the worst case, could lead to the arrest, detention or deportation of sex workers (Malloch 2016). Ethical considerations must be at the heart of investigations into the trafficking-technology nexus since poor research can have serious consequences for the people involved in the sex market.

To summarise, technological changes throughout society have contributed to abundant digital data. Novel analytical methods are often required to make sense of patterns in vast collections of digital traces, leading to an epistemological shift. At this atheoretical turn, prediction and inductive analysis are perceived as favourable to the traditionally deductive and theoretically informed epistemologies associated with social scientific inquiry. These changes have also impacted research into the trafficking-technology nexus, where the obsession with model prediction obscures the crucial role that theory plays in understanding the online dimension of exploitation. Because most research in this domain is directed towards the policing of trafficking, the inadequate understandings underpinning much of the research are deeply problematic. Research into the trafficking-technology nexus must be theoretically grounded and sensitive to the many complexities associated with exploitation, or risk causing more harm than benefit to the populations involved in the sex market.

References

Antonopoulos GA, Baratto G, Di Nicola A, Diba P, Martini E, Papanicolaou G, Terenghi F (2020) Technology in Human Smuggling and Trafficking: Case Studies from Italy and the United Kingdom, 1st edn. Springer, Cham

Bechmann A, Bowker GC (2019) Unsupervised by Any Other Name: Hidden Layers of Knowledge Production in Artificial Intelligence on Social Media. Big Data Soc 6(1):1–11. https://doi.org/10.1177/2053951718819569

Benbouzid B (2019) To Predict and to Manage. Predictive Policing in the United States. Big Data Soc 6(1):1–13. https://doi.org/10.1177/2053951719861703

Bolin G, Andersson Schwarz J (2015) Heuristics of the Algorithm: Big Data, User Interpretation and Institutional Translation. Big Data Soc 2(2):205395171560840. https://doi.org/10.1177/2053951715608406

Bornakke T, Due BL (2018) Big–Thick Blending: A Method for Mixing Analytical Insights from Big and Thick Data Sources. Big Data Soc 5(1):1–16. https://doi.org/10.1177/2053951718765026

Boyd D, Crawford K (2012) Critical Questions for Big Data: Provocations for a Cultural, Technological, and Scholarly Phenomenon. J Inf Commun Soc 15(5):662–679

Brayne S (2020) Predict and Surveil: Data, Discretion, and the Future of Policing. Oxford University Press, New York

Breiger RL (2015) Scaling Down. Big Data Soc 2(2). https://doi.org/10.1177/2053951715602497

Bunnik A, Cawley A, Mulqueen M, Zwitter A (2016) Introduction to Big Data Challenges. In: Bunnik A, Cawley A, Mulqueen M, Zwitter A (eds) Big Data Challenges: Society, Security, Innovation and Ethics, 1st edn. Palgrave Macmillan, Basingstoke, pp 1–8

Burrell J (2016) How the Machine 'Thinks': Understanding Opacity in Machine Learning Algorithms. Big Data Soc 3(1):1–12. https://doi.org/10.1177/2053951715622512

Castells M (2010) The Rise of the Network Society, 2nd edn. John Wiley & Sons, Ltd., Chichester

Christin A (2017) Algorithms in Practice: Comparing Web Journalism and Criminal Justice. Big Data Soc 4(2):1–14. https://doi.org/10.1177/2053951717718855

De Vries I, Cockbain E (2023) Governing Through Indicators: Structural Biases and Empirical Challenges in Indicator-Based Approaches to Human Trafficking Research and Policy. In: Faulkner E (ed) Modern Slavery in Global Context. Bristol University Press, Bristol

Deeb-Swihart J, Endert A, Bruckman A (2019) Understanding Law Enforcement Strategies and Needs for Combating Human Trafficking. In: Proceedings of the 2019 CHI Conference on Human Factors in Computing Systems, Chicago, pp 1–14

DiMaggio P (2015) Adapting Computational Text Analysis to Social Science (and Vice Versa). Big Data Soc 2(2):1–5. https://doi.org/10.1177/2053951715602908

Dourish P (2016) Algorithms and Their Others: Algorithmic Culture in Context. Big Data Soc 3(2):1–11. https://doi.org/10.1177/2053951716665128

Dourish P, Gómez Cruz E (2018) Datafication and Data Fiction: Narrating Data and Narrating with Data. Big Data Soc 5(2):1–10. https://doi.org/10.1177/2053951718784083

Dubrawski A, Miller K, Barnes M, Boecking B, Kennedy E (2015) Leveraging Publicly Available Data to Discern Patterns of Human-Trafficking Activity. J Hum Traffick 1(1):65–85. https://doi.org/10.1080/23322705.2015.1015342

Eusebi A, Vasek M, Cockbain E, Mariconti E (2022) The Ethics of Going Deep: Challenges in Machine Learning for Sensitive Security Domains. IEEE European Symposium on Security and Privacy Workshops. Genoa, In, pp 533–537

Gradecki J, Curry D (2017) Crowd-Sourced Intelligence Agency: Prototyping counterveillance. Big Data Soc 4(1):1–7. https://doi.org/10.1177/2053951717693259

Hovy E, Bryan NM, Philpot A, Silva DR, Sundararajan A (2014) Data Integration from Open Internet Sources and Network Detection to Combat Underage Sex Trafficking. In: Proceedings of the 15th Annual International Conference on Digital Government Research

Hughes DM (2002) The Use of New Communications and Information Technologies for Sexual Exploitation of Women and Children. Hastings Women's L J 13(1):127–146

Hundman K, Kejriwal M, Gowda T, Boecking B (2018) Always Lurking: Understanding and Mitigating Bias in Online Human Trafficking Detection. In: Proceedings of the 2018 AAAI/ACM Conference on AI, Ethics, and Society, pp 137–143

Kaufmann M, Egbert S, Leese M (2019) Predictive Policing and the Politics of Patterns. Brit J Criminol 59(3):674–692. https://doi.org/10.1093/bjc/azy060

Kearns I, Muir R (2019) Data-driven Policing and Public Value. The Police Foundation, London

Kennedy E (2012) Predictive Patterns of Sex Trafficking Online. Carnegie Mellon University

Kitchin R (2014) Big Data, New Epistemologies and Paradigm Shifts. Big Data Soc 1(1):1–12. https://doi.org/10.1177/2053951714528481

Kjellgren R (2022) Good Tech, Bad Tech: Policing Sex Trafficking with Big Data. Int J Crime Justice Soc Democr 11(1):149–166. https://doi.org/10.3316/agispt.20220412065553

Lewis K (2015) Three Fallacies of Digital Footprints. Big Data Soc 2(2):1–4. https://doi.org/10.1177/2053951715602496

Lopez JJ, Truesdale-Moore S (2020) The Use of Spatial Statistics to Control Human and Sex Trafficking. Int J Soc Sci Humanit 10(2):57–61. https://doi.org/10.18178/ijssh.2020.10.2.1014

Malloch M (2016) Criminalising Victims of Human Trafficking: State Responses and Punitive Practices. In: Malloch M, Rigby P (eds) Human Trafficking: The Complexities of Exploitation. Edinburgh University Press, Edinburgh, pp 175–193

McKinley N (2017) Our Generation and the Fight Against Slavery. Huffpost, 6 December. https://www.huffpost.com/entry/our-generation-and-the-fi_b_9996634

Milivojevic S, Segrave M (2017) Gendered Exploitation in the Digital Border Crossing? An Analysis of the Human Trafficking and Information Technology Nexus. In: Gender, Technology and Violence. Routledge, pp 28–44

Mittelstadt BD, Allo P, Taddeo M, Wachter S, Floridi L (2016) The Ethics of Algorithms: Mapping the Debate. Big Data Soc 3(2). https://doi.org/10.1177/2053951716679679

Musto JL, Boyd D (2014) The Trafficking-Technology Nexus. Soc Polit Int Stud Gend State Soc 21(3):461–483. https://doi.org/10.1093/sp/jxu018

Mützel S (2015) Facing Big Data: Making Sociology Relevant. Big Data Soc 2(2). https://doi.org/10.1177/2053951715599179

Nagpal C, Miller K, Boecking B, Dubrawski A (2017) An Entity Resolution Approach to Isolate Instances of Human Trafficking Online. Carnegie Mellon University, Pittsburgh

Reid D (2016) Man vs. Machine: The Battle for the Soul of Data Science. In: Bunnik A, Cawley A, Mulqueen M, Zwitter A (eds) Big Data Challenges: Society, Security, Innovation and Ethics, 1st edn. Palgrave Macmillan, Basingstoke, pp 11–22

Resnyansky L (2019) Conceptual Frameworks for Social and Cultural Big Data analytics: Answering the Epistemological Challenge. Big Data Soc 6(1):1–12. https://doi.org/10.1177/2053951718823815

Scoular J, Pitcher J, Sanders T, Cunningham S, Campbell R (2019) Beyond the Gaze and Well Beyond Wolfenden: The Practices and Rationalities of Regulating and Policing Sex Work in the Digital Age. J Law Soc 46(2):211–239

Shahrokh Esfahani S, Cafarella MJ, Baran Pouyan M, DeAngelo G, Eneva E, Fano AE (2019) Context-specific Language Modeling for Human Trafficking Detection from Online Advertisements. In: Proceedings of the 57th Annual Meeting of the Association for Computational Linguistics, pp 1180–1184

Skidmore M, Garner S, Desroches C, Saggu N (2018) The Threat of Exploitation in the Adult Sex Market: A Pilot Study of Online Sex Worker Advertisements 1. Policing 12(2):210–218. https://doi.org/10.1093/police/pax007

Smith GJD (2018) Data Doxa: The Affective Consequences of Data Practices. Big Data Soc 5(1):1–12. https://doi.org/10.1177/2053951717751551

Törnberg P, Törnberg A (2018) The Limits of Computation: A Philosophical Critique of Contemporary Big Data Research. Big Data Soc 5(2):1–12. https://doi.org/10.1177/2053951718811843

Volodko A, Cockbain E, Kleinberg B (2019) "Spotting the Signs" of Trafficking Recruitment Online: Exploring the Characteristics of Advertisements Targeted at Migrant Job-Seekers. Trends Organ Crime 23:7–35. https://doi.org/10.1007/s12117-019-09376-5

Voloshin D, Derevitskiy I, Mukhina K, Karbovskii V (2016) Identifying Venues for Female Commercial Sex Work Using Spatial Analysis of Geocoded Advertisements. Procedia Comput Sci 80:345–355. https://doi.org/10.1016/j.procs.2016.05.349

Wang H, Cai C, Philpot A, Latonero M, Hovy EH, Metzler D (2012) Data Integration from Open Internet Sources to Combat Sex Trafficking of Minors. In: Proceedings of the 15th Annual International Conference on Digital Government Research

Methods in Practice: Designing an Effective Workflow in Computational Criminology

Introducing Computational Criminology

Tensions between the disciplines of social science and big data, or data science, in claiming dominion over knowledge production in the social world, are nothing new (Burrows and Savage 2014). In some corners of the debate, it has even, controversially, been suggested that the social sciences have become obsolete in light of rapid advances in big data analytics (Anderson 2008; Mayer-Schönberger and Cukier 2013). The social sciences certainly have a lot to benefit from integrating methods associated with big data analytics, or, more broadly, data science. Nevertheless, it is difficult to see how any meaningful research into the social world can be done without the integration of social theory, epistemology or any form of sociological imagination (Mills 2000). Indeed, Mills (2000, pp. 3, 6) argued:

> Neither the life of an individual nor the history of a society can be understood without understanding both … The sociological imagination enables us to grasp history and biography and the relations between the

R. Kjellgren, *Internet-Mediated Exploitation in the Scottish Online Sex Market*, Transnational Crime, Crime Control and Security,
https://doi.org/10.1007/978-3-032-09275-5_6

> two within society. That is its task and its promise. To recognize this task and this promise is the mark of the classic social analyst.

A significant challenge of contemporary social science is how to apply this sociological imagination to understand how both the lives of individuals and the development of society are shaped by the influence and adoption of networked technologies—such as the internet and smartphones. With much of our day-to-day life mediated, to varying extents, by networked technologies, many of these contemporary challenges are interdisciplinary in nature, requiring both technical skills for working with novel and huge volumes of data and the sociological imagination and theoretical foundation necessary to provide a broader context in which the data can be successfully analysed and interpreted. It is at this intersection that computational social science emerged as a unique field which "leverages the capacity to collect and analyze data with an unprecedented breadth and depth and scale" (Lazer et al. 2009, p. 3). It is this particular fusion of a theory-driven social scientific approach, with the methods and tools from the computer sciences, including programmatic approaches to problem-solving, web scraping and crawling for data collection, and machine learning and artificial intelligence for analysing or making sense of the data, that makes computational social science exceptionally well-suited to respond to emerging socio-technical challenges (Keuschnigg et al. 2018; Brooker 2020).

As criminologists, our primary interest is in studying the contexts, causes and consequences of crime and criminality. Just as networked technologies in many respects have transformed how we live our lives, they have also had a profound impact on crime. Of course, the internet has affected crimes differently. Some types of crime may have been largely unaffected, such as threatening or abusive behaviour, or other forms of public disorder crime, since the internet and networked technologies may be irrelevant to committing such crimes. The internet has also led to new types of crimes in which the internet is required to carry out the crime (i.e., *internet-dependent crime*), for instance, hacking and the spread of malware (McGuire and Dowling 2013). Crimes may also be reconfigured by the emergence of the internet. These types of internet-mediated crimes can be very diverse in nature since they are defined on the basis of involving the internet at some point in the process of committing the crime. Sex trafficking is such a crime: the internet is by no means essential to carry out the crime of sex trafficking, but, depending upon the precise context and situation, it may be beneficial for offenders to use the internet, whether to recruit and groom victims, arrange transportation, advertise victims online or monitor their lives and enforce compliance. Understanding how exploitation in contemporary sex markets is mediated by the internet can be described as a socio-technical challenge, which computational criminology may be uniquely positioned to respond to.

Computational criminology is located at the intersection of digital criminology and computational social science. Whereas both computational criminology and digital technology are focused on studying the influence of technologies, such as the internet, upon crime, criminalisation, law enforcement and the wider justice system, the former integrates methods that are most commonly associated with the computer and data sciences. Internet-mediated exploitation can certainly be studied with methods associated with digital criminology, such as digital ethnography, netnography or more traditional social scientific methods such as qualitative interviewing; however, a central tenet of this book is the importance of fusing criminological and social theory and computational explorations and analysis of data, which can be used to advance our understanding of internet-mediated crime. Recall from chapter "Digital Traces, Big Data and Epistemological Shifts" how it was argued that much of current criminological research on internet-mediated exploitation was underwhelming due to being unable to identify patterns within the sex market, and, conversely, that big data-oriented research on the topic fundamentally misunderstands and misrepresents the social context of the data. The limitations in how the two methodological and disciplinary approaches have attempted to make sense of exploitation illustrate why computational criminology is so important.

The Ethical Challenges of Scraping and Using Open-Source Data

Web scraping is the systematic collection of online data. In its simplest form, it is a way to computationally extract information from a website. Whereas many forms of digital research may involve the researcher browsing, exploring and manually collecting information from websites, and storing it on a computer for future analysis, the obvious limitation of this approach is that it is inefficient when there is a large amount of information to collect. This is where social science can learn valuable lessons from the computer sciences. What is needed is an approach to collect online information which is scalable, and this can be achieved by programming. Using statistical programming and workflow management in the quantitative social sciences is certainly nothing new (Turner and Lambert 2015), but the use of programming to collect data is less common. Imagine that we want to adopt a dog from the local animal shelter, and before making our decision, we want to collect information on the name, age, sex and breed of each dog on the webpage. In order to do this, a simple programmatic approach to collecting this information may involve the following steps:

1. Navigate to the webpage containing a listing of all the animals for adoption, and store the Uniform Resource Locator (URL) as a variable in your programming environment.
2. Instruct your computer to access the URL.
3. Instruct your computer to extract the Hypertext Markup Language (HTML) from the webpage and store that as a new object in your programming environment.
4. Instruct your computer to extract the information of interest from the HTML object.
5. Process the information into a format suitable for analysis (like a dataframe where each row represents one dog and the columns the variables of interest).

Now, this is a very basic example, but the same logic and set of instructions can be modified and used on a much larger scale through the application of programming. An important extension to web scraping is *web crawling*. A crawler, spider, or bot, in this context, is essentially a small program designed to traverse webpages by following the hyperlinks contained within each URL, and then indexing the webpages visited. Combining a crawler with web scraping can thus be a very powerful tool for data collection. An excellent example of how web crawling can be applied to real-world criminological problems is the *Project Arachnid*,[1] in which web crawling is a critical component of their work to detect and combat the spread and proliferation of child sexual abuse materials (CSAM) online. The spider automatically navigates the web to identify and flag CSAM, and using a technique called image and video hashing, the digital footprints of the CSAM can be stored and matched against future instances when the materials are detected online, thus creating valuable actionable intelligence for law enforcement.

For the current case study presented in this book, web crawling was used to systematically collect online escort adverts and store them in an encrypted database. The particular details of how this was implemented will be discussed in later sections. However, it is very important to bear in mind that web scraping and crawling—just as other methods of data collection—pose unique ethical challenges. The use of these technologies in social research is, compared to traditional social scientific methods, a relatively recent addition to the methodological repertoire of social scientists. The ethical issues associated with web scraping are, of course, not unique to the social sciences, but needless to say, they are not always recognised as ethical challenges by others who are using web scraping. Consider Google—a tremendously useful search engine which is underpinned by web crawling and the indexing of hyperlinks and URLs—and we certainly would not be 'googling' if it were not for these emerging technologies. However, a more problematic example includes how some nefarious actors may use web scraping to harvest email addresses, which can be used to try to defraud people through elaborate (or not so elaborate) scams. Even in academia, this questionable practice can be observed

[1] https://projectarachnid.ca/en/.

as researchers get hundreds of unsolicited emails from predatory academic journals that rely on email addresses of academics harvested through crawling and scraping. More recently, the emergence of generative AI provides further testimony to how web scraping is fundamentally connected to contemporary modes of knowledge production, since large language models require huge amounts of textual data, which are sourced online—irrespective of whether the author agrees with this or not. The common denominator of how web scraping technologies are used in these examples is that they are—arguably—motivated and driven by generating profits by harvesting online data. Whereas this can be, to say the least, ethically questionable, what about using these technologies to advance social research? If data are published online and publicly available to everyone, does that mean that anyone can use that data for research?

Any research using web scraping applied to what has previously been termed 'found data' (Connelly et al. 2016), or in other words, data occurring as a result of social processes and not created for the purpose of research, needs to reflect upon such ethical questions. Unlike a survey, in which informed consent by research participants would be gained in advance, this was not possible with regard to the online escort adverts. However, whereas a survey, for instance, would collect data on individuals, the escort adverts collected for this research did not pertain to individuals per se, but rather, the professional lives of sex workers and other actors in the sex market. In other words, the data collected represented digital traces associated with marketing strategies, which were posted online on publicly accessible platforms, and there is, as such, not necessarily a perception or expectation of privacy with regard to the data posted. Whilst the data collected are not *personal data* per se, they were nevertheless treated as such, to protect the integrity and anonymity of the individuals posting the adverts. Even so, this does not mean that the scraping and analysis of online escort adverts is unproblematic.

Indeed, the analysis of online escort adverts is inevitably a form of surveillance. UK police forces are already either monitoring or using adverts as part of their investigations into exploitation, and as established in the literature review, academics and NGOs—both within and outwith the UK—have been collecting and analysing escort adverts for several years. The problem, however, both with regard to policing and research, is that the uncritical collection and analysis of online adverts poses serious risks of causing harm to both individual sex workers and, more widely, sex worker and migrant communities. Individual sex workers—particularly migrant sex workers—risk having their adverts targeted by law enforcement as being indicative of potential trafficking. The consequences can be varied, from unwanted attention to detention and deportation. As for the wider sex worker communities, and as argued elsewhere (e.g., Kjellgren 2022), poor research involving online data on the sex market, often motivated by particular anti-sex work ideologies, risks producing seriously misleading estimates or drawing simplistic conclusions and committing a particular form of digital fallacy: conflating online information and behaviours as reflecting an independent offline reality. Caution should always be used when analysing online escort adverts, and this research attempts to both improve upon how the police utilise open-source intelligence from adverts and, furthermore, to critically examine the value of escort adverts for social inquiries into the sex market.

Because of the serious harms that can stem from poor research or over-policing, a decision was made not to make the code developed for this research public. The main rationale for this is that there must be strong reasons for scraping and analysing escort adverts. As was clear from the literature review, many who collect and analyse escort adverts have extremely limited knowledge of the sex market, and it is questionable that their efforts are in the best interests of those affected by issues relating to exploitation and sexual labour. The same argument can, of course, be made in relation to the current research too. It is my belief that the findings from this research are beneficial to our understanding of the organisation of the sex market, and the analysis of online escort adverts can help dispel commonly repeated myths regarding online sex trafficking. This research has strong implications for the policing of sex trafficking, and the aim has always been to provide a more inclusive and responsible policing approach, which is sensitive to the plethora of experiences associated with the sex market. Since this research involves web scraping and the design of a novel methodology for analysing patterns in escort adverts, some extra caution is warranted. One of the issues, of course, is the risk that a technology developed for a specific purpose is used differently than initially intended. An example of this could be targeting particular groups based on the characteristics found within open-source intelligence, irrespective of any evidence implying a need for intervention. In the worst case, this could lead to punitive actions in the name of anti-trafficking.

Notwithstanding that technology can be used inappropriately, there is also an issue about the indirect consequences that technology can cause simply by increasing technological surveillance capabilities. As Brayne (2020) eloquently points out, so-called *dragnet surveillance*—the collection and analysis of the digital traces of everyone rather than specific groups under suspicion—is a serious concern. In other words, as big data-oriented technology becomes more accessible to law enforcement, there has been a more widespread shift from reactive to predictive policing (Brayne 2020). This is extremely problematic in this research context since it increases the possibility that pre-emptive action is taken in the absence of identified criminality or safeguarding concerns. Such actions can easily lead to the arrest, detention or deportation of sex workers, even though there may be no evidence to suggest any involvement of organised crime. This research strongly supports the notion that predictive policing in a trafficking context is deeply problematic and should be avoided. Similarly, and as will be clear in later chapters, this research advocates for a targeted approach to policing sex trafficking, in which open-source intelligence plays a highly specific role.

It is always difficult to shield against risks relating to how technology is used in practice. In this particular case, police interviewees demonstrated a great level of awareness of the risks involved with new technologies, and the need to avoid hoarding data and increasing surveillance capabilities in situations where it is not warranted (e.g., where there is no evidence of criminality). It is also important to point out that technology is not essential to engaging in unethical forms of policing; online escort adverts can be targeted irrespective of methodologies used to identify patterns. Similarly, police forces across the UK are already monitoring adult services websites, but their approaches are often spasmodic and not necessarily informed by research and evidence (Scoular et al. 2019). The use of web scraping and analysis of open-source data in research can therefore make a valuable contribution by providing a more critical lens to policing internet-mediated sex trafficking, and hopefully contribute to more inclusive and comprehensive responses to exploitation within the sex market.

Making Sense of Open-Source Data: Designing an Effective Workflow

The process involved in conducting a mixed-methods, computational criminology research project can be quite complex, and this necessitates a well-designed and effective workflow. This is particularly important in projects which involve web scraping and open-source data, given the multitude of decisions that need to be made when writing algorithms to collect and process data into a format which is suitable for statistical analysis. Workflow is a cornerstone of social statistics and quantitative social sciences, and it helps the researcher to structure and document all their work—which is invaluable for identifying errors—but it is also, more widely, vital for facilitating reproducibility, replicability and transparency (Freese 2007; Turner and Lambert 2015). What complicated the workflow development of this research was, of course, that a decision had to be made not to publish the code and data online, given the potential harm that could stem from the research being misused. As such, ethical approval (granted by the University of Stirling) was contingent upon not publishing the code and data online, which is otherwise something that should be encouraged, for the reasons mentioned above.

The most fundamental building block of a statistical workflow is computer code (or syntax), contained within scripts, which then form the workflow, or audit trail, which enables the researcher to reproduce their work. For this research, three different software, or programming languages, were used. Python was used for web scraping and initial data cleaning, R for data wrangling and the bulk of the analysis, and Stata for multilevel regression models. For long projects (such as this one), it is imperative to thoroughly document the analytical decisions made, for the very simple reason that it is impossible to accurately remember everything.

In the workflow underpinning this research, which is presented below, I have also chosen to integrate other components of the research which are not part of a statistical workflow per se, but are imperative to the mixed-methods foundation of the case study. The reasons for this are to provide a more rigorous and detailed overview of the research project, and in recognition of the fact that any statistical workflow is underpinned by epistemological and methodological choices, which inevitably affect how the research is carried out in practice. The workflow presented below can be seen as a template of how to design and structure a mixed-methods computational criminology project.

Case Study Design and Workflow

What is potentially distinctive about this case study is that it combines more traditional sociological methods, such as semi-structured interviews, statistical modelling and network analysis, with methods more commonly associated with the data sciences, including data mining, web scraping and quantitative text analysis. However, combining such a wide variety of methods and data is challenging. This necessitated a clear plan of research, and the primary purpose of this section is to introduce the reader to the various research stages of this case study.

The following section, Research Questions and Context, will briefly highlight the research questions this case study seeks to address, in addition to the broader context of the research. The nature of the research questions requires a more elaborate epistemological discussion, which is provided in the section "Epistemological Considerations". The research process is explained in greater detail under section "Research Process", which begins with a high-level summary of the research stages and how each relates to the research questions. It then proceeds to provide more detailed explanations of the individual stages.

Research Questions and Context

In light of the insights from the previous chapters, it is clear that there are gaps regarding the role of technology in facilitating exploitation and, more specifically, the extent to which we can understand processes related to the sex market through the analysis of online data. There is limited research on sex trafficking from the perspective of Scottish stakeholders, and even though research has begun to emerge in the UK, which highlights online patterns related to the sex market, none is particularly rigorous. Indeed, this research is more ambitious in that it seeks to apply more critical theoretical frameworks relating to exploitation, sexual labour and big data, with a fusion of methods suitable to understand some of the complexities associated with the online sex market. The research can be considered exploratory; there were no clear hypotheses at the start of the research process, and given the unique blend of methods and data, it was aimed equally at solidifying our knowledge on internet-mediated exploitation and understanding the best approaches to research it. In geographical terms, the research was specifically designed to be relevant to the Scottish context. However, because of the nature of trafficking and exploitation in the sex market, which often transcends borders and involves stakeholders from across the UK, efforts were made to make it more broadly relevant to the wider UK context.

The questions were constructed to strike a balance between contributing to our current understanding of exploitation and technology within the sex market, and building upon those findings to improve responses to exploitation:

1. How are online technologies used within the off-street sex market?
2. How do criminal networks and OCGs use online technologies to facilitate their operations, specifically with regard to advertising victims and connecting with sex buyers?
3. To what extent is it possible to identify networks operating within the off-street sex market, and patterns of vulnerability and exploitation, from online data?

4. To what extent could any identifiable patterns and network structures be useful for law enforcement and partner agencies?

Questions 1 and 2 were designed to specifically address crucial knowledge gaps regarding the role of technology within the sex market and, particularly, how criminal networks use technology in this context. Question 3 is more exploratory and epistemologically relevant to how we can identify and understand online patterns in this context. Finally, question 4 is largely designed to capture the relevance of the identified patterns in practitioner contexts. There is a natural progression in the questions, in which insights from questions 1 and 2 feed into the exploration of online data. Subsequently, the identified online patterns were interrogated against the qualitative data.

Epistemological Considerations

The fusion of online, open-source data and qualitative offline data is a challenging task. As with any mixed methods research, this necessitates careful epistemological reflection. In the context of the social sciences, using data gleaned from online sources is a fairly recent development, in contrast to more well-established methods such as qualitative interviewing and survey analysis (Savage and Burrows 2007). As such, it is important to recognise some of the epistemological limitations of working with more novel forms of data. This is particularly pertinent in relation to this case study, as it is trying to understand patterns in online escort adverts, which are very different compared to other forms of online data. There are three key considerations to address, namely what is the actual object of study; how can we study it; and how can we harmonise findings from vastly different data sources?

With regard to the first question, the object of study is the sex market, or perhaps more specifically, the relationship between the online and offline dimensions of the sex market. As such, the units of analysis in this research context consist of two elements, online escort adverts and qualitative data related to the experiences of stakeholders. The entire sex market is arguably performative in the sense that what is being commodified is a performance (Abel 2011). Services such as the pornstar or girlfriend experience are essentially performances, and successfully appealing to the desires and fantasies of clients is associated with increased revenue, since these transactions occur within a market context (Brents and Hausbeck 2007). Escort adverts, as such, represent the digital traces of marketing strategies, created to attract clients within the market. Consequently, they are not necessarily truthful, nor representative of the lived realities of the individuals posting them, in terms of age, nationality or ethnicity, or the words they use to describe themselves. This has implications for how we understand escort adverts as research data: they do not allow us to understand the experiences, qualities and characteristics of sex workers, only the marketing strategies or choices they use online, within this highly performative market. In the context of this book, the online data analysis consists of an evaluation of marketing strategies, and it seeks to understand how these relate to vulnerability and exploitation. There certainly is a continuum of vulnerability and exploitation within the sex market; however, our capacity to observe and understand it, based on online escort adverts, is limited. This is primarily because the data represents performative marketing strategies rather than lived experiences.

Considering these complexities, it is important to consider how we can best study the online sex market within the confines of one research project. A combination of ethnographic accounts, peer-led research and online data analysis would no doubt have been the preferred way, but what could realistically be achieved within the given timeframe was limited. Since the research specifically looks at the online dimension of the sex market, it was certainly important to include a strong quantitative component, capable of identifying patterns within the sex market. However, given the complexities discussed earlier, regarding the performative role of online escort adverts, the importance of more rich, contextual, qualitative data was also recognised. Therefore, interviews with stakeholders experienced in responding to harms relating to vulnerability, migration and exploitation were deemed appropriate and necessary. This would lend a certain degree of external validity to the online patterns if triangulation could be achieved successfully, which brings us to the final consideration: triangulating and harmonising data of such vastly different epistemological qualities.

It is recognised that quantitative and qualitative analyses are equally important to this project. Arguably, relying solely on one of the two approaches would lead to severely limited findings. Without qualitative insights, it would be impossible to determine the meaning, validity and significance of online patterns. Conversely, drawing exclusively on qualitative data would not allow us to understand the scale and complexity of patterns and networks within the online sex market. Harmonising and triangulating insights from such different sources, however, is not straightforward.

Part of what informed a more critical perspective on both the sex market and online data stems from the research reviewed in previous chapters; in other words, the sex market is complex, as is the very nature of online data. Using online data to understand the sex market is exceptionally complicated. There are also vastly different epistemologies underpinning the specific methods used, which adds further complications. Qualitative interviewing is often associated with more constructivist or interpretivist epistemologies, and big data-oriented research utilising online data tends to be largely atheoretical (Anderson 2008; Edwards and Holland 2020). The conundrum at the heart of this project, and indeed all research examining the online dimension of the sex market, is that escort adverts are, epistemologically speaking, a very poor source of data. Nevertheless, they are essential because they allow us to examine aspects of the market that we otherwise would be unlikely to appreciate. Additionally, it is especially important to unpack assumptions associated with escort adverts, given their role in the contemporary policing of harms within the sex market.

This research relied on a continuous and iterative strategy of inquiry. The meaning of the online patterns was reflected upon in the context of the qualitative findings; conversely, the qualitative findings were examined in relation to the identified online patterns. To provide a more concrete example of why this was necessary, consider how a person with Italian heritage who might consider their national identity Scottish in everyday life may advertise as Italian; there may be clear benefits in doing so to differentiate oneself within the market. Now, a quantitative examination would lead us to conclude that the person *is* Italian because that is what can be observed from the advert. A more critical reading of the data, informed by qualitative insights and with the aforementioned epistemological considerations in mind, would suggest the person's ethnicity to be *unknown*. After all, the context in which the data are produced is often very different compared to what we can observe online; we can only observe a performance mediated by a technological infrastructure. Every analytical decision part of this research had to be met with such continuous scepticism and critical scrutiny.

This strategy reinforces the notion that 'big', granular and fragmented data *cannot* readily be interpreted without understanding the context in which the data are produced (Törnberg and Törnberg 2018). Bornakke and Due (2018, p. 13) proposed a framework for blending big and 'thin' data with more contextually 'thick' data. The authors summarise blending as

> the contribution from two (or more) separate input spaces containing, respectively, thick and big data analytical insights which share some conceptual associations in a generic space.

The notion of blending thick and thin data guided the analytical process within this project. Even though the two data sources are epistemologically distinct, they are nevertheless crucial to understanding the processes underpinning the posting of online adverts and how various processes are manifested online. Because of the epistemological complexities associated with this project, the research process had to be carefully designed to maximise the strengths of both data sources and how they could be blended to produce novel insights. This process will be described in more detail in the following section.

Research Process

This research has, since its inception, been a mixed-methods project. The complexity of the topic warranted the use of triangulation and blending of thick and thin data, which was achieved by combining qualitative interviews with key stakeholders and applying quantitative methods to online, open-source data. A variety of methods were combined to address the research questions, and how the specific methods used relate to the questions is shown in Table 1.

Table 1 Summary of research questions, methods and outputs

Research question	Methods	Research output
1, 2, 4	Semi-structured interviews	Qualitative interview data
	Thematic analysis	Qualitative data organised into themes and codes
3	Web crawling	Quantitative dataset
	Principal component analysis	Assess network complexity
	Quantitative text analysis	Derive similarity measures
	E-I index analysis	Examine network homophily
	Quadratic assignment procedure	Examine predictors of tie formation
	Multilevel modelling	Examine network-level influences on advert-level outcomes

While combining such a wide variety of methods and vastly different data sources is challenging, the research process was carefully structured to ensure that each method was applied when appropriate. The process followed a logical flow; each stage was linked and contributed to systematically addressing different elements of the research questions. As such, it flowed from fairly broad in scope to highly specific, before all insights were blended and triangulated, the results of which are presented in the final chapter of this book.

The remainder of this section explains the stages of the research process more thoroughly as they unfolded throughout the project. A high-level overview of the entire process is provided in Fig. 1. The technicalities of individual methods are kept to a minimum; more detail is present in their respective analytical chapters (see chapters "Complexity, Similarity and Tie Formation in Advert Networks", "Network Influences on Extreme Service Advertisement" and "Key Messages and Conclusions: Future Directions in the Computational Criminology of Internet-Mediated Exploitation"). An exception to this is section "Stage 7: Automated Network Identification", which highlights the development of the automated methodology used in this research, where a more thorough discussion is required.

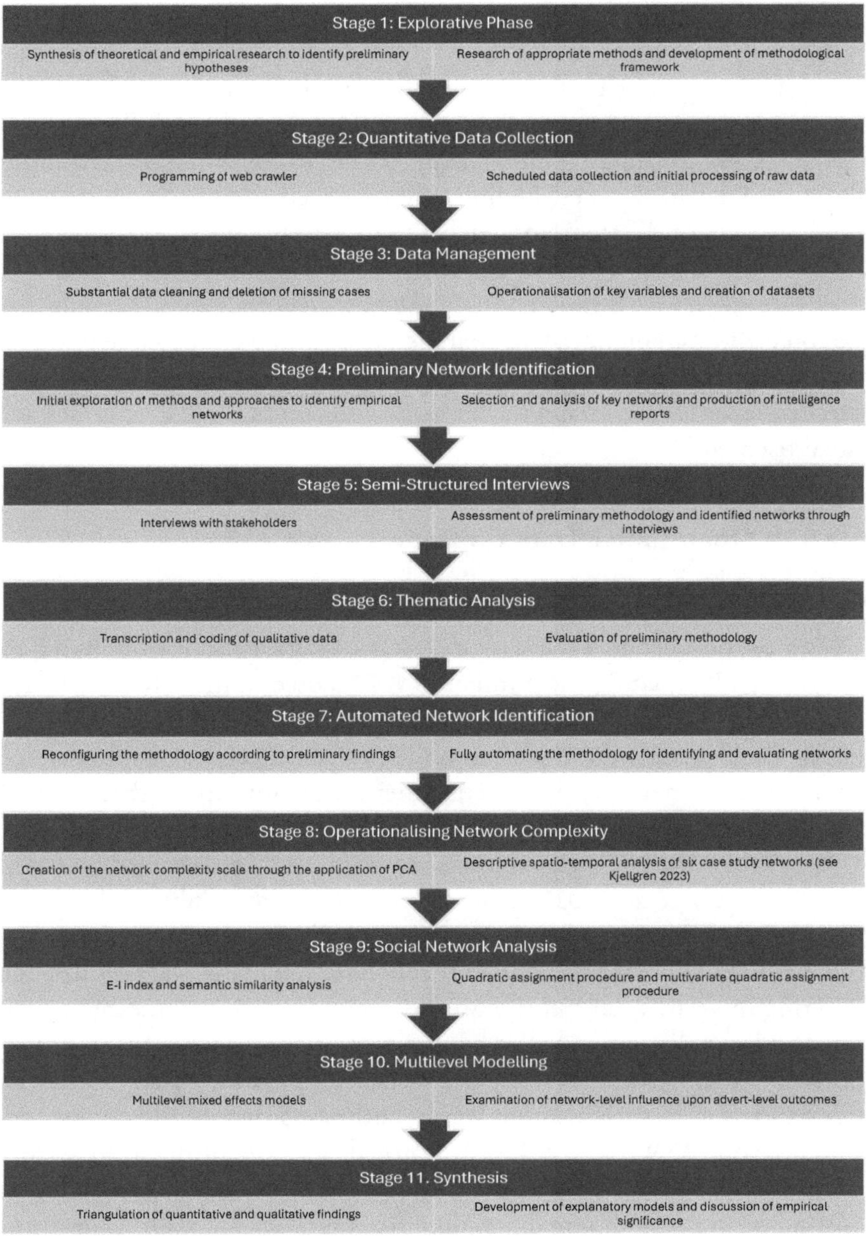

Fig. 1 Flowchart of research process

Stage 1: Explorative Phase

The initial stage was closely associated with the literature review. After reviewing theoretical, empirical and methodological research, the key challenge was considering the best approaches to collecting and analysing the different data sources. Preliminary tests were conducted to evaluate the feasibility of different approaches, and a clear plan was drawn up to define the parameters of the case study. In addition, the insights from the literature review culminated in different hypotheses that could be explored through quantitative analysis. Most notable was the hypothesis that a network's online structure may influence the marketing strategies used in adverts (see chapter "Network Influences on Extreme Service Advertisement").

Stage 2: Quantitative Data Collection

The quantitative data consisted of escort adverts posted on one of the UK's most popular adult services websites (ASWs; henceforth referred to as ASW 1). Estimating the number of ASWs used in the UK is challenging. As Cunningham et al. (2017) have previously observed, ASWs are not homogenous, and range from online escort directories, multi-service adult entertainment platforms, customer review forums (with dedicated spaces for marketing sexual services), and online classifieds, to name but a few. From their mixed-methods research on internet-mediated sex work, Sanders et al. (2018) noted how sex workers only used a small handful of ASWs to market their services. ASW 1 is one of the platforms that has been consistently popular throughout the years. The rationale for selecting this particular website was informed by previous research in the UK. Additionally, some ASWs require more rigorous verification procedures for posting adult services adverts, such as providing passport details (see Sanders et al. 2018), and it was hypothesised that criminal networks would favour ASWs where they can provide as little information as possible, and ASW 1 is one such site. The poster is required to pay a fee to post an advert, which remains online for a limited time. Other features increasing visibility can also be paid for, as well as the automatic renewal of the advert. The site in question includes several subcategories of adult services. Since this research is focused on the exploitation of adult women, the category relating to escort services provided by women was used as the basis for data collection. Approximately 9000–12,000 online adverts were active on each of the occasions of data collection.

When online platforms are used as a basis for data collection, there is always a question about cross-platform generalisability. One of the issues in this context is that different platforms are structured differently and contain different functionalities, which means that it can be difficult to compare findings across platforms. Another issue relating to generalisability, which is more difficult to account for, is that there is currently limited knowledge on whether specific groups of sex workers and networks are more prone to advertise on particular platforms. With regard to the first issue, the methods used in this research will likely be transferable to any platform which contains information similar to ASW 1 (specifically, phone numbers and user accounts). In relation to the second issue, whether or not the *findings* can be generalised to other platforms, is more questionable. In addition, platforms change over time—new features are added, and others removed—which further affects the future generalisability of any findings. Nevertheless, future research should ideally include more than one ASW to further examine issues of generalisability.[2]

A web crawler was developed in Python (v. 3.8.5) using the *scrapy* package[3] to collect the online data required for the analysis. This crawler was designed only to capture relevant variables whilst complying with the instructions in ASW 1's *robots.txt* file, which is a set of instructions websites provide to crawlers, or bots, concerning what parts of a website are allowed to be scraped. To create a minimal load on the server of ASW 1, the crawler was configured only to scrape an advert every few seconds.

[2] This research received ethical approval to examine the two leading ASWs in the UK, and the initial aim was to do so to better understand cross-platform differences and generalisability; however, due to time constraints, a decision was made to focus on one platform.

[3] https://docs.scrapy.org/en/latest/index.html.

XPath and Cascading Style Sheets (CSS) selectors were used to scrape relevant elements from the HTML code.[4]

In the development stages, adverts from particular locations in the UK would be scraped and compared to the counts of adverts on the websites. Following successful tests, the crawler was deployed across the whole of the UK and compared to the counts of public-facing adverts on the website. Once the crawler was functional, it was scheduled to scrape adverts every fortnight. Due to occasional disruptions and technical glitches, sometimes adverts were scraped less frequently, and other times more frequently for error-checking purposes. All adverts scraped were stored in an encrypted MongoDB database. Adverts were scraped between 29/01/2021 and 20/04/2022. On average, 10,208 adverts (SD = 2716) were collected on each occasion. One reason for particularly low counts on some occasions was that adverts were collected during the peak of the COVID-19 pandemic. Occasionally, adverts were not successfully scraped (for various reasons); hence, the final dataset does not contain every single advert posted during this time.

In total, 685,007 records were collected during this time. However, a significant number of these were duplicates, due to the simple reason that one advert could be live across several points of data collection. As such, the actual number of unique records was 413,880. Strictly speaking, this is not directly translatable to the actual number of adverts. Throughout time, adverts may be reposted, and details may change, such as the location, the services offered or the phone numbers used. It is thus natural for adverts to evolve over time, reflective of underlying processes of posting and moving around in the sex market. The result is that there are actually more records of adverts than there are *unique* adverts. The precise structure of the data will be described in more detail in *Stage 3: Data Management*.

In total, 18 elements were scraped from each advert. This is not equal to the number of variables derived from these elements, nor the number of variables used in the final analysis, however. Table 2 shows an overview

[4] It is important to point out that no images or metadata related to the images in the adverts were scraped. This was both an ethical and technical decision; scraping the images themselves would have involved the possibility of accidentally scraping indecent images of children (IIOC). Second, the images themselves were not of analytical value for this research.

Table 2 Summary of scraped advert elements, descriptions and analytical purposes

Element	Description	Analytical purpose
Advert ID	An identifier unique to an advert posted; the same identifier will remain constant over time, even if the content within the advert changes.	Used as a clustering identifier in the multilevel models to denote unique adverts and account for changes occurring throughout time. It also served as the primary unit of analysis in the social network analysis.
Age	The advertised age of the sex worker.	Recoded into different functional forms and used as a control in models and the E-I index analysis.
Title	The title of the advert.	Combined with the 'description' element to form the basis of the quantitative text analysis, which primarily involved estimating semantic similarity.
Description	A textual description written by the poster.	
Agency	The name of the escort agency posting the advert (if the sex worker is not advertising as independent).	This was initially collected to be part of network identification but was not included in the final network methodology.
Ethnicity	Predefined ethnic categories: African/ Caribbean, Arabic, Asian, Caucasian, Indian, Latina, Mixed and Other.	Combined together with the 'nationality' element to create more nuanced variables relating to ethnicity (including dummies to differentiate between British and Non-British adverts).
Rate for in-calls	Rates in pounds for in-calls (15 minutes, 30 minutes, 1 hour, 2 hours, 4 hours, overnight).	The rate variables were going to be used as control variables in modelling, but due to a large degree of missing data, they were excluded.
Rate for out-calls	Rates in pounds for out-calls (15 minutes, 30 minutes, 1 hour, 2 hours, 4 hours, overnight).	

(continued)

Table 2 (continued)

Element	Description	Analytical purpose
Coordinates	The coordinates pertaining to where the adverts were posted.	These were primarily used to calculate the geographical dispersion of adverts within networks. They were also used for the purpose of linking the adverts to higher-level geographical units such as data zones, intermediate data zones and local authorities.
Mode	Whether the advert is listed as being posted by an independent sex worker or an agency.	Used as a dichotomous control variable in the multilevel models.
Nationality	The advertised nationality, or national identity, of the sex worker. In total, 217 different nationalities were observed.	Combined with ethnicity (see above).
Phone number	The phone number listed in the advert.	One of the two variables (the other being User ID) used to identify and create empirical networks. It was later on deleted from the dataset.
Location and outcode	The name and postcode outward code of where the advert was posted (e.g., Aberdeen AB25).	Used to count the number of unique locations a network had been posting adverts in.
First date posted	The date in which the advert was first posted. Note that this can go back quite far in time due to the fact that the same advert may be reposted, and it can therefore cover a period that extends the scraping period.	Used to calculate the number of days in which a network had been operating on ASW 1. Used as a control variable in some models.

(continued)

Table 2 (continued)

Element	Description	Analytical purpose
Services	A list of the services offered (total number of possible services was 23).	Operationalised both into dummy variables and a continuous variable indicating how many services were being advertised. Chapters "Complexity, Similarity and Tie Formation in Advert Networks" and "Network Influences on Extreme Service Advertisement" used six specific dichotomous service variables as part of the statistical modelling.
Status	Whether the poster has paid extra for any of the three special features of the advert: VIP, Featured, Highlight. This would be done to increase visibility and marketability.	Used as control variables in the statistical models.
URL	The URL of the advert.	This was collected for purposes of verification throughout the early stages of the development of the web crawler, to examine adverts where data were not being successfully scraped.
User ID	A unique identifier of the account from which the advert was posted.	One of the two variables (the other being phone number) which was used as a basis to identify and create empirical networks.

of all the elements scraped from the adverts and their main analytical purpose. A common feature of online data is that it is often structured in formats unsuitable for statistical analysis and includes both textual and non-textual data. For instance, of relevance to this research were both nominal variables, such as nationality and location, continuous variables, such as rates charged for services, and textual string data, such as advert descriptions. These different variable types generally require a non-trivial amount of data management. The first iteration of data cleaning was done using Python as part of the data collection. All scraped adverts were processed through a pipeline which involved formatting each element, such as removing HTML tags and other unwanted features, before sending the cleaned advert to MongoDB. The more substantial data management process was done in R and will be described in more detail below.

Stage 3: Data Management

A significant number of steps were involved in the data management process. All processing was done in R (v. 4.2.1) and documented in an RMarkdown file for reproducibility.[5] Parts of the data management were straightforward and involved tasks commonly performed in quantitative social sciences; others included more complicated processes requiring further explanations.

Data Cleaning

A variety of steps were necessary to process the data into a form suitable for quantitative analysis. Principally, it involved coding and recoding variables into the desired functional forms and levels of measurement. All scraped elements were first examined to check for anomalies. This, for instance, included the identification of non-informative digits entered into the phone segment of the advert (e.g., 00000000) or phone numbers involving fewer than the usual number of digits. Some variables, including phone numbers, also required harmonisation since those were often specified in different ways (e.g., +44 or 0044). Regular expressions were used to rectify and harmonise such variables. The two most critical variables were phone numbers and user IDs, since these were used to construct networks (more on this in *Stage 4: Preliminary Network Identification*). Once the cleaning was completed, all phone numbers were replaced with numerical identifiers. Following the final stage of network identification (see section "Stage 7: Automated Network Identification"), this variable was dropped from the dataset altogether.

[5] In normal circumstances, all the code should be made publicly available to allow for verification and replication; this, however, is problematic due to the nature of this research. Indeed, it is not appropriate to publish since covert data collection and analysis inevitably is a form of surveillance of the sex market.

Missing Data

As is common in research involving online data, a significant challenge was the high rates of missing values across variables. Some variables contained unexplainable missing values, and it was difficult to understand what caused this since the error could have occurred based on irregularities on ASW 1's platform, due to some glitch in the crawler, or simply omitted by the poster of the advert. Table 3 provides an overview of missing values on the scraped elements of the dataset:

There was a huge number of missing values across the variables pertaining to the rates charged for services, which meant they had to be excluded from the analysis. A substantial amount of missing values can also be seen for the nationalities variable. This is because nationality, like rates charged for services, is an optional element of escort adverts. Some workarounds were used for particular modelling exercises, such as combining ethnicity and nationality to create more theoretically sensible variables.

There is always the question of the veracity of the information contained in some of the variables. For example, nationality will, in some instances, reflect what marketing choices are deemed desirable or lucrative in the situational context of the market. As such, listwise deletion of cases across all variables with missing data was considered inappropriate. However, some variables were crucial for this analysis, and a listwise deletion of cases was therefore performed in relation to the following variables: phone numbers, user IDs, coordinates and ethnicity. Regarding the latter, there were only a handful of missing cases, and it was therefore considered appropriate to do so.

The Final Dataframe

Following data cleaning and initial data management, the dataset consisted of 213,699 advert records. As mentioned earlier, these records are snapshots of adverts in time, meaning that whilst the records are unique, they are not unique adverts. There was a natural hierarchy within the data: (1) advert records were nested in (2) unique adverts that, in turn,

Table 3 Summary of missing values across scraped variables

Element	Missing values
Advert ID	0
Age	0
Title	97
Description	53
Agency	0
Ethnicity	13
In-call rate: 15 minutes	194,069
In-call rate: 30 minutes	110,022
In-call rate: 1 hour	89,567
In-call rate: 2 hours	353,654
In-call rate: 4 hours	375,127
In-call rate: Overnight	366,825
Adverts with no in-call rate	88,957
Out-call rate: 15 minutes	393,641
Out-call rate: 30 minutes	374,472
Out-call rate: 1 hour	167,892
Out-call rate: 2 hours	351,194
Out-call rate: 4 hours	375,084
Out-call rate: Overnight	362,652
Adverts with no Out-call rate	165,890
No data on any rate variable	3342
Coordinates	6
Mode	0
Nationality	182,984
Phone number	11,212
Location and postcode outcodes	258
First date posted	62
Services	0
Status	0
URL	0
User ID	1

were nested in (3) user accounts. It was acknowledged that there was also a fourth level—the network level—but the algorithm to define group membership had not yet been created. The statistical analyses in this case study used (2) unique adverts[6] as the primary unit of analysis, because it is the most plausible representation of an *actual* individual that can be

[6] Note that unique adverts are abbreviated in some tables in chapters "Complexity, Similarity and Tie Formation in Advert Networks" and "Network Influences on Extreme Service Advertisement" as ADID, since this is the identifier which denotes their uniqueness.

identified from the data. One might suggest user accounts might more plausibly map on to actual individuals. This is not the case, however, as it is fairly common that one account may control adverts for several individuals, which would be the case for escort agencies, sex worker collectives or the criminal networks that this project focuses on. It should be noted that all statistical analyses were replicated with (1) advert records as the unit of analysis, and the results were compared to (2) unique adverts. A comparison of the results favoured treating (2) unique adverts as the primary unit of analysis. This was favourable for two reasons: statistically speaking, focusing on unique adverts reduces some of the bias towards advert posting patterns. This is most pertinent in relation to the social network analysis. Networks based on records of adverts would create a false layer of complexity, which would be somewhat misleading when evaluating the structure and homophily of advert networks. A scenario where one sex worker posts and reposts the same advert may lead to 30 records of adverts, simply because data collection is longitudinal. Basing networks on unique adverts instead would in that case mean that one advert represents that one sex worker. Second, and from a substantive point of view, we can be more certain that unique adverts are *more likely* to correspond to unique individuals than advert records themselves. Whereas some further data management was required for specific parts of the different analyses, the dataframe described here formed the basis of all of them. The specific details of how the analytical datasets were produced are described in more detail in the subsequent sections of this chapter.

Stage 4: Preliminary Network Identification

This stage of the project was focused on theoretically and methodologically examining how online networks on the sex market could be identified. The specific challenges at this stage were first to define what should be considered networks and then develop a methodology capable of identifying and operationalising networks in practice.

Defining Networks

How to best define and operationalise networks is far from an arbitrary question, since all statistical analyses in this case study are contingent upon how networks are constructed. Moreover, applicability is also of critical importance; networks must make sense from a policing perspective and be of operational value. The fact that online networks are the subject of study makes it even more complicated. Some online networks, typically associated with social media, have been demonstrated to correlate with offline networks (Subrahmanyam et al. 2008), but this is certainly not the case in this research context. Online networks on the sex market are more likely to correspond to distinct advertising patterns, and we do not know the extent to which online connections map onto offline connections between individuals. In other words, we cannot automatically assume that one unique advert represents one unique individual. In some circumstances, this will be the case, such as independent sex workers, whereas it is unlikely to be the case in more complex configurations on the sex market (sex worker collectives, escort agencies, and criminal networks, for instance).

A reasonable starting point in defining networks for this research was to revisit the literature reviewed as part of chapter "*Criminal Networks, Opportunity Structures and the Process of Exploitation*" to consider what makes criminal networks unique as a form of organisation. As Morselli (2009, p. 1) explains:

The scope, forms, and contents of criminal organizational systems vary across an extended continuum. They range from simple co-offending decisions to seize an available and attractive criminal opportunity to sophisticated designs to monopolize a given market or geographical territory. They may be based on the incentives offered by a one-time partnership to execute a criminal venture or framed within a bureaucratic-like infrastructure that demands and enforces exclusivity on the actions and productivity of members.

From this perspective, we would expect a considerable diversity in the scale and structure of criminal networks involved in the sex market; from situations where only one perpetrator may exploit a victim to transnational organisations facilitating large-scale exploitation. However, what makes criminal networks particularly difficult to study is that we often have limited or missing data on key actors and the activities they are involved in (von Lampe 2009). As such, the possibility of accurately capturing the precise structure of criminal networks by analysing online data was deemed minimal. From an epistemological perspective, there was limited information to construct empirical connections (especially compared to the rich investigative data usually part of the study of criminal networks).

Given previous research into the sex market (Kjellgren 2018, 2019), three specific variables were used to form edges: (1) phone numbers, (2) user accounts and (3) semantic similarity. Phone numbers and user accounts are by far the most reliable indications of any form of underlying organisation within online networks, since they both are central to brand-building processes and maintaining a consistent presence within the sex market. Semantic similarity is more ambiguous, but at this stage of the project, it was still deemed important to identify connections that could imply a certain degree of cooperation and organisation. This decision was in line with previous research that suggested it could be used to identify networks within the sex market (Kjellgren 2018; Li et al. 2018). As will be explained in section "Stage 7: Automated Network Identification", connections based on similarity were removed altogether after a more thorough evaluation of the preliminary methodology with law enforcement investigators. It was used prior to these discussions to inform network operationalisation but later excluded due to the high probability of identifying spurious connections. Whereas phone numbers and user accounts are the most reliable variables to be used in network operationalisation in this context, it should nevertheless be recognised that they do not necessarily inform us of the underlying relations (i.e., the individuals part of a network and the extent to which they are connected). They are, however, useful from a policing perspective since this information can be used in triangulation with other intelligence, and this was a guiding insight in the operationalisation of these networks. Whilst the decision to use phone numbers and user accounts can be considered appropriate and justifiable for these reasons, it should also be noted that the decision to rely on these two particular variables for forming edges fundamentally affects *all* statistical analyses conducted in this research. In other words, substantially different results from the statistical modelling could be a possibility if different criteria for edge formation were applied.

As defined in this research, a network emerges organically as part of underlying processes relating to how adverts are posted within the online sex market. More specifically, the networks should be referred to as *advert networks*, since we do not possess any tangible information on the offline network. An advert network, then, is defined as a collection of adverts that are connected by empirical ties. This means an advert network may only involve one individual; their online footprints make it an advert network, regardless of the number of offline people involved. For brevity, advert networks are henceforth referred to simply as *networks*. In some instances, criminal networks are mentioned, which is explicitly reserved for the conversations with police respondents who had identified criminality within the investigative networks under discussion.

Initial Methodology and Intelligence Reports

With a workable definition of networks, the next step in the research process was developing a methodology to identify networks automatically. There were two reasons for doing this. The first was that it was necessary to do so in order for subsequent stages of the analysis, which required adverts to be nested within empirical networks. It was also necessary to produce intelligence reports on specific networks, which would be systematically discussed with investigators. This was done to aid the interpretation of the online patterns and to understand what type of information and intelligence is useful from a policing perspective.

A fairly simple, iterative algorithm was developed to extract networks from the dataframe. In brief, a phone number or user account was put into to the algorithm, which then proceeded to query the database and extract adverts based on empirical connections. It continued to iterate until exhaustion (i.e., no new connections could be identified). It then produced visualisations and statistics on the network and summarised

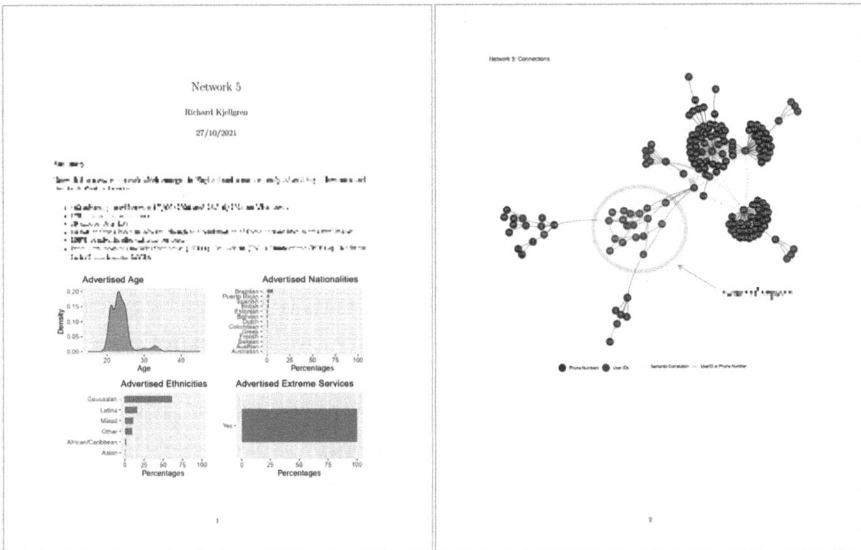

Fig. 2 Example extract of intelligence report

them in a PDF document, which served as a basis for discussion in interviews with investigators. Figure 2 provides a snapshot of what these intelligence reports looked like.

Stage 5: Semi-Structured Interviews

All qualitative data in this research were collected through semi-structured interviews. These interviews had two very specific purposes. First, they were designed to collect the data required to answer research questions 1 and 2 (how online technologies are used within the sex market, specifically by criminal networks). Second, the interviews conducted with police respondents also involved systematic discussions of the intelligence reports. The purpose of this was to address research question 4 (to better understand patterns in online data, and what information would be useful from an investigative perspective).

Respondent Sampling and Recruitment

Researching the sex market and, in particular, issues of vulnerability, exploitation and sex trafficking is challenging due to the ethics and logistics involved. This research is focused upon the policing of, and responses to, exploitation, and it therefore seemed a sensible approach to focus on recruiting stakeholders responding to harms within the sex market.[7] This decision had been made prior to the start of this research project, and relying on interviews with stakeholders takes us further away from understandings of exploitation informed directly by lived experience; this is considered a significant limitation of this research.

Whilst the research is primarily relevant to a Scottish context, a decision was also made to include respondents outwith Scotland. Police Scotland was particularly suitable since it is the second largest police force within the UK, spanning the largest geographical area, including both urban and rural spaces. This allowed for a much more nuanced perspective on responding to exploitation, compared to what could have been gained from a police force that is more or less exclusively metropolitan. However, in recognition that most investigations will transcend police force boundaries, respondents from police forces other than Police Scotland were also approached to provide a better balance. Whilst the findings are not generalisable, they still provide a solid foundation for our understanding of exploitation, and given that criminal networks are likely to circulate the UK, the findings will likely be relevant to other police forces as well.

Two specific inclusion criteria were applied in the recruiting process. Police respondents were required to have recent experience in sex trafficking investigations or work specifically in a position relating to sex trafficking investigations. Non-governmental organisations (NGOs) that supported or advocated for the rights of one or more of the following groups were considered for recruitment: (1) sex workers, (2) trafficking

[7] Whilst it would have been invaluable to consult people with lived experience of these issues and to involve them in the research design, this was deemed as too great a challenge for my PhD, which this book is based on, particularly since it involved a quite ambitious quantitative element, and that I, as a researcher, had no prior connections to either sex worker communities or other communities potentially affected by issues related to migration and exploitation.

victims and (3) migrants. The recruitment of police respondents was largely respondent-driven, in the sense that the initial respondents within Police Scotland approached suitable candidates on my behalf. In total, nine respondents from Police Scotland were identified, five of whom belonged to the National Human Trafficking Unit (NHTU). Four officers served as Human Trafficking Champions in different police divisions across Scotland. These Human Trafficking Champions have special responsibilities regarding responding to and investigating human trafficking in their divisions. The NHTU coordinates and provides support to divisional Human Trafficking Champions and investigates some of the more complex and large-scale human trafficking cases in Scotland.

In addition to the police respondents from Police Scotland, one detective from a larger metropolitan English police force was also recruited to complement Scottish perspectives. This was particularly pertinent given the significance of the link between Scotland and the English region in question, regarding the flows of criminal networks. Taken together, police respondents covered a substantial geographical area, which allowed for regional comparisons in the qualitative analysis. It is also worth mentioning that many detectives served in specialised trafficking-related capacities such as senior investigating officers, coordination, intelligence and internet investigation. As such, the police sample involved people of varying ranks, responsibilities and niche expertise—all related to sex trafficking.

The other four respondents represented different NGOs. These were recruited specifically to introduce non-policing perspectives on the issues pertinent to this research. Twelve NGOs were identified as suitable candidates through a combination of desk-based research and snowball sampling. These consisted of nine sex worker rights or support organisations, two NGOs specifically supporting trafficking victims and one organisation supporting vulnerable and often exploited migrants. The overall response rate was quite low (33%). The organisations that either declined or did not respond to the research requests were all groups supporting and advocating for sex workers. The low response rate was perhaps not surprising, given that recruitment coincided with the peak of the COVID-19 pandemic. In addition, the very notion that a researcher is researching sex trafficking or exploitation can be sufficient to dissuade sex work-oriented NGOs from partaking in research. This is not surprising given how exploitative the anti-trafficking discourse has been historically, often depriving sex workers of their agency, despite claiming to work in their interest (see, for instance, Ellison 2017 for a more thorough discussion). With that said, the four NGOs that accepted the invitation to interviews had varied experience with regard to specifically responding to sex trafficking, though nevertheless provided invaluable perspectives on wider issues relating to sexual labour, migration, vulnerability and exploitation. Respondents were incredibly generous with their time, despite facing ongoing challenges within their organisations. Indeed, all stakeholders were either considered essential workers or provided essential services throughout a very turbulent period of recent history and had limited availability to engage with academic research. The final list of respondents can be found in Table 4.

Table 4 Summary of respondents by role and organisation

Respondent	Organisation	Details
Detective Constable 1	English Police Force	Modern Slavery Unit
Detective Constable 2	Police Scotland	National Unit
Detective Sergeant 1	Police Scotland	National Unit
Detective Sergeant 2	Police Scotland	National Unit
Detective Sergeant 3	Police Scotland	Divisional
Detective Inspector 1	Police Scotland	National Unit
Detective Inspector 2	Police Scotland	National Unit
Detective Inspector 3	Police Scotland	Divisional
Detective Inspector 4	Police Scotland	Divisional
Detective Chief Inspector 1	Police Scotland	Divisional
NGO Worker 1	Sex Worker Support (Scotland)	Managerial Position
NGO Worker 2	Trafficking Victim Support (Scotland)	Managerial Position
NGO Worker 3	Migrant Support (Scotland)	Managerial Position

Data Collection and Interview Schedules

Data collection was carried out using semi-structured interviews. Since this occurred during the pandemic, all interviews were conducted online using Microsoft Teams. The interviews were recorded (only audio was captured) directly onto the researcher's encrypted hard drive. The audio recordings were then used to manually produce transcripts in NVivo 12. Two different interview schedules were used, one for each group of stakeholders. The interview schedule for NGO participants focused on the barriers faced by migrants and victims in seeking services and support and, subsequently, how our responses to these issues can be improved. The interviews with police officers primarily focused on their experiences investigating sex trafficking and its online dimension. All interviews were conducted one-to-one, except for one interview involving two police officers from the same divisional unit (Detective Inspector 4 and Detective Sergeant 3). The length of the interviews ranged from 41 to 83 minutes, with an average of 57 minutes.

The interview process was designed differently for police officers, which involved systematic discussions on past or ongoing sex trafficking cases and an evaluation of the intelligence reports produced as part of the research. These intelligence reports highlighted networks specific to the geographical area where the detectives were based (and for the national unit, large-scale networks operating across the country). The networks themselves were selected because of their perceived complexity. Following semi-structured questions around the policing and online dimension of sex trafficking, and their investigative experiences, these reports were shared with the participants during the interview. Discussions were focused on how they interpreted the patterns, their usefulness from an investigative point of view and the extent to which the methodology could be useful in practice. The findings specific to the methodological assessment are presented in the section titled "Stage 7: Automated Network Identification".

Stage 6: Thematic Analysis

The rationale for conducting the thematic analysis at this particular stage of the research process was that qualitative insights were required to progress further. In other words, further development of the quantitative methodology depended on the qualitative findings, specifically the preliminary methodological assessment. Braun and Clarke's (2006) thematic analysis was the method used to analyse the qualitative data. More precisely, the analysis involved an inductive or 'bottom-up' approach (Braun and Clarke 2006, p. 28). This flexible method is particularly well-suited to identifying patterns in qualitative data and ensuring the themes constructed are firmly connected to the data. As such, there was no predefined coding frame; rather, codes were constructed through an iterative process. The analytical process itself was directly informed by the work of Braun and Clarke (2006) and involved the following steps:

1. First reading of all the data to note particular keywords, trends or ideas and note-taking.
2. Compiling the notes to generate initial codes.
3. Second reading of the data involving text segmentation and the first round of coding.
4. Review codes to identify contrasts, similarities and potentially distinct or related themes.
5. Review of all the themes and a third reading of the data and re-coding as necessary.
6. Define the final themes and formally define the boundaries and relationships between themes.

Whilst the approach was inductive, it is unrealistic to think that the analysis was not influenced by the theoretical orientation and epistemological assumptions underpinning this research; however, working iteratively throughout the process ensured that all themes were firmly and coherently embedded in the data. An exception to this inductive form of thematic analysis was in relation to the specific discussions held with police officers regarding the efficacy of the methodology, in which the analysis took a deductive turn: the purpose of this particular exercise was to evaluate responses strongly linked to some very specific interview questions, specifically regarding whether the developed methodology was considered useful, what information was useful, and what potentially could make it more useful.

Stage 7: Automated Network Identification

Following the qualitative data analysis, the next step was to consider how the emergent findings could inform the methodological development critical to this research. Constructing a solid methodology and automated workflow was crucial for two reasons. First, the statistical analyses in this project required the observations to be nested within networks, and the dataframe thus had to be transformed into a relational matrix (i.e., a dataset which describes the relations between adverts). Second, the methodology could prove useful in investigative contexts itself, given its focus on large-scale, automated data processing and capability of identifying networks and patterns, and scalability was therefore important.

Assessment of Methodological Validity and Utility

This section briefly highlights the findings related to the qualitative assessment of the preliminary methodology. The discussions with investigators were largely focused on the validity of the identified networks and online patterns in terms of how they mapped onto participants' experiences of online sex trafficking investigations. The assessment of the validity and utility of the developed methodology was based on police respondents' previous investigative experiences, and focused on how the online networks in the sex market that they had previously investigated compared to the networks identified as part of this research, in terms of their structure and spatio-temporal patterning. The methodology used to identify these networks was explained in detail throughout the semi-structured interviews with investigators, and the utility of the information and identified patterns were also discussed.

Validity, in this context, refers to the extent to which the patterns and networks identified in this research were similar to police respondents' observations of criminal networks part of sex trafficking investigations. With no exception, the networks presented were highly similar to what investigators would normally encounter (and try to identify) as part of their inquiries:

> what you've shown there in the map, that's been replicated in multiple inquiries, current ones that I have just now, and historic ones … so that is pretty accurate, what you're showing there. (Detective Inspector 1)

> I would imagine you would see that replicated repeatedly. Yep. In whatever the area, whatever the nationality. (Detective Sergeant 2)

> The fact that those figures you're showing me there—285 adverts, 70 unique phone numbers—yeah, that's what we've already seen. There is a suggestion just from looking at that, that potentially there will be involving people who are exploiting females, or at least controlling them. (Detective Inspector 2)

> I'm looking at that, Richard, with fascination, genuine fascination … because I actually recognise, and it doesn't surprise what you've kind of highlighted there—it doesn't surprise me what you're identifying. (Detective Inspector 4)

From an investigative point of view, the comments from detectives add merit to the validity of the methodology used to identify these networks and their relevance to trafficking investigations. However, just because the patterns are relevant to sex trafficking investigations does not *prove* that the methodology is effective at identifying sex trafficking: there is still a high risk of false positives unless the patterns and networks are triangulated with other, more substantial evidence. It is also important to point out that what was perceived as adding validity to the methodology had relatively little to do with information on sociological characteristics (e.g., ethnicity, age, nationality), as these were acknowledged to be spurious more often than not. Rather, it was the representation of the networks themselves, and the spatio-temporal patterns, that were deemed similar to what is likely to be encountered during investigations and, moreover, what is useful from an investigative point of view.

In terms of the value of the methodology, participants were also positive and highlighted various ways in which it would add value to their current efforts of generating intelligence on sex trafficking. First, the methodology was described as valuable for proactive policing in local contexts. There is often limited intelligence on local off-street sex markets, and from "a proactive perspective, it's brilliant, because we can very quickly kind of focus our resources in that area" (Detective Chief Inspector 1). In particular, it was described how it could be beneficial to monitor large-scale networks establishing themselves in local communities, and that intelligence could then be triangulated against other local intelligence to identify safeguarding concerns. Resources are precious, and when there is a prolonged presence of a network, the intelligence produced by the methodology can be useful in helping to "see where I need to train officers, and get them awareness, and get more of an intelligence picture" (Detective Constable 1). If the network has a presence in other divisional areas, it will also allow for easier sharing of information between divisions:

I think that's really handy, and would result in a lot of conference calls because you'd be pulling together, you know, numerous forces, and saying, "we've clearly got the same group operating here, what do you know?" and then that sharing of information. (Detective Inspector 3)

Besides the proactive benefits, however, the primary value is likely linked to reactive policing efforts, as the intelligence produced can add a digital layer of information to ongoing inquiries. It is important to note that the police can produce similar intelligence themselves, "through more complicated telecom work", but collecting, analysing and establishing links between entities is a resource-intensive process, and a clear benefit is "how quickly you could get that information" (Detective Inspector 3). As one investigator noted, "it would certainly cut down a lot of hours of research and sometimes days of research" (Detective Sergeant 2). Such research also requires a certain amount of technical and analytical expertise, which is not always readily available on short notice:

That's not something that we could do, what you've shown me just now, ourselves. We would have to get an analyst to do that. It's difficult to get analysts, they're like hen's teeth in the police, so we do get them on operations, but we, unless we get an analyst to do what you've shown me here, we wouldn't get that product. (Detective Inspector 2)

The value of the developed methodology is that because it is largely automated, intelligence can be produced very quickly and "through a simple system" (Detective Inspector 3). In addition, because the algorithm used—and subsequent analysis—rely on accounts and phone numbers, the links established were considered 'factual', as opposed to hypothetical relationships between observed similarities or indicators used to *suggest* the presence of control and exploitation:

because it's fact—it's absolute—these are the phone numbers, these are the connections that we've made, and these are the areas that they are located in. (Detective Sergeant 3)

This is an important point: the methodology does not produce factual information on exploitation, but it can provide a modicum of evidence on the structure of an actual network, without making presumptions about the presence or absence of control and exploitation:

the simplest way of putting this, so in terms of what you're producing there, there's no two ways about it, if we got evidence and you overlay, I mean, when you overlay factual, I mean, the very nature of what we do in terms of any crime type, and any crime investigation, factual information is factual information and that [intelligence report is] excellent to have. (Detective Inspector 4)

As such, the intelligence produced through the methodology is valuable for guiding operational and investigative decisions and providing information on "where we should be looking next perhaps" (Detective Sergeant 1). The intelligence produced through the methodology "would be a pivotal starting point to start research[ing]" (Detective Sergeant 2) the information underlying the adverts, to eventually "decide how and where to disrupt that" (Detective Chief Inspector 1), since the truly valuable information, or evidence, will be the information that is not publicly accessible but only available to the police themselves:

if there's a product, or an algorithm or whatever you want to call it, can then input data and look at [ASWs] over a period of time, to say, by the way, there's a common number, maybe we could look at that and see, right, who does that number belong to, and it makes me, it would make my job and every other SIO [Senior Investigating Officer], so much easier, because you would then get that picture of you know, where is that number, it's at Glasgow, Liverpool. We then can put our investigative strategies in place. (Detective Inspector 1)

In addition to its value in giving a technological steer to an ongoing investigation, it can also be useful to illustrate spatio-temporal movement patterns. Because "human trafficking is all about the movement" (Detective Chief Inspector 1), being able to present such information clearly and concisely is key:

it gives us a really clear human trafficking case ... So if we can show that movement, as you've done here, it gives us a much easier tool to give to the Fiscal for example. Their whole issue is evidencing the movement of people. So yeah, that's a really valuable tool from that perspective. (Detective Chief Inspector 1)

Being able to present complicated information in an easily digestible and concise format is absolutely critical, and as some pointed out, the implications of that may go beyond the investigative stage and prove useful in other judicial contexts as well:

ultimately I suppose, allow it in a court context, a jury to understand what we're talking about, and to be convinced of the information that we're presenting as being credible information that a crime has occurred and has been ... and the information that you've got there is factual information, which, when we overlay with witness statements or whatever information from other sources of data, then it can be combined ... provide a compelling case for us to get evidence for a warrant, or whatever it may be. (Detective Inspector 4)

To summarise, the methodology was identified as being capable of identifying networks that are similar to what investigators have previously encountered throughout various inquiries and also relevant to the policing of sex trafficking. It may have the most practical value in overlaying ongoing investigations with a real-time, digital dimension of network structures and spatio-temporal patterns. Because so much information in online adverts will be spurious, there are clear benefits in relying on empirically established connections rather than using indicators to deem what adverts may or may not be of interest in an investigation. If the methodology could be developed into a scalable, easy-to-use tool aimed at law enforcement, it could have some very clear benefits in terms of freeing up time and resources for other crucial activities. There are always questions regarding the credibility and validity of online intelligence, but the findings indeed suggest that the triangulation of open-source intelligence with intelligence from other sources can be valuable in both national and divisional contexts.

Methodological Refinement

Following the preliminary methodological assessment, the next step of the research process sought to draw on the findings from the semi-structured interviews to improve the methodology. One issue of the research process relates to the circularity of methodological validation. In other words, because a set of initial patterns and networks was presented and discussed with practitioners, in which there is no information available to confirm what the patterns actually represent, the very nature of the conversations was speculative and based on their experience. There is, therefore, a danger that the credibility and validity of the identified patterns are reaffirmed rather than carefully evaluated in light of more substantial evidence. This is a valid point of criticism, and it certainly would have been beneficial to work with more robust data pertaining to offline networks and their online dimension. However, in the absence of such data, the evaluation was highly valuable for two specific reasons. First, whilst it could not confirm that exploitation per se was a feature of the identified networks, the conversations clearly demonstrated what type of information was valuable from an investigative point of view. Second, irrespective of what the patterns and networks were actually representing, the interviews provided much clarity on how online data are best used as part of investigations—an invaluable insight in the context of the methodology development.

In more concrete terms, an important change to the methodology was related to the observation that the only useful connections—from a policing perspective—were the phone numbers and user accounts. The idea of forming connections based on semantic similarity was therefore abandoned because of the risk of generating false-positives. It should be noted, however, that the decision not to rely on semantic similarity was not solely a consideration regarding operational relevance. Indeed, there is currently limited information regarding the extent to which advert plagiarism may occur in online escort advertising; it is conceivable that individuals or networks could copy the textual descriptions from adverts that they deem relevant, especially if English is not their first language. On a different note, it might also be expected that adverts *may* be similar simply because the descriptions are all focused on the same topics (e.g., description of physical characteristics and services offered). Defining a cut-point for when two adverts should be considered similar is therefore not straightforward. Epistemologically speaking, utilising semantic similarity would introduce a lot of uncertainty due to the (potentially) high risk of generating false-positives, simply because we cannot be certain that a tie based on semantic similarity actually represents a meaningful offline tie; phone numbers and user accounts, on the other hand, provide a much more robust way of inferring the presence of an offline tie between two adverts.

The findings from the assessment inevitably shifted the focus away from the more sociologically meaningful variables—such as age, nationality and ethnicity—to instead focus on what investigators perceived as most useful, namely, the structure and geography of the networks. The methodology thus needed to be capable of automatically identifying all empirical connections between adverts that were based upon phone numbers and user accounts. All of this was achieved in R with a variety of packages, but most importantly, the *igraph* (Csardi and Nepusz 2006) and *Tidyverse* (Wickham et al. 2019) packages. This also involved defining several custom functions and algorithms that could then be pieced together to build a scalable workflow.

The algorithm relied on the dataframe created earlier (see *Stage 3: Data Management*), and two edge lists were created through a series of merges; one was created based on shared phone numbers, and one was based on user accounts. These two edge lists were then combined into one, representing all observed ties between adverts in the dataset, and with one variable denoting edge type (i.e., phone number or user account). In computational terms, this resulted in the transformation of the original dataframe into a graph, or relational matrix. As defined in this research, a network would be a component (a collection of nodes unconnected to other groups) within the graph. For the purpose of identifying

Table 5 Summary of networks and the number of unique adverts

N	Range	Mean	SD	Median
15,016	1–1544	8.23	34.6	2

components, edge type was ignored, and the network was simplified by removing loops, that is, one edge with the same node as the two end-points. Multiple edges were also removed. This resulted in a final edge list representing an undirected and unweighted network of all adverts in the dataframe. Once this was completed, it was possible to identify all distinct components in the overarching network. Each distinct network (i.e., component of the graph) was assigned a unique group identifier, which was then appended to each advert in the original dataframe. In total, 123,537 unique adverts were found to be clustered within 15,016 distinct networks. The distribution of adverts, as shown in Table 5, is in line with what we would expect; the majority of advert networks represent independent sex workers, with fewer networks containing a disproportionate number of adverts. Besides the process of identifying and constructing networks, the algorithm was also designed to calculate network-level statistics, which will be described in the following section.

Adding Network-Level Variables

A series of functions was defined to obtain geographical and network statistics for each network in the dataframe. The network statistics included density, average shortest path, transitivity (or clustering coefficient), diameter, closeness, degree, eigenvalues and betweenness. The metric distance between adverts in a network was calculated to estimate the geographical dispersion within each network. Each advert contained geographical coordinates, and using the *geosphere* package in R[8] functions were defined to calculate the average, median and standard deviations in kilometres between all adverts in a network, and these were then appended to the original dataframe.

[8] https://CRAN.R-project.org/package=geosphere.

The Final Data Structure

Before highlighting the actual analysis, it is worth describing the structure of the final dataset. To be more precise, the original dataframe had been transformed into two objects. The primary unit of analysis of both was unique adverts, and the first was constructed as a hierarchical dataframe where the second level consisted of the networks the adverts were nested in. The second object was an edgelist which specified the relations between all unique adverts. Network-level variables consisted of the structural and relational characteristics of the networks, such as geographical dispersion and the network statistics mentioned earlier. It also included simple network-level count variables, such as the number of unique adverts, the number of advertised locations, and the total number of nationalities listed within the adverts. It also contained advert-level variables (see 3.4.10 for the variables included in the final analysis) pertaining to the marketing strategies used within the actual adverts.

Stage 8: Operationalising Network Complexity

With all the data management and processing completed, the data were in a format suitable for statistical analysis. The first part of the analysis, which is published and described elsewhere (Kjellgren 2023, 2025), was focused on using principal component analysis (PCA) to distil a series of theoretically interesting network-level variables into a combined measurement of the scale and structure of networks, argued to be an indicator of the underlying network complexity. Network complexity was argued to be a result of three different dimensions relating to a network: the scale, geographical distribution and structure. Table 6 shows the variables that were used in this exploration, and the full results are reported in Kjellgren (2023, 2025). For now, it is sufficient to know that each network was ranked, in terms of its complexity, on a scale ranging from 1 to 10, and this measure formed the basis of analyses conducted in chapters "Complexity, Similarity and Tie Formation in Advert Networks" and "Network Influences on Extreme Service Advertisement". The distribution of networks on the complexity scale is shown in Fig. 3.

Table 6 Operationalisation of network complexity scale, from Kjellgren (2023)

Dimension	Variable	Operationalisation	Description
1. Network scale	Number of user accounts	Count of the number of distinct user accounts used by the network.	Gives a reasonable indication of the scale of a network. It is unlikely to directly translate to the number of people involved; however, a larger number of user accounts could likely indicate that more people are required to maintain the operation of the network
1. Network scale	Number of advertised ethnicities.	Count of the number of distinct ethnicities (of 12 possible) advertised by the network	Whereas, ethnicity certainly can be considered a marketing strategy, a larger number of advertised ethnicities could indicate that more than one person is involved
2. Geography	Geographical dispersion	The standard deviation of the distance between each pair of adverts within a network, as measured in kilometres. A standard deviation of 0 would indicate no dispersion and a larger standard deviation indicates larger geographical dispersion	This is important to both understand the geographical scale of a network and the potential movement patterns involved

(*continued*)

Table 6 (continued)

Dimension	Variable	Operationalisation	Description
3. Network structure	Density	The prevalence of dyadic relationships, in which a value of 1 indicates that all theoretically possible combinations of ties are formed and lower values indicate unformed combinations of ties	Density provides a measure of how densely connected a network is. A high density means that adverts are largely connected by the same phone numbers and user accounts, which likely would be the case for independent sex workers. The opposite may be true for more distinct forms of offline organisations
3. Network structure	Average shortest path	The average of the shortest paths between all pairwise combinations of adverts within a network. A lower number would indicate a cohesive network, whereas a higher number means that it is more dispersed	An important measure of network topology that captures how dispersed a network is, in terms of its connections
3. Network structure	Diameter	The longest of all shortest paths between all pairwise combinations of adverts within a network. A higher number indicates both a dispersed and potentially larger network	Another important topological measure that also feeds into the network size

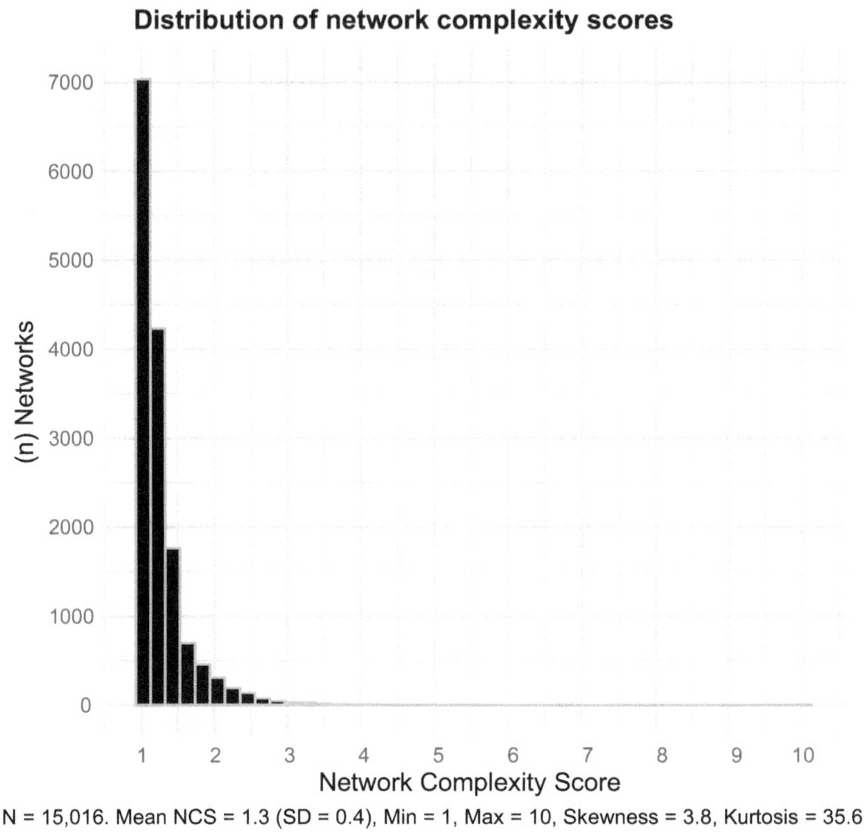

Fig. 3 Distribution of network complexity scores

It should be noted that this combined measurement—or *principal component*—which is referred to as the *network complexity scale* throughout the analyses in subsequent chapters is the result of the linear combinations of the values of the input variables specific to the dataset used (Härdle and Simar 2019). In other words, if the same method were applied, using the same input variables, but on a different and unrelated dataset, the derived values would be different. For example, the most complex network identified in the current dataset (with a score of 10 on the current network complexity scale) will differ in complexity from another network with the same score in a different dataset. As such, the distribution of values across the input variables used is what drives the identification of principal components, and subsequently, affects how they are interpreted. In terms of transferability, whereas the different dimensions of complexity (network scale, geography and structure) are theoretically valid and transferable, the *empirical* contributions of each of the input variables for measuring complexity will be variable. Consequently, even though the operationalisation and interpretation of network complexity is a result of the empirical patterns within the data used in this research, the conceptualisation of complexity as consisting of the dimensions of network scale, geography and structure is transferable to other empirical investigations.

Stage 9: Social Network Analysis

A core analytical aim was to examine the structure of the identified networks. The social network analysis presented in chapter "Complexity, Similarity and Tie Formation in Advert Networks" relied exclusively on relational data and used three specific methods. Homophilous processes, or group-embedding, were examined through a comparison of each network's external-internal index (E-I index; Krackhardt and Stern 1988). To examine the textual similarity of adverts, the cosine distance was calculated, both in relation to all adverts *within* a network and between networks. Finally, a series of quadratic assignment procedures (QAP), and its multivariate counterpart, MRQAP, were conducted. This method was used to test relational hypotheses and examine the factors contributing to tie formation in the empirical networks. A more thorough explanation of the respective methods, and how to interpret the results, are provided in chapter "Complexity, Similarity and Tie Formation in Advert Networks".

Stage 10: Multilevel Modelling

An early hypothesis to emerge from this case study was that network structure might predict the marketing strategies used in individual adverts. Testing this hypothesis was the principal aim of chapter "Network Influences on Extreme Service Advertisement". Because of the nested structure of the data, multilevel modelling or mixed effects models were particularly well-suited for this task. A series of regression models were constructed to examine the association between network-level characteristics and advert-level marketing strategies, especially in relation to what is often highlighted as extreme services (e.g., Skidmore et al. 2018). The analysis was focused upon statistical patterns in marketing strategies associated with networks within the sample that could be considered 'typical'. After some initial regression diagnostics of the first set of models, the most complex network displayed a high degree of leverage. The removal of this observation made the magnitude of the estimated effects weaker, but arguably provided a better representation of tendencies within 'typical' online networks in the sex market. In terms of the interpretation of the patterns identified from the statistical modelling, it is worth remembering that they represent 'typical' networks, and that there is a potential that the patterns may actually be stronger in more complex networks (as was the case with the excluded network). Table 7 provides a brief overview of the analytical variables specifically used within the models, and some of these also formed the basis of the analysis conducted in chapter "Complexity, Similarity and Tie Formation in Advert Networks".

Stage 11: Socio-Ecological Synthesis

Finally, once all of the different empirical analyses had been conducted, the final part of the research process involved the synthesis of findings from across the different chapters. The findings were framed in light of a socio-ecological framework consisting of four interlinked levels: individual, relationship, community and societal (Dahlberg and Krug 2006). This bore much resemblance to the thematic analysis conducted earlier; whether quantitative, qualitative or more theoretically oriented, each finding was extracted, coded and categorised under themes relating to the original research questions, and the four socio-ecological levels. Links were established between the findings themselves, but also with regard to previous research. This was largely an iterative process which culminated in the triangulation of several important insights, the most important of which are presented and discussed in the final chapter of this book.

Table 7 Analytical variables used in the multilevel models

Type	Variable	Definition
Dependent Variable	OWO (oral without protection)	The percentage of advert records within an advert identifier that offers unprotected oral sex.
Dependent Variable	A Levels	The percentage of advert records within an advert identifier that offers anal sex.
Dependent Variable	PSE (pornstar experience)	The percentage of advert records within an advert identifier that offers a pornstar experience. This can potentially encapsulate a wider array of services that can be considered more extreme.
Dependent Variable	WS (water sports)	The percentage of advert records within an advert identifier that offers acts involving urine.
Dependent Variable	All Extreme (AE)	The percentage of advert records within an advert identifier that offers all four of the services listed above (OWO, A Levels, PSE and WS).
Dependent Variable	GFE (girlfriend experience)	The percentage of advert records within an advert identifier that offers a girlfriend experience. This was included as a service that potentially stands in contrast to the more extreme services and, particularly, the pornstar experience, which may be more associated with rougher forms of sex. The girlfriend experience, conversely, tends to be associated with (the illusion of) intimacy.
Dependent Variable	Dining	The percentage of advert records within an advert identifier that offers dining as a service. Similar to the GFE, this is potentially different since it involves escorting without intercourse.

(*continued*)

Table 7 (continued)

Type	Variable	Definition
Dependent Variable	Extreme Scale	A combination of the PSE and WS variables, in which the sum of these was calculated and the combined variable later rescaled to range from 1 to 10. The choice of these two variables was based on the first set of models, in which the results suggested these required a more in-depth analysis based on some commonalities in the patterns identified. It should be noted, however, that other attempts were made, with factor analysis and principal component analysis, to identify a latent dimension of more extreme services. The simplest solution, in this case combining the two variables, appeared to offer the best fit to the data.
Independent Variable	Age	The mean age of the advert records nested in the advert identifier (i.e., unique adverts).
Independent Variable	VIP	The percentage of advert records within an advert identifier that had the VIP status, which is a feature that can be paid for to increase the visibility and reach of an advert.
Independent Variable	Featured	The percentage of advert records within an advert identifier that had the 'featured' status which, similar to the VIP status, increases visibility and reach.
Independent Variable	Highlighted	The percentage of advert records within an advert identifier that had the 'highlighted' status, and as the two variables above, is a paid feature to increase the visibility and reach of an advert.

(*continued*)

Table 7 (continued)

Type	Variable	Definition
Independent Variable	Ethnicity	The modal ethnic category of the advert records nested in an advert identifier. It is a combination of the ethnicity and nationality variables from the scraped data. An attempt was made to construct a more sociologically meaningful operationalisation of nationality and ethnicity similar to the recommendations of the Office for National Statistics. For the purposes of this analysis, it was deemed important to not only focus on ethnic identity, but also to be able to control for nationality, since both the literature and qualitative findings of this research highlight migrants as particularly vulnerable to exploitation.
Independent Variable	Region	The modal International Territorial Level 1 (ITL) region of the advert records nested in an advert identifier. This comprises the nine regions of England and Scotland, Wales and Northern Ireland.
Independent Variable	Network Complexity Scale	The scale intended to measure the complexity of a network. It was treated as a level 2 variable in the random effects models
Independent Variable	Network Complexity Scale Quintiles	The network complexity scale mentioned above partitioned into quintiles. This was used in the first instance of models to allow for more complex networks to be directly compared to the 20% least complex networks.
Independent Variable	Network Services	The percentage of adverts within a network that are advertising all services except for PSE and WS. This measurement was used as a control variable in the final model to examine the extent to which it is predictive of PSE and WS.
Independent Variable	Network Mean Services	The average number of services (out of a total of 23 unique services) offered by networks.

Concluding Remarks

This chapter has introduced computational criminology and the central ideas underpinning workflow management and provided an overview of the methodological design of the mixed-methods research, which provided the foundation for the research conducted for this book. Rather than being overly prescriptive, the structure of this chapter, and the methodological details, considerations and discussions, are meant to serve as a template or example for guiding future students of computational criminology. It has also provided sufficient methodological detail to allow the reader to understand the logical connections between the different components of this research, whilst also serving as a roadmap for the remainder of this book.

References

Abel GM (2011) Different Stage, Different Performance: The Protective Strategy of Role Play on Emotional Health in Sex Work. Soc Sci Med 72(7):1177–1184. https://doi.org/10.1016/j.socscimed.2011.01.021

Anderson C (2008) The End of Theory: The Data Deluge Makes the Scientific Method Obsolete. In: Wired Magazine

Bornakke T, Due BL (2018) Big–Thick Blending: A Method for Mixing Analytical Insights from Big and Thick Data Sources. Big Data Soc 5(1):1–16. https://doi.org/10.1177/2053951718765026

Braun V, Clarke V (2006) Using Thematic Analysis in Psychology. Qual Res Psychol 3(2):77–101. https://doi.org/10.1191/1478088706qp063oa

Brayne S (2020) Predict and Surveil: Data, Discretion, and the Future of Policing. Oxford University Press, New York

Brents BG, Hausbeck K (2007) Marketing Sex: US Legal Brothels and Late Capitalist Consumption. Sexualities 10(4):425–439. https://doi.org/10.1177/1363460707080976

Brooker PD (2020) Programming with Python for Social Scientists. SAGE Publications Ltd.

Burrows R, Savage M (2014) After the Crisis? Big Data and the Methodological Challenges of Empirical Sociology. Big Data Soc 1(1):1–6. https://doi.org/10.1177/2053951714540280

Connelly R, Playford CJ, Gayle V, Dibben C (2016) The Role of Administrative Data in the Big Data Revolution in Social Science Research. Soc Sci Res 59:1–12. https://doi.org/10.1016/j.ssresearch.2016.04.015

Csardi G, Nepusz T (2006) The Igraph Software Package for Complex Network Research. Int J Complex Syst 1695(5):1–9

Cunningham S, Sanders T, Scoular J, Campbell R, Pitcher J, Hill K, Valentine-Chase M, Melissa C, Aydin Y, Hamer R (2017) Behind the Screen: Commercial Sex, Digital Spaces and Working Online. Technol Soc 53(1):47–54. https://doi.org/10.1016/j.techsoc.2017.11.004

Dahlberg LL, Krug EG (2006) Violence a Global Public Health Problem. Cien Saude Colet 11(2):277–292. https://doi.org/10.1590/S1413-81232006000200007

Edwards R, Holland J (2020) Reviewing Challenges and the Future for Qualitative Interviewing. Int J Soc Res Methodol 23(5):581–592. https://doi.org/10.1080/13645579.2020.1766767

Ellison G (2017) Criminalizing the Payment for Sex in Northern Ireland: Sketching the Contours of a Moral Panic. Br J Criminol 57(1):194–214. https://doi.org/10.1093/bjc/azv107

Freese J (2007) Replication Standards for Quantitative Social Science: Why Not Sociology? Sociol Methods Res 36(2):153–172. https://doi.org/10.1177/0049124107306659

Härdle WK, Simar LO (2019) Applied Multivariate Statistical Analysis, 5th edn. Springer International Publishing, Cham

Keuschnigg M, Lovsjö N, Hedström P (2018) Analytical Sociology and Computational Social Science. J Comput Soc Sci 1(1):3–14. https://doi.org/10.1007/s42001-017-0006-5

Kjellgren R (2018) Connecting the Dots: Mapping Networks, Vulnerability and Exploitation within the Off-Street Sex Market. University of Stirling, Stirling

Kjellgren R (2019) Deciphering Digital Networks: Using Open-source Data to Assess the Role of Ethnicity and Nationality in Structuring the Off-street Sex Market. University of Stirling, Stirling

Kjellgren R (2022) Good Tech, Bad Tech: Policing Sex Trafficking with Big Data. Int J Crime Justice Soc Democr 11(1):149–166. https://doi.org/10.3316/agispt.20220412065553

Kjellgren R (2023) "Dark Spaces of Precarity": Networks and Complexity in the Off-street Sex Market. PhD Thesis, University of Stirling.

Kjellgren R (2025) The Geographies and Complexities of Online Networks in the Off-street Sex Market. Criminol Crim Just 25(1):81–103. https://doi.org/10.1177/17488958241245287

Krackhardt D, Stern RN (1988) Informal Networks and Organizational Crises: An Experimental Simulation. Soc Psychol Q 51(2):123–140. https://doi.org/10.2307/2786835

Lazer D, Pentland A, Adamic L, Aral S, Barabási A-L, Brewer D, Christakis N, Contractor N, Fowler J, Gutmann M, Jebara T, King G, Macy M, Roy D, Van Alstyne M (2009) Computational Social Science. Science 323(5915):721–723. https://doi.org/10.1126/science.1167742

Li L, Simek O, Lai A, Daggett M, Dagli CK, Jones C (2018) Detection and Characterization of Human Trafficking Networks Using Unsupervised Scalable Text Template Matching. In: 2018 IEEE International Conference on Big Data (Big Data), Seattle, WA, USA

Mayer-Schönberger V, Cukier K (2013) Big Data: A Revolution That Will Transform How We Live, Work, and Think, 1st edn. John Murray Publishers, London

McGuire M, Dowling S (2013) Cyber Crime: A Review of the Evidence Chapter 1: Cyber-dependent Crimes. Home Office, London

Mills CW (2000) The Sociological Imagination. Oxford University Press

Morselli C (2009) Inside Criminal Networks, 1st edn. Springer, New York

Sanders T, Scoular J, Campbell R, Pitcher J, Cunningham S (2018) Internet Sex Work: Beyond the Gaze, 1st edn. Springer Nature, Cham

Savage M, Burrows R (2007) The Coming Crisis of Empirical Sociology. Sociology 41(5):885–899. https://doi.org/10.1177/0038038507080443

Scoular J, Pitcher J, Sanders T, Cunningham S, Campbell R (2019) Beyond the Gaze and Well Beyond Wolfenden: The Practices and Rationalities of Regulating and Policing Sex Work in the Digital Age. J Law Soc 46(2):211–239

Skidmore M, Garner S, Desroches C, Saggu N (2018) The Threat of Exploitation in the Adult Sex Market: A Pilot Study of Online Sex Worker Advertisements. Policing 12(2):210–218. https://doi.org/10.1093/police/pax007

Subrahmanyam K, Reich SM, Waechter N, Espinoza G (2008) Online and Offline Social Networks: Use of Social Networking Sites by Emerging Adults. J Appl Dev Psychol 29(6):420–433. https://doi.org/10.1016/j.appdev.2008.07.003

Törnberg P, Törnberg A (2018) The Limits of Computation: A Philosophical Critique of Contemporary Big Data Research. Big Data Soc 5(2). https://doi.org/10.1177/2053951718811843

Turner KJ, Lambert PS (2015) Workflows for Quantitative Data Analysis in the Social Sciences. Int J Softw Tools Technol Transfer 17(3):321–338. https://doi.org/10.1007/s10009-014-0315-4

von Lampe K (2009) Human Capital and Social Capital in Criminal Networks: Introduction to the Special Issue on the 7th Blankensee Colloquium. Trends Organ Crim 12(2):93–100. https://doi.org/10.1007/s12117-009-9067-z

Wickham H, Averick M, Bryan J, Chang W, McGowan LD, François R, Grolemund G, Hayes A, Henry L, Hester J, Kuhn M, Pedersen TL, Miller E, Bache SM, Müller K, Ooms J, Robinson D, Seidel DP, Spinu V, Takahashi K, Vaughan D, Wilke C, Woo K, Yutani H (2019) Welcome to the Tidyverse. J Open Source Softw 4(43):1686. https://doi.org/10.21105/joss.01686

Exploitation and the Policing of Contemporary Sex Markets in Scotland

Introduction

This chapter presents the findings from a thematic analysis of data gathered through qualitative interviews with the police and other stakeholders. The analysis focuses on the Scottish context of policing and responding to exploitation. Thirteen out of fourteen participants were located in Scotland. Nine detectives were currently serving in Police Scotland, either in the National Human Trafficking Unit (NHTU) or as human trafficking champions in various police divisions throughout the country. Four participants represented four different Scottish non-governmental organisations (NGOs), all supporting or advocating for the rights of trafficking victims, migrants or sex workers. However, given the propensity of criminal networks to operate across borders, one detective from a northern English police force was also included, to provide a unique cross-national perspective. The analysis was inductive and structured around Braun and Clarke's (2006) thematic analysis. It consisted of six distinct stages of coding and the construction of themes, the details of which are presented in *Methods and Analytical Approach*.

R. Kjellgren, *Internet-Mediated Exploitation in the Scottish Online Sex Market*, Transnational Crime, Crime Control and Security,
https://doi.org/10.1007/978-3-032-09275-5_7

The role and impact of technology is an overarching theme within this analysis, interwoven with other areas related to migration, sexual labour, exploitation and policing. There is a natural progression in how the findings are presented and discussed, moving from broader sociological issues related to the sex market to the details of the investigative process. The findings also relate to the organisation of exploitation and the challenges of policing sex trafficking. The analysis is divided into three broader sections, which represent three overarching themes: (1) migration, sexual labour and exploitation; (2) technological change and the organisation of exploitation and (3) the complexities associated with policing criminal networks operating in the sex market.

Migration, Sexual Labour and Exploitation in Late Capitalism focuses upon the nature of sexual labour and the extent to which sex work is inherently exploitative. Here, the role of agency is discussed in more detail, particularly concerning migration for sexual labour. It also highlights the spectrum of working conditions found within the sex market. The section examines how sexual labour is organised in various ways and how sex workers mobilise capital to reduce the risk of exploitation. The discussion also focuses on commonalities in the experiences of victims of exploitation. This also covers the recruitment process and the strategies criminal networks use to achieve control and compliance over their victims.

Findings relating to the theme of technological change will be presented in *Technological Changes and the Organisation of Exploitation*. The analysis focuses on how online technologies have led to paradoxical developments in the sex market; it simultaneously reduces some risks associated with sex work and contributes to "dark spaces of precarity", which possibly are conducive to exploitation. The implications of technological change for how criminal networks operate in the sex market are also a significant component of this theme.

Policing Criminal Networks in the Sex Market highlights findings pertaining to the challenges associated with policing sex trafficking and, more broadly, criminal networks operating in the sex market. Here, issues relating to police demand, resources and prioritisation are highlighted. The epistemological qualities of escort adverts as a form of data and intelligence are discussed in more depth, in addition to how open-source intelligence is situated within the broader context of investigating sex trafficking. The final section "Concluding Remarks" summarises the key findings from the qualitative analysis.

Methods and Analytical Approach

All qualitative data in this research were collected using semi-structured interviews. These interviews had two very specific purposes. First, they were designed to collect the data required to answer the following questions:

1. How are online technologies used within the off-street sex market?
2. How do criminal networks and organised crime groups use online technologies to facilitate their operations, specifically with regard to advertising victims and connecting with sex buyers?

Second, the interviews conducted with police respondents also involved systematic discussions of intelligence reports. These intelligence reports were described in more detail in chapter "Methods in Practice: Designing an Effective Workflow in Computational Criminology" (section "Stage 7: Automated Network Identification"). Essentially, intelligence reports on networks operating in the detectives' local areas were generated algorithmically (based on scraped, open-source data), and part of the analysis was focused on interpreting the patterns, based on their investigative experiences.

Respondent Sampling and Recruitment

Researching the sex market and, in particular, issues of vulnerability, exploitation and sex trafficking is challenging due to the ethics and logistics involved. This research is focused upon the policing of, and responses to, exploitation, and it therefore seemed a sensible approach to focus on recruiting stakeholders responding to harms within the sex market. This decision was prior to the start of this research project; however, relying on interviews with stakeholders takes us further away from understandings of exploitation informed directly by lived experience—this is considered a significant limitation of this research and will be discussed in more detail in chapter "Key Messages and Conclusions: Future Directions in the Computational Criminology of Internet-Mediated Exploitation".

Whilst the research is primarily relevant to a Scottish context, a decision was also made to include respondents outwith Scotland. Police Scotland was particularly suitable since it is the second largest police force within the UK, spanning the largest geographical area, including both urban and rural spaces. This allowed for a much more nuanced perspective on responding to exploitation, compared to what could have been gained from a police force that is more or less exclusively metropolitan. However, in recognition that most investigations will transcend police force boundaries, respondents from police forces other than Police Scotland were also approached to provide a better balance. Whilst the findings are not generalisable, they still provide a solid foundation for our understanding of exploitation, and given that criminal networks are likely to circulate the UK, the findings will likely be relevant to other police forces as well.

Two specific inclusion criteria were applied in the recruiting process. Police respondents were required to have recent experience in sex trafficking investigations or work specifically in a position relating to sex trafficking investigations. Non-governmental organisations (NGOs) that supported or advocated for the rights of one or more of the following groups were considered for recruitment: (1) sex workers; (2) trafficking victims and (3) migrants. The recruitment of police respondents was largely respondent-driven, in the sense that the initial respondents within Police Scotland approached suitable candidates on my behalf. In total, nine respondents from Police Scotland were identified, five of whom belonged to the National Human Trafficking Unit (NHTU). Four officers served as Human Trafficking Champions in different police divisions across Scotland. These Human Trafficking Champions have special responsibilities regarding responding to and investigating human trafficking in their divisions. The NHTU coordinates and provides support to divisional Human Trafficking Champions and investigates some of the more complex and large-scale human trafficking cases in Scotland.

In addition to the police respondents from Police Scotland, one detective from a larger metropolitan English police force was also recruited to complement Scottish perspectives. This was particularly pertinent given the significance of the link between Scotland and the English region in question, regarding the flows of criminal networks. Taken together, police respondents covered a substantial geographical area, which allowed for regional comparisons in the qualitative analysis. It is also worth mentioning that many detectives served in specialised trafficking-related capacities such as senior investigating officers, coordination, intelligence and internet investigation. As such, the police sample involved people of varying ranks, responsibilities and niche expertise—all related to sex trafficking.

The other four respondents represented four different NGOs. These were recruited specifically to introduce non-policing perspectives on the issues pertinent to this research. Twelve NGOs were identified as suitable candidates through a combination of desk-based research and snowball sampling. These consisted of nine sex worker rights or support organisations, two NGOs specifically supporting trafficking victims and one organisation supporting vulnerable and often exploited migrants. The overall response rate was quite low (33%). The organisations that either declined or did not respond to the research requests were all groups supporting and advocating for sex workers. The low response rate was perhaps not surprising, given that recruitment coincided with the peak of the COVID-19 pandemic. In addition, the very notion that a researcher is researching sex trafficking or exploitation can be sufficient to dissuade sex work-oriented NGOs from partaking in research. This is not surprising given how exploitative the anti-trafficking discourse has been historically, often depriving sex workers of their agency, despite claiming to work in their interest (see, for instance, Ellison 2017 for a more thorough discussion). With that said, the four NGOs that accepted the invitation to interviews had varied experience with regard to specifically responding to sex trafficking, though nevertheless provided invaluable perspectives on wider issues relating to sexual labour, migration, vulnerability and exploitation. Respondents were incredibly generous with their time, despite facing ongoing challenges within their organisations. Indeed, all stakeholders were either considered essential workers or provided

Table 1 Respondent details

Respondent	Organisation	Details
Detective Constable 1	English Police Force	Modern Slavery Unit
Detective Constable 2	Police Scotland	National Unit
Detective Sergeant 1	Police Scotland	National Unit
Detective Sergeant 2	Police Scotland	National Unit
Detective Sergeant 3	Police Scotland	Divisional
Detective Inspector 1	Police Scotland	National Unit
Detective Inspector 2	Police Scotland	National Unit
Detective Inspector 3	Police Scotland	Divisional
Detective Inspector 4	Police Scotland	Divisional
Detective Chief Inspector 1	Police Scotland	Divisional
NGO Worker 1	Sex Worker Support (Scotland)	Managerial Position
NGO Worker 2	Trafficking Victim Support (Scotland)	Managerial Position
NGO Worker 3	Migrant Support (Scotland)	Managerial Position
NGO Worker 4	Trafficking Victim Support (Scotland)	Managerial Position

essential services throughout a very turbulent period of recent history and had limited availability to engage with academic research. The final list of respondents can be found in Table 1

Data Collection and Interview Schedules

Data collection was carried out using semi-structured interviews in the autumn of 2021. Since this occurred during the pandemic, all interviews were conducted online using Microsoft Teams. The interviews were recorded (only audio was captured) directly onto the researcher's encrypted hard drive. The audio recordings were then used to manually produce transcripts in NVivo 12. Two different interview schedules were used, one for each group of stakeholders. The interview schedule for NGO participants focused on the barriers faced by migrants and victims in seeking services and support and, subsequently, how our responses to these issues can be improved. The interviews with police officers primarily focused on their experiences investigating sex trafficking and its online dimension. All interviews were conducted one-to-one, except for one interview involving two police officers from the same divisional unit (Detective Inspector 4 and Detective Sergeant 3). The length of the interviews ranged from 41 to 83 minutes, with an average of 57 minutes.

The interview process was designed differently for police officers, which involved systematic discussions on past or ongoing sex trafficking cases and an evaluation of the intelligence reports produced as part of the research. These intelligence reports highlighted networks specific to the geographical area where the detectives were based (and for the national unit, large-scale networks operating across the country). The networks themselves were selected because of their perceived complexity. Following semi-structured questions around the policing and online dimension of sex trafficking, and their investigative experiences, these reports were shared with the participants during the interview. Discussions were focused on how they interpreted the patterns, their usefulness from an investigative point of view, and the extent to which the methodology could be useful in practice. The findings specific to the methodological assessment are presented in chapter "Methods in Practice: Designing an Effective Workflow in Computational Criminology" (section "Stage 7: Automated Network Identification").

Thematic Analysis

The rationale for conducting the thematic analysis at this particular stage of the research process was that qualitative insights were required to progress further. In other words, further development of the quantitative methodology depended on the qualitative findings, specifically the preliminary methodological assessment. Braun and Clarke's (2006) thematic analysis was the method used to analyse the qualitative data. More precisely, the analysis involved an inductive or 'bottom-up' approach (Braun and Clarke 2006, p. 28). This flexible method is particularly well-suited to identifying patterns in qualitative data and ensuring the themes constructed are firmly connected to the data. As such, there was no predefined coding frame; rather, codes were constructed through an iterative process. The analytical process itself was directly informed by the work of Braun and Clarke (2006) and involved the following steps:

1. First reading of all the data to note particular keywords, trends or ideas and note-taking.
2. Compiling the notes to generate initial codes.
3. Second reading of the data involving text segmentation and the first round of coding.
4. Review codes to identify contrasts, similarities and potentially distinct or related themes.
5. Review of all the themes and a third reading of the data and re-coding as necessary.
6. Define the final themes and formally define the boundaries and relationships between themes.

Whilst the approach was inductive, it is unrealistic to think that the analysis was not influenced by the theoretical orientation and epistemological assumptions underpinning this research; however, working iteratively throughout the process ensured that all themes were firmly and coherently embedded in the data. An exception to this inductive form of thematic analysis was in relation to the specific discussions held with police officers regarding the efficacy of the methodology, in which the analysis took a deductive turn: the purpose of this particular exercise was to evaluate responses strongly linked to some very specific interview questions, specifically regarding whether the developed methodology was considered useful, what information was useful, and what potentially could make it more useful.

Migration, Sexual Labour and Exploitation in Late Capitalism

The Spectrum of Working Conditions

Sexual labour was suggested to be organised for a variety of reasons. In the context of organised forms of sex work—such as working cooperatively, in partnerships or through intermediaries—there is potentially a broad spectrum of possible working conditions. Before examining this in more detail, it is important to note that there were diverging views about sex work as a form of labour or as inherently exploitative. In other words, some respondents argued that prostitution, by definition, is a form of exploitation in the context of patriarchal gender structures, whereas others had a more nuanced view. For instance, one NGO worker emphasised exploitation as a feature of late capitalism and argued that while the sex industry certainly involves risks, the reality of sexual labour is perhaps more mundane and not simply an expression of patriarchal domination or violence against women:

> I think in a capitalist society, many of us are in management relationships that feel exploitative and that is without the added element of criminalisation of that relationship. (NGO Worker 1)

In contrast, others expressed ambivalence regarding women's agency and whilst "they may have become involved in prostitution of their own volition, for lack of a better descriptor" (NGO Worker 2), the extent to which there truly is a 'choice' to engage in sexual labour was questioned. Whether or not an individual may actually end up exploited, many perceived the migration for sexual labour as an active choice made by women to improve their lives:

> I'd say they have their own plans, but you know that sort of short-term pain, I think they're willing to take, to try and set themselves up. (Detective Inspector 3)

However, these choices were described as often being made in structurally constrained contexts. Participants pointed out how several intersecting factors "can really push women to the margins" (NGO Worker 2), such as socio-economic deprivation, the feminisation of poverty and the potential to earn money in a short amount of time. A central component of this theme is how various forms of capital were suggested to influence the working conditions of sex workers. The lack of economic capital was often perceived as a motivator to either engage in sex work or seek opportunities abroad, which later may transcend into exploitation. Human capital, including language skills, experience of working in the sex industry and location-specific knowledge, were described as central to working safely in the sex market. Social capital was also outlined as equally important and, in this context, relates to the networks and connections available to sex workers, in which they can mobilise resources to negotiate their situation. From this, it can be argued that human and social capital mediate the opportunities for sex workers to work independently and the type of social support available. By extension, migrant sex workers may therefore have minimal capital to draw upon to both facilitate their labour and avoid relying on potentially exploitative relationships:

> they need money, they're then being given this really good opportunity to make some serious money and so, the money on offer and the fact that they're in a foreign country with no support mechanism around them. (Detective Inspector 3)

A precarious migrant status was outlined by respondents as an additional barrier, and some migrants were described as particularly vulnerable due to "their inability and access of recourse to public funds and therefore mainstream supports" (NGO Worker 2). Regarding vulnerability to exploitation, NGO workers unanimously agreed that the UK's current hostile immigration system significantly contributes to increased vulnerability. It is conceivable that with limited opportunities for legal migration, many migrant sex workers in the UK may have a precarious legal status. This is not only problematic because women may have to rely on a third-party to work—including sexual labour—but also, if they have been victimised, as pointed out by several respondents, the fear of deportation "prevents them from coming forward" (NGO Worker 1). This could also mean that they may be reluctant to engage with official services, such as the National Referral Mechanism, if they are victims of trafficking, since a situation of exploitation may be preferable to deportation:

they maybe make a judgement call that they are better off staying in that situation, than potentially getting deported. (NGO Worker 3)

Some respondents suggested there is a tendency amongst migrant sex workers to form informal co-operatives along national or ethnic lines to overcome some of the challenges associated with limited capital. One participant explained that the person most proficient in English may be tasked with administrative tasks such as banking, distributing earnings within the cooperative, posting adverts and communicating with clients: "it's good business to be able to share the workload" (NGO Worker 1). In some scenarios, the respondent explained, the administrator, whether or not the person is engaging in sex work themselves, may charge a fee in exchange for the duties they perform. From this, it can be observed that there are clear benefits to working cooperatively—both in terms of increasing revenue and reducing risks associated with working alone—sex workers may nevertheless be criminalised for doing so:

all of those relationships come with an element of risk, in terms of facilitating one another's prostitution, working together, running a brothel, so, the kind of idea of a collective is very informal, and I think it could be made much more formal, which would be great. (NGO Worker 1)

Whereas informal collectives based on trustworthy ties were suggested to have a positive effect on working conditions, it was also highlighted how sex workers with limited capital might have to rely upon more exploitative relationships that potentially transgress the spectrum into exploitation or sex trafficking:

I think many migrant sex workers have to depend on relationships with traffickers, if that's how you want to call them ... they have to rely on people in order to not only bring them across borders into the country, but then they have to rely on people to, you know, facilitate their work to get up an advert, and to organise their bookings when often they can't speak English on the phone to clients. (NGO Worker 1)

Of course, as one respondent pointed out, migration status is not the only factor that contributes to exploitation; the current laws in Scotland surrounding sex work "put people into positions of vulnerability to exploitation" (NGO Worker 1). The criminalisation of sexual labour, particularly brothel-keeping laws, always means a risk is involved when sex workers work together. Migrants were described as often having to rely on working together because of language barriers and a lack of familiarity with working in the UK. Those in a managerial position, it was argued, take a risk when they, in some capacity, facilitate the sexual labour of others due to the current laws:

> managers themselves know that they are criminalised and they're taking a risk, so in order to make that risk worthwhile and to pay off, they will charge quite exorbitant fees … workers' rights might not be their main priority, you know their priorities are to make a profit. (NGO Worker 1)

Police respondents highlighted that in situations where a criminal network facilitates sexual labour, the working conditions are also variable. One detective reflected upon a recent sex trafficking investigation and the surprise of not finding "male OCG members in the actual premises" (Detective Inspector 2), and the absence of oversight from those higher up in the criminal network. It was also suggested that the working environments and, by extension, means of control vary along national or ethnic lines. From these narratives, it appears that those in more exploitative working environments exercise agency and engage in self-coercion[1] and are thus "allowed to move about freely" or so "ingrained or trusted" (Detective Sergeant 3) that more controlled working environments are not required.

Experiences of Control and Exploitation

With the challenges associated with migration for sexual labour in mind, and the variable working conditions associated with the sex market, both

[1] The prominent role of self-coercion in exploitative situations has previously been noted in relation to sex trafficking; see, for instance, Igbinomwanhia (2021) for a more extended discussion.

as discussed in *The Spectrum of Working Conditions* and in chapter "The Nature and Organisation of the Sex Market", it is crucial to consider the experiences of victims of exploitation specifically. Of course, this research is limited in what can be concluded regarding this, since the interviews were based on second-hand accounts (e.g., law enforcement and NGOs), as opposed to lived experience. While popular discourse on sex trafficking often would have us believe that women are primarily deceived, forced or threatened into exploitation, the realities of entering the sex market can be more complex. Choice, coercion and deception are complicated by the often liminal agency of migrant sex workers. A crucial question to consider is whether victims (as identified by the police or service providers) knew, prior to migration, that they would engage in sexual labour. From the experiences of investigators and service providers, victims appear to have had varying levels of knowledge of what labour they were going to perform:

> I've definitely come across a mixture, I've come across people who have said that they know they're coming across as an escort, and as part of that, they knew there would be sexual working involved in that. (Detective Inspector 3)

> It's more likely than not they didn't know that that was going to happen, from what they disclose to us. (NGO Worker 2)

If women knew they were coming to the UK to engage in sex work, it was argued that they would have certain expectations of what the situation of labour may look like, and they may have been promised making "more money whilst seeing fewer punters" (NGO Worker 2) and greater control over their working environment. Some of the conversations with the respondents suggest the existence of prior ties between victims and offenders, which facilitated the recruitment process. A criminal network may "engage with females that they know in their local area" (Detective Inspector 1) to recruit women into the sex industry, and "there's probably elements of word-of-mouth through friends or family that they get involved" (Detective Inspector 3). It was suggested that these pre-existing ties are not only useful for recruitment, but when a criminal network has a local presence in the victim's community, it is also easier to achieve and maintain control over a person:

> [They] have got family and associates back in [the country of origin], so they've got both ends covered. They've got people in [the country of origin] where they're recruiting these females, and then they've got people here, which makes it much easier. (Detective Inspector 2)

Criminal networks were described as offering victims "a false promise of a new life in the UK" (Detective Chief Inspector 1) or a "better way of life … so they can send money back to relatives" (Detective Sergeant 1). Respondents described deception as key in situations when women had limited prior knowledge of what they would do in the UK. Some women were described as believing they came to the UK to be au-pairs, cleaners, to work in a café or a restaurant, and having an opportunity to improve their English skills. Once they have arrived in the UK, they might be told "that the job fell through" (NGO Worker 2) and "that's when it all starts" (Detective Inspector 1).

From the perspectives of respondents, deception is not limited to offering non-existent or misleading job opportunities, it also plays a part in other recruitment strategies. One such strategy that was described is the "loverboy" technique, in which the offender forms a romantic relationship with the victim and convinces them to engage in sexual labour. This technique was described as central in some previous sex trafficking cases, in which "the female thinks she's in a relationship with this male, and they're going to come over to the UK and have this wonderful opportunity" (Detective Sergeant 2). The deception may not only be limited to false promises of a better life and new opportunities, but it was also suggested that deception may continuously play a role throughout a more extended period of an exploitative relationship:

> we've definitely seen examples, where the only reason that a girl has decided to go to the police is because the relationship's broken down, you know, where they've maybe find out that their partner has four or five other girls who he treats … the same as her, but she thought she was the only one involved in it, you know. If it hadn't been for that breakdown in the rela-

> tionship with her exploiter, she probably would never have contacted law enforcement, and that is more than once I've seen that happen. (Detective Inspector 3)

Despite it being quite frequently argued in popular discourse that the internet is important for recruiting women into sex trafficking, there was little evidence from the qualitative interviews to suggest that has been the case in this research context. The police and other stakeholders often have less information about the recruitment process than the exploitation phase, since this often occurs elsewhere. Unless women openly describe how they were recruited or the police cooperate with police forces in the origin country, respondents pointed out that it will be difficult to gauge how recruitment occurred. Nevertheless, one NGO worker described how narratives surrounding social media are starting to emerge:

> we're beginning to hear women who talk about being targeted online on Facebook and other places, and recruited, and in that way groomed into a relationship, or an online relationship, and then the individual joins them and then they're sold on and exploited in that way. (NGO Worker 2)

Like many other aspects of modern life, online technologies may simply be one way of communication, and whilst they may be relevant in the recruitment process, there was no suggestion from the qualitative interviews that they were widely used for this purpose. From the perspective of respondents, recruitment processes were considered variable and depending upon whether women knew beforehand they were migrating to engage in sexual labour specifically. Even so, some respondents pointed out that deception may still be involved in that false promises may be offered, regarding what they can expect from their labour situation and level of control over their lives. At other times, deception appears to have been more blatant, and women were described as being under the impression that they were migrating to do something completely different than sex work. The individuals encountered were often described by respondents as having experienced different forms of socio-economic deprivation. One detective reflected upon their experiences in one investigation:

> generally what you find is that most of the females that are being kept are from a really poor background. Broken families, mother and father may not work, they're very poor, and most of them were recruited quite young, at thirteen, fourteen. (Detective Inspector 2)

This criminal network recruited young girls in their home country and forced them into commercial child sexual exploitation, and "then once they're an adult, they get moved to various countries throughout Europe" (Detective Inspector 2). Another respondent also mentioned that the victim in one investigation had been known to local authorities in her home country as being vulnerable, and that "she kind of ended up making the wrong associations and was then trafficked on the back of that" (Detective Chief Inspector 1).

Socio-economic vulnerability was described as acting as a driver for victims to migrate for sexual labour to improve upon the conditions in their home countries, and some regions characterised by widespread deprivation were argued to be used as recruiting pools into the sex industry:

> the areas where these vulnerable females are targeted, you know, there is deprivation, there is poverty. (Detective Inspector 1)

As such, based on the perspective of respondents, socio-economic needs were described to be exploited by networks recruiting women into the sex industry, and women may simultaneously also make a conscious decision to migrate to engage in sexual labour for the financial incentives involved:

> the driver is that they're making money that they couldn't make back in their home country; they couldn't because of the economics over there. And even though they are receiving a very small amount of money, if anything, that is still greater than they would get back home. So that's our main barrier, driver, or factor. (Detective Sergeant 1)

Others also mentioned how some women encountered in investigations or referred to their services had very complicated backgrounds and pre-existing vulnerabilities. For instance, one respondent pointed out that

> Many of the women we support were vulnerable to being trafficked because they were fleeing another form of violence against women. Many are survivors of domestic abuse, some women were fleeing, or are survivors of [female genital mutiliation], honour-based violence, childhood sexual abuse – many women are survivors of sexual abuse and familial abuse as children. (NGO Worker 2)

Because of the complicated relationships between victims and offenders, and that women in exploitative situations may choose to remain in them due to the absence of viable options, many respondents agreed that a significant issue is that many individuals encountered do not perceive themselves as victims. This was expressed as a challenge both by investigators and support services who, at times, find women not to readily self-identify as victims:

> they're saying they don't want our support and assistance, even though there are a number of red flags around her and we are concerned for her and her situation. (NGO Worker 2)

However, as another respondent argued, the reasons why someone might not identify as a victim of trafficking are complex. Indeed, it was highlighted by one participant how sex workers and, in particular, migrant sex workers may have pre-existing vulnerabilities or be fleeing different forms of abuse, and a more exploitative situation may be preferable to more alarming circumstances in their home country:

> The other thing is, *many people also don't want to be identified*, and I think that that's a really big thing that law enforcement and even anti-trafficking organisations don't understand, is that the alternative, in that the country of origin, and the issues that arose there for somebody, they may be running away due to being LGBTQ+, they may have migrated because there's no opportunities, they may need to come and make money for family back home, so on, then there's no other way. (NGO Worker 1, added emphasis)

This is perhaps one of the most difficult conundrums at the heart of trafficking: the realities of exploitation are often more complex than what legal definitions of trafficking capture, and the *choice* to remain in an exploitative situation may simply be the lesser of two 'evils'. The reasons that someone may not self-identify as a victim are manifold, and these may intersect—such as a fear of their exploiters in combination with the risk of losing what little income they have:

> Sometimes fear of those that are controlling them, sometimes they don't perceive themselves to be victims, some of them do make a bit of money out it and they don't want to see that money lost. (Detective Chief Inspector 1)

Related to this point, investigators also described a divergence in the presentation of the 'self' and the reality of the situation. In other words, whilst women encountered in police investigations may present themselves as relatively satisfied with their situation and not divulge any criminality, investigators may eventually uncover evidence suggesting a different situation involving coercion, control or violence. Detectives described how such evidence would normally be obtained by interrogating communication devices such as phones and laptops, which often showed "a story behind that version of events … which isn't always as accurate as they would like you to believe" (Detective Inspector 1), such as not having enough money to buy food or being subjected to violence. The concept of agency is important in this context, and detectives recognised agency as contributing to this skewed presentation of the self since some individuals may *willingly* remain in such situations because it is preferable to other (potentially more desperate) circumstances:

> But one thing we found was, when we started to review their mobile phones, there was a different story; we've actually seen what was taking place. So there's no doubt that these females – a lot of the females – find themselves, to a certain extent, in a better position because they're making a bit more money. But there's absolutely no doubt that there is fear, certainly from our OCG, threats, intimidation, violence. There is absolutely no doubt that that's there. (Detective Inspector 2)

What adds further complexity to the situation is that different forms of exploitation can occur concurrently or consecutively. Perhaps this is also one of the reasons for victims' ambivalence regarding how they perceive their situation. One respondent explained that someone might experience exploitation within the sex market, but that does not necessarily mean it is *sexual exploitation* per se, and recalled how they have primarily encountered individuals in the sex market who described their situation as "economic exploitation and labour exploitation" (NGO Worker 1). In contrast, another NGO worker described that most of their service users "would identify as being victims of sexual exploitation" (NGO Worker 2). Another scenario was also described in which someone would willingly migrate to engage in sexual labour but end up in an exploitative situation:

> For some other women … they would say it was financial exploitation, and they were aware they were coming to be involved in prostitution … but they didn't get to hold any of the money, it was taken by their pimp, their trafficker, their partner, in those cases, so they would see that as financial exploitation. (NGO Worker 2)

There may be selection effects in operation here: some women may be more likely to approach or be referred to certain services or organisations based on their experiences of exploitation. Similarly, the police are potentially more likely to open an inquiry where safeguarding issues can be identified, even though they are likely to encounter less vulnerable sex workers during wellbeing visits.

Some participants also described situations which may involve elements of sexual exploitation, even though it is not necessarily sex trafficking per se. For instance, someone "might have been kept as a domestic servant, but at the same time sexually exploited" (NGO Worker 3), or "a woman who has been subjected to forced labour or forced begging or something like that in the daytime, would also be sexually exploited at some other point" (NGO Worker 4). A police respondent similarly highlighted that because some migrants may "have a greater story coming over here" (Detective Inspector 3), in terms of the risks involved with smuggling, sexual exploitation may be part of their migration journey. In that case, sexual exploitation is not necessarily motivated by financial gain, "it might be through gratification of the exploiters" (Detective Inspector 3).

Because exploitation can be intertwined in various ways, it is perhaps not surprising that those considered victims of exploitation may feel ambivalence in how they understand their situation. Conceivably, the motivations to migrate and seek economic opportunities abroad may contribute to this form of 'self-coercion', in which someone would rather remain in an exploitative situation than make their situation known to the authorities, which could always end in detention or deportation. Perhaps it is not surprising that such concerns contribute to low engagement and limited trust in authorities and service providers, and based on the interviews conducted, it seems that low engagement is central to the challenges associated with investigating and responding to sex trafficking.

A relatively common narrative from the interviews conducted was the centrality of debts and debt bondage in contributing to situations of exploitation. As was discussed in chapter "Journeys into the Precariat: Migration, Exploitation and Trafficking", debts may occur naturally as part of the financial costs of migration, but debts can also pre-date migration, such as the victim or their families owing significant amounts of money to organised crime groups in their country of origin. It was argued by respondents that the presence of debts potentially serves to constrain women's agency, which may force them to remain in exploitative situations and "essentially being owned by their trafficker until the debt's repaid" (Detective Chief Inspector 1). Since the only way to repay large debts—or remit crucial money to relatives—may be to remain in a situation of exploitation, criminal networks can be in a strong position to exercise control further:

> they can't refuse men, they can't say no, they've been told you owe money, and sometimes that idea of a debt is sufficient for women to say, "well, this is all my own fault, alright, okay", or maybe the debt is held by family members at home, and women are concerned if they don't remit money, then harms that would come to them individually, from their trafficker,

> but the gang behind the trafficking will *also* be knocking on their mum's door looking for money. (NGO Worker 2)

Whilst debt in itself creates dependency upon facilitators, one participant also mentioned how they had encountered a criminal network providing controlled drugs to the victims to create further dependency, as "it helps the traffickers to increase the debt and their reliance on the trafficker" (Detective Chief Inspector 1). This suggests that creating a sense of dependency and using subtle control mechanisms may be a more effective strategy to ensure compliance than violence and physical control. Related to this, it was highlighted in chapter "Criminal Networks, Opportunity Structures and the Process of Exploitation" (section "Unpacking the Sex Trafficking Crime Script") how using violence or physically restraining an individual's freedom is a costly strategy, as it can draw unwanted attention from the public. Indeed, from the conversation with respondents, some reported that if violence was present, it was usually used as a last resort:

> the violence only starts when they refuse to sell sex, so when they refuse to be prostituted ... the violence for women tends to happen at that early stage, when she refuses and says no, and then women describe being assaulted, and then in an effort to make the assaults stop, they then agree ... to survive and stop the assaults happening. That tends to be a quite common story. (NGO Worker 2)

One investigator pointed out that it is challenging for the police to obtain evidence that there has in fact been violence. Police respondents described how it may not be that uncommon to receive intelligence or reports about possible violence, but the issue is, as one investigator put it, "we've never had the evidence to support it" (Detective Chief Inspector 1). Even if violence has been a feature of a situation of exploitation, individuals were described as still being reluctant to engage "whether that's through the fear of the individuals or the fear of what might happen to friends or family back home" (Detective Inspector 3).

From the interviews, it appears that threats are more commonly used, as it is possibly a less costly tactic than resorting to violence. It was suggested that criminal networks with a presence in both the origin and destination country can “exploit these geographical locations and threaten friends and family back home as well” (Detective Inspector 3). Some also reported how criminal networks exploit victims’ precarious migration status:

> telling women that they’re here illegally, and that they’ll denounce them to the authorities and they’ll be deported. (NGO Worker 2)

It was also pointed out how various forms of control appear to intersect and “create a situation of dependency” (NGO Worker 2). As one investigator put it, “the immediate control is still there, the financial control is still there, and there’s obviously threats to family back home as well” (Detective Sergeant 2). This situation of dependency seems, according to the perspective of participants, to make victims compliant and less likely to engage with the police and support services.

Based on the qualitative interviews and the experiences of respondents, there is a suggestion that migrants and victims often have complicated lives, and that the decision to migrate for sexual services entails certain perils, which can be a direct result of how both migration and sex work are regulated. Whereas these accounts of experiences of sexual labour, migration and victimisation are limited due to being secondary accounts of highly complex issues, they nevertheless offered important insights into how these issues are perceived from law enforcement or service providers’ perspectives. Respondents pointed out how migrant sex workers may have little choice but to put their faith in facilitators to both cross borders and successfully engage in sexual labour, and this increases the risk of exploitation. It is important to consider how wider technological change has affected these underlying processes, and the following section will focus on this.

Technological Changes and the Organisation of Exploitation

This part focuses on how online technologies have reconfigured the sex market and its consequences for how exploitation is organised and facilitated. Because the respondents had substantial experience, often having worked on issues relating to policing harms in the sex market or providing services to victims for several years, they were in a good position to elaborate upon the changes they had observed.

Technological Change: Dark Spaces of Precarity

As was discussed in chapter "The Nature and Organisation of the Sex Market", the global sex market has changed tremendously due to the introduction of the internet and communication technologies. There was a widespread perception amongst participants that this was indeed also the case in the UK. Perhaps the most obvious indication of change, according to respondents, would be the decline of street-based prostitution and that in previous decades "you saw prostitution on the street predominantly", whereas more recently, "the business has moved online, like so much" (Detective Chief Inspector 1). There was a suggestion from these accounts that there has been a stratification of the overall sex market in which those more fortunate can benefit from new technology, while street-based sex workers "tend to be local, very vulnerable females" (Detective Sergeant 1).

Many respondents highlighted that it is not simply that there has been a shift from street-based sex work to an off-street market, but that the overall market for sexual services has expanded significantly. Two particular elements could be attributed to this "burgeoning market" (Detective Sergeant 2): increased availability and accessibility. Sexual services were previously advertised in magazines or newspapers, and "it was only a limited amount of people that would access ... that media" (Detective Inspector 1). As a result of online marketing, sexual services were perceived as more readily accessible:

> I think it's fair to say that it's had a massive impact ... and somebody only now has to go on their mobile phone on to [ASW 1], [ASW 2], whatever one site, and it's as simple as a click on a button and making contact with a girl ... they're on a plate for them, and very simple, and it's made as simple as possible. (Detective Inspector 3)

If the sex market indeed has expanded, a crucial question is whether this has led to a diversification in terms of the transactions that occur within the marketplace, and if there have been changes in expectations of the services offered. One participant highlighted that extreme services were seemingly more commonplace nowadays in comparison to previous decades:

> the demands for the services placed on them have changed, and have increased and become more extreme over the course of the years, and what's expected and what's a "normal" sexual service sale has changed. (NGO Worker 2)

Parallel developments in the increased availability and accessibility of online pornography were offered as a partial explanation of why the sex market has become more extreme:

> I suppose, in my sense, some of that is linked to pornography. You know, so punters will talk about wanting a porn star experience, "but I can't do that with my partner, so I'll pay for it", you know, and how porn has changed over the years and become more extreme - that's what men are seeing and thinking and looking for as well. (NGO Worker 2)

Nevertheless, another respondent pointed out that drawing the line between what can be considered 'extreme' varies from person to person and "everybody has ... different boundaries and barriers and one thing that may seem extreme to one person, might not seem extreme to another" (NGO Worker 1). However, what was highlighted as something that could potentially be considered as deviating from the norm would be if extreme services were advertised at no extra cost:

> I guess my gut instinct is that if extreme services were being advertised at a low price, or a price that was in line with non-extreme services, then yes, I think that could potentially be an indicator and one that wouldn't quite seem in the norm. (NGO Worker 1)

Some detectives also highlighted that providing extreme services could indicate vulnerability or one of the "indicators of trafficking" (Detective Sergeant 1). Victims of exploitation were argued to likely be pushed to offer these services since these would mean "more money for the organisation" (Detective Sergeant 2).

Online technologies were described as having led to somewhat paradoxical developments within the sex market. As was highlighted in chapter "The Nature and Organisation of the Sex Market", sex work can be conducted more safely due to screening mechanisms, staying in contact with others, and advertising online rather than working on the streets. One respondent pointed out how sex workers have always been savvy, and technology provides the infrastructure to work more safely; as an example, sex workers

> tend to be very well-versed in keeping themselves safe and keeping themselves networked, and there's a lot of online resources that are by and for sex workers that, you know, sign-point to resources, sign-point to what's the norm, what's not the norm, so I think that much of the protective factors around exploitation have actually been developed by sex workers themselves to keep each other safe. (NGO Worker 1)

However, encrypted communication and the anonymity offered by the internet were also identified by respondents as potentially contributing to some market segments which help facilitate exploitation. It was highlighted how sex workers historically were involved in the informal policing of the sex market when it primarily occurred on the streets, by keeping minors away and sharing local knowledge of harmful clients. While such practices—coordinated by sex workers themselves for their own safety—still occur online, due to the shift to an expanding online market, sex workers were also described as being "put into these kinds of dark spaces of precarity" (NGO Worker 1). In these online spaces, "it's easier to remain invisible and anonymous as a punter" (NGO Worker 2), and there's "very little safeguarding" (Detective Sergeant 2) in combination with a lesser sense of repercussion:

> I think that it has created access to sex workers that maybe perhaps, potentially, there wasn't so much before when it was mainly on-street, because people can sit behind, in private, completely anonymously, and reach out to people and offer certain things that maybe involve an element of exploitation, without that sense of repercussion. (NGO Worker 1)

This feeds back into the previously discussed increase in the availability and accessibility of sexual services, and due to the impersonal transactions associated with the online world, it is conceivable that there may be increasing opportunities to push someone's boundaries. However, online spaces may not only lack the signals present in other markets that more clearly define the boundaries of acceptable vis-à-vis non-acceptable behaviour, but according to respondents, these 'dark spaces of precarity' may also provide an environment benefiting those seeking to control and exploit others. In sum, online spaces were perceived as valuable for sex workers to work more safely and simultaneously useful for networks trying to conceal their online identity or organised nature.

The Organisation of Exploitation

In light of the preceding discussion on expanding precarious online spaces, this section looks more closely at how exploitation is organised and how online technologies relate to this. In particular, the themes in this section provide a rich context and description of how contemporary criminal networks on the sex market operate, as described from the perspectives of respondents.

From the discussions with the research participants, some perceived sex trafficking to offer a low-risk, high-reward opportunity to generate substantial profits. The motivation behind these criminal networks was unanimously perceived to be financial. As one respondent put it, "they don't actually care what type of exploitation it is, as long as that individual is generating some form of income" (NGO Worker 2). Some detectives drew parallels to other forms of organised crime, in which "it's always been about making the money" (Detective Inspector 1), whether the group is controlling the supply of guns, substances or, as in this case, human beings. Participants highlighted how women, through processes of commodification, become valuable assets to criminal networks:

> there's a version that we've got, everybody's treated, you know, really badly, and I know it sounds a strange thing to say, but when you remove the sex work, I think some of the girls probably get looked after because they're a valuable commodity. So I think there's probably two aspects, I think you probably got those who are mistreated, but I think you probably got some who are well looked after, to keep them on board, and make the group or the other individuals involved as much money as they can. (Detective Inspector 3)

This is an important point that alludes to how complex the relationship between offender and victim appears to be in situations of exploitation. The experiences of participants suggest that it is within the criminal network's interest to minimise conflict and the need to resort to threats and violence, and it is conceivably advantageous if compliance can be achieved in other ways. The accounts of the respondents suggest that individuals may be in exploitative situations, but unless they are seriously mistreated and still receive remuneration for their labour, this process of commodification may foster a sense of loyalty to the exploiters. Again, this could potentially be due to a lack of capital to work independently, thus making sex workers reliant on a third-party to facilitate their labour.

If criminal networks involved in the sex market are perceived as motivated purely by financial incentives, it also follows that they may engage in other illegal activities to supplement their income. A criminal network may—strictly speaking—not be conducting sex trafficking but, in one way or another, have a presence in the sex market, such as controlling a brothel. They may also operate and direct other forms of serious and organised crime aside from their operations in the sex market. As one detective put it in relation to the link between sex markets and drug markets,

> I'm confident the crossover is significant, I think, my experience is, if they're involved in sexual exploitation, there will probably be an element of drug dealing involved in that as well. (Detective Chief Inspector 1)

This was partially explained by the fact that a criminal network may have pre-existing supply lines for a specific commodity, and in turn, those involved can mobilise capital to more easily "move other commodity" (Detective Inspector 3). There were, for instance, crossovers between cannabis cultivation and exploitation in the sex market in some criminal networks observed throughout investigations.

From the interviews, it appears online technologies have affected how criminal networks organise their operations. It is not as simple as that it would be *impossible* to engage in sex trafficking and exploitation without technology, but it simply allows a network to streamline its business. This seems to be particularly important for larger networks spanning significant geographical areas and involving a high number of individuals. For instance, one detective explained: "we only scratched the surface … we encountered 30 females, but there's no doubt there's an awful lot more" (Detective Inspector 2). Such a large-scale network was perceived as being reliant on technology to manage its operations effectively:

> We've certainly seen patterns when we start to analyse the information and intelligence around phones and adult services websites, that they play a large factor in facilitating, if you like, being able to carry out that kind of operation. (Detective Sergeant 1)

Online marketing was suggested by police respondents as instrumental to having the most commercial success and reaching the greatest number of customers. Whereas some online criminal activities—such as procuring illicit substances—were described as confined to the darker corners of the web, "you don't have to go on the dark web to find somebody to buy sex from" (Detective Inspector 3). Transactions of sexual services between consenting adults are not criminalised, and the internet affords criminal networks access to an otherwise legitimate, though unregulated, market. There was a widespread agreement that *if* sex trafficking is currently occurring in the UK, victims are almost certainly going to be advertised on the same platforms used by independent sex workers: advertising online "is their main tool to generate that income ... you've got to use that technology to get your business model running" (Detective Inspector 1).

These new technologies were not only believed to be central to marketing, but they were also perceived as increasing a network's capacity to exercise control. When both offenders and victims alike are equipped with communication technology, it was argued that it is easier to surveil and monitor the activities of the victims, thus potentially reducing the need for physical control mechanisms such as violence or confinement:

> women have talked about traffickers using Facebook and other apps as a means to exert their control over women. So women may on the surface be on her own, be going out and about, you know, no indicators of force or coercion, but via Facebook, traffickers are monitoring what's going on and their whereabouts as well. (NGO Worker 2)

Given the importance of mobility in the sex market, mobile technology allows criminal networks to assert control even if they are geographically distant from their victims: "if female victims are allowed out to travel, they will be in contact with their exploiters" (Detective Sergeant 1). Respondents pointed out how any non-compliance can quite easily be monitored, and if there are deviations from criminal networks' instructions, such as not being in a place at a certain time, "then, you know, the threat will be carried out" (NGO Worker 2).

Online technologies were also perceived to increase a network's administrative capacity. Some activities are easier to do online rather than offline; online technologies make booking short-term accommodation such as Airbnb's or arranging transportation easier. Similarly, others also mentioned how online banking and monetary transactions are becoming more widespread. The value of communication technology was described as "invaluable" to these groups, and one investigator summarised it well:

> they're extremely important because they can continually maintain their presence, but evolve in their immediate communication, it's invaluable to them, and they can pop up, obviously, and have an instant marketplace, in

> whatever area, it's not exactly word-of-mouth or anything, so it's very much they got an instant customer base wherever they go, due to the availability of these sites. (Detective Sergeant 2)

Technologies were perceived as allowing criminal networks to become more sophisticated in their operations, however, as one detective pointed out, the level of sophistication "varies dramatically depending upon the organisation you're looking at" (Detective Constable 2).

For a criminal network to be successful in the sex market, transience was argued by police respondents as crucial. Three reasons were highlighted by participants as to why these networks need to be flexible and in constant flux. First, for the same reasons sex workers tour the country to appeal to new markets, criminal networks must also penetrate and extend their geographical reach to different markets to increase their profits. Second, frequently moving victims around the country is also a form of control mechanism, as it increases the dependence on the facilitators and significantly reduces the victim's situational awareness. From respondents' experiences, a common narrative when interacting with potential victims is that they have very little knowledge about their whereabouts. This constant movement prevents victims from establishing ties with local communities but also reduces their capacity to develop social capital within the network:

> If you asked them what city they were staying in, they didn't know that, and it's because they're being moved around all the time, and it's to stop them getting familiar with that location and other females that they're living with. (Detective Inspector 2)

However, the lack of situational awareness was also described as being manifested in other ways. Participants described women as having very little control over their situation; some are unaware that they are being advertised online and "don't even know when clients are arriving" (Detective Constable 1) or the amount of money changing hands, "all they know is they were maybe given twenty quids at the end of the week" (NGO Worker 2).

Finally, criminal networks in the sex market were argued to be transient because it reduces their visibility to law enforcement and draws less attention from the public. This included several aspects, such as constantly changing phones, phone numbers and email accounts, and making the electronic trail more difficult to follow. One investigator highlighted how criminal networks, as a result of using technology, have become better at concealing their activities and that it becomes more challenging "to pin down and attribute the criminality to the top-line perpetrators" (Detective Sergeant 2). Based on the experience of investigators, the networks part of investigations were unlikely to stay in the same place for a prolonged period to avoid "neighbours start[ing] to pick up on men coming and going" (Detective Inspector 3), because if too much attention is drawn to a particular address, they might attract the attention of the police. It was also pointed out how some individuals may only be at an address for a few days or a week and often travel between cities throughout the entire UK. This constant rotation of women across different addresses and different regions of the country was believed to be a considerable challenge for the police to "stay ahead of the game" (Detective Chief Inspector 1). By the time the police receive intelligence on suspicious activities, the criminal network might already have moved on, "so enforcement and sort of disruption opportunities aren't easy to come by" (Detective Inspector 3). Technologies, as such, can be perceived as central to operating as a transient network:

> in terms of the internet and technology, I mean, what I would probably say with that is that it's continuous, so you can start off at the beginning of a day trying to address something, and sometimes you might not know it, but over the course of the day, that situation may have altered because there's continuous communication, instant communication, and instant ability to alter a situation through the internet and technology. (Detective Inspector 4)

If networks in the sex market are transient, where would criminal networks be expected to operate? As several respondents pointed out, "it's all about demand" (Detective Inspector 1), and the greatest demand for sexual services tends to be in larger cities: "it's like any other business—they go where the customer is" (Detective Sergeant 3). Cities like Glasgow, Edinburgh and Aberdeen have larger off-street sex markets than other areas in Scotland, and it might therefore be expected that criminal networks target those locations. Again, reinforcing the notion of transience, one detective explained:

> The organised crime groups that we've come across, they just don't have one locality. As I said, their motivation for this is financial gain, so they'll be working out of various locations, and they'll have females all over the place. (Detective Inspector 2)

This is an important point because law enforcement or service providers occasionally come across victims, or potential victims, in more rural areas or smaller cities where "there wouldn't be a kind of a known off-street industry" (NGO Worker 2). It was suggested by participants that one possible reason for this is the fierce competition associated with large markets across major cities where "there's more people involved in the trade" (Detective Chief Inspector 1). Therefore, criminal networks were perceived as consciously deciding to relocate to more rural areas or smaller cities with a less competitive market. In addition, it was also suggested that networks may adopt a 'commuting' model in which their operations might be organised from a larger city, but adverts are being placed online in neighbouring towns and cities within commuting distance. For instance, a network based in Stirling could easily appeal to the markets in both Glasgow and Edinburgh "because it's an easy commute" (Detective Inspector 1).

Based on the experiences of participants, it was highlighted how the norm for larger criminal networks is to operate across all countries in the UK, and that it would not be uncommon to see a network spanning significant geographical distances. The longer a network has been operating, the more likely it is that they have visited several locations:

> all of the women we work with have experienced some sort of movement if the trafficking situation has been going on longer than a couple of weeks. (NGO Worker 2)

For larger networks originating outside of the UK, it also appears common that the group might have operated in other countries throughout Europe and "Scotland is just one of these countries where they came in for a period of time" (Detective Inspector 1). In light of a wider transition into an expanding off-street sex market, "it's less likely to be traditional brothels and saunas where women we work with have been exploited in" (NGO Worker 2). Instead, typically transient accommodation options—such as short-term lets and Airbnb's—appear favoured by criminal networks. This seemingly fits well with their business model and allows them to "do their business for maybe a week and then move on to another property" (Detective Sergeant 2). Respondents proposed that criminal networks may perceive it as less risky to operate from short-term accommodation in residential urban areas than a hotel, where irregular activities may get reported faster. Besides the typical short-term holiday rentals, criminal networks were described as using privately rented accommodation, and some respondents mentioned a tendency of these groups to "use the same landlords all the time" (Detective Inspector 2). A network may have rented several flats from the same landlord, either within a city or across cities, and women were described as being moved between the different properties. Larger networks renting several flats—especially if they are in the same stairwell—might have an on-site person in charge "controlling what's happening" (Detective Inspector 1). Some respondents referred to what they termed "alpha females":

> who is generally a female who has kind of worked her way up the ranks, I suppose, or maybe is older, or whatever, but she's involved more in the recruiting side of things, so [the OCG] have a level of trust in 'er, so they'll use her details for a lot of travel bookings, financial transactions, all that kind of things. (Detective Sergeant 2)

Others also found when visiting premises that the 'alpha female' would instruct officers that they were the only one speaking English and hence doing all the talking with the police. This creates a potentially exploitative situation since it would allow the person in charge "to control what's being said" (Detective Inspector 2) and what information may or may not be shared. From the discussion with participants, in some of the more extensive criminal networks that had been investigated, there may be additional hierarchical structures of the network, and one investigator described it well:

> you tend to find you've got, in each address, you'll have a female who is potentially an alpha female, but then you'll get other alpha females who are above those. They're maybe in control to a certain extent of females at that address, but you can also have alpha females that sit above that and maybe control a few addresses, and then you would have the OCG members. But that's not always the case, but we did find that quite a lot. (Detective Inspector 1)

This seems to suggest the possibility of a continuum of organisation within the sex market and the possibility of hierarchically structured criminal networks. No more than one person might, of course, facilitate exploitation, but to effectively manage and control several women, it is conceivable there may be a need for a stricter division of labour and a more extensive network.

Given the transient and mobile nature of organised exploitation, criminal networks were described as requiring online technologies to access local markets. Besides having a geographical presence, they will also, according to investigators, likely have a digital presence. These will, in the vast majority of the time, be ASWs. Detectives described the networks under investigation to have used a variety of ASWs, though two of the larger ASWs were much more commonly used.[2] It was also suggested that criminal networks also "tend to go across" (Detective Constable 2) different ASWs and not limit themselves to one platform. One thing appears quite clear, however: no one had any experiences of victims being identified on the dark web, and it was explained that,

> generally, the people who are trawling for, to buy sexual services, may not have access or have the knowledge to access the dark web. So, it may well be that there is a degree of organisation behind exploitation going on in the dark web. But not the sort of trawling for, looking for sexual encounters. (Detective Sergeant 1)

[2] ASW 1, which this case study is focused on, was one of the two main ASWs.

According to the experiences of participants, the websites used by independent sex workers are also the same ASWs targeted by criminal networks operating in the sex market. However, in contrast to independent sex workers or smaller co-operatives of sex workers, the discussions with investigators suggest that operating as large-scale networks across significant geographical areas requires no small amount of coordination. For instance, some investigators described how some of the more extensive networks encountered used "call centres" to manage communication with potential clients, like any other legitimate business. In other words, the person answering the phones is not necessarily the same person who will provide the service:

> you're going to get multiple adverts for the same group of females, and then there'll be persons managing these phones, like a call centre, because when we go to search these addresses, and there'll be, you know, 10, 15, 20 mobile phones, all with a number and maybe a name on the back of it. (Detective Inspector 1)

It can be argued, based on the discussions with investigators, that role specialisations—such as someone being in charge of posting adverts or answering phones—increase the administrative capacity of a network, and they can, therefore, more easily reach a wider pool of clients and establish themselves across a multitude of local markets:

> they kind of have that base down in London and just keep controlling them all over ... we don't know enough at the moment, they might have a cohort of fifty women, who they're constantly changing around the country, so it makes sense that they have got one base somewhere, and they got these links in all over. (Detective Constable 1)

Taken together, the findings from qualitative interviews seem to suggest that the organisation of exploitation in the sex market is multifaceted; the transience of criminal networks and complicated relationships between victims and offenders make exploitation in the sex market challenging to investigate. Migrants, sex workers, victims of exploitation and criminal networks were described as occupying the same offline and online markets. A challenge for criminal networks is to adapt their marketing strategies to blend in with independent sex worker adverts, and strike a balance between concealing their identity and successfully attracting clients. The amalgamation of diverse actors occupying the same space appears to pose serious challenges for law enforcement in policing the sex market. The police have limited resources, and trafficking investigations are incredibly resource-intensive, especially since there are two dimensions to account for: the offline network and the evidential trail they leave online. The following section will shift the analysis to describe the challenges faced by the police and how they make sense of digital traces that are part of contemporary trafficking investigations.

Policing Criminal Networks in the Sex Market

This section builds upon the previous discussions to provide a deeper understanding of the contemporary challenges of policing sex trafficking and criminal networks within the sex market, as experienced by participants. Every police force and division has limited resources, and effectively reviewing incoming intelligence is critical. This section begins with a description of these challenges before proceeding to examine how investigators make sense of the digital traces of criminal networks. Based on the respondents' experiences, this section aims to review the role of open-source intelligence in the investigative process and the extent to which online escort adverts are important to contemporary investigations.

Police Demand, Priorities and Resources

Every police force—or division—has different demands. Trafficking may not necessarily be a high priority everywhere, investigators argued, since other crimes may require a more urgent response, such as other forms of serious and organised crime, where there may be immediate safeguarding issues. Inquiries of most concern related to trafficking involve immediate safeguarding issues; these would be situations where there is evidence to suggest the presence of potential harm. Resources are limited for both national and divisional units, which necessitates the police to be very targeted in deciding which cases to pursue.

Participants described numerous ways in which potential instances of sex trafficking come to the attention of the police, such as the National Referral Mechanism, other agencies, NGOs, the Home Office, the Modern Slavery Helpline, CrimeStoppers or internally, as a result of other policing activities. A significant portion of intelligence will have come through police incidents, such as disturbance calls, noise complaints, anonymous calls from the public or suspicious activity reports, and "if it's strong enough to take overt action on, we'll get that information in and then develop it" (Detective Sergeant 2). Both NGOs and the police receive tips from sex buyers from time to time, with clients reporting that the person they were scheduled to meet may seem "quite vulnerable, perhaps didn't want to be there" (NGO Worker 1), or that they were not "as happy or willing to engage in the services as they would have liked" (Detective Sergeant 1).

Whilst the discussions with police respondents suggested there may be no shortage of leads or intelligence warranting further investigation, the police do, after all, have limited resources and "obviously we can't investigate everything ... but we would have to assess everything and look at what we can deal with" (Detective Inspector 2). Investigating human trafficking is "incredibly resource-intensive" (Detective Sergeant 1), and the National Human Trafficking Unit (NHTU) has more resources to develop intelligence than local police divisions throughout Scotland. Even so, given the volume of information received relevant to human trafficking, the NHTU themselves need to prioritise effectively in the context of limited resources. In public discourse on human trafficking, the issue is often framed as a problem of a wider lack of awareness and thus that the activities of criminal networks go unnoticed. That may partially be true, however, the discussions with investigators suggested there is no shortage of information available to the police; what sometimes is lacking is the resources to develop intelligence and identify criminality:

> There is a large amount of information out there that we could utilise if we had the resources to do that. (Detective Sergeant 1)

Police divisions and the NHTU are forced to make difficult choices, and police respondents described how they target threats where there are "obvious issues" (Detective Inspector 4) and evidence to warrant urgent action. The large-scale networks operating across borders and divisional boundaries are the primary focus of the NHTU, whereas either location-specific or smaller inquiries can be directed to local divisions. Prioritisation, across both police divisions and the NHTU, was argued by respondents to be guided by safeguarding concerns:

> if there was ever information that somebody has been exploited, including sexually, then that would be a priority to identify and get that person safe. (Detective Inspector 3)

However, what may be perceived as 'safeguarding concerns' from a police perspective may conceivably be very different from how those being targeted experience their situation. One detective went on to explain how each case is different, and if there is no immediate identifiable criminality, it may not be viable to initiate an inquiry but rather, link in with partners and offer support:

> unless we identify a crime right there and then when we walk through that door, it then takes a twist and it all becomes about protecting, so, if they say, "no, I'm not been forced to be here, I'm here of my own volition, I am in involved in the sex trade, but it's my choice", if we can't identify criminality that we can disrupt, it's linking in with partners. (Detective Chief Inspector 1)

From these discussions, it appears to be a very delicate balance between the policing of harm and the need to not over-police sex workers working out of their own volition and not under anyone's control:

> You've got to consider as well, there's consent issues and your human rights issues that, what the girls do is not a crime. It's the management of them that is a crime. So unless that's highlighted to us as a crime, then we'll not be carrying out an investigation into it. (Detective Sergeant 3)

Put differently, it might be very difficult to justify pursuing a lead where there are no immediate safeguarding concerns but in which criminality *may* occur, rather than focus precious resources on other ongoing issues where there may be clear safeguarding issues or identifiable harms. Nevertheless, 'safeguarding issues' or 'identifiable harms' can of course be subject to variable interpretations, and there is always a risk that situations that the police judge as requiring intervention may in fact cause more harm than good to sex workers. The policing of exploitation in the sex market thus requires a highly targeted approach in which potential harms and safeguarding issues are always considered against the rights of sex workers to engage in sexual labour safely.

Based on the interviews with investigators, it was also clear that additional challenges also occur because the sex market is augmented with an online dimension. Sex trafficking investigations will likely involve the need to assess digital traces and online intelligence. This is challenging for several reasons, including the resources required to analyse open-source intelligence and due to the epistemological uncertainties associated with online escort adverts. The next section will describe these challenges in more detail.

Understanding Digital Traces

With the widespread adoption of the internet and communication technologies within the sex market, police respondents highlighted that contemporary criminal networks involved in sex trafficking in the UK are likely to have an online presence. However, interpreting data generated in the sex market was highlighted as neither easy nor straightforward. Broadly speaking, and as described in more detail in chapter "Digital Traces, Big Data and Epistemological Shifts", indicators are usually employed to infer the presence of trafficking from online data, but indicators themselves are highly problematic for several reasons. The online world does not accurately reflect offline behaviours; transactions within the sex market occur in a market context, and much of the online data are thus reflective of marketing strategies rather than any form of *objective* reality of sex work.

Despite the fact that the internet renders interaction between clients and sex workers more anonymous, most online activities tend to generate digital traces. Since this presents an opportunity for police intervention, criminal networks were described as having to adapt their modus operandi to leave as little information as possible behind; even so, reaping the benefits of online advertisement comes at the cost of leaving a digital footprint:

> if you're the person paying for those adverts, it doesn't make it the most anonymous service, whereas previously you know, you wouldn't have had to supply any information, whereas now, there's still a footprint, there's still somebody who's paid for that advert, which leads to a phone number, so there's still telecoms work that can be done. (Detective Inspector 3)

Similarly, it was also highlighted how bank transactions produce an evidential trace that can be followed to understand various aspects of a potential trafficking operation. Clients were reported as increasingly paying online, which presents an opportunity to "go back and engage with the punter" (Detective Inspector 1) to proceed with an inquiry. Digital traces in this context may transcend borders, as the money is "transferred to the main man … who's sitting in a house in [the country of origin]" (Detective Inspector 1). However, as another detective pointed out, criminal networks are also employing strategies to conceal the footprint they leave behind:

> The perpetrators are becoming very adept at leaving very little official footprints anywhere, whether that's financial or anything, so they will have accounts, communication devices, addresses, any overt footprints that would be on the sort of searchable systems, they will have it in [the] girls' names. (Detective Sergeant 2)

In relation to escort adverts, it was suggested by respondents that criminal networks tend to market women as independent sex workers, "because, it's like everything, if something's independent, you'd think you're getting a better service" (Detective Inspector 3). To be successful, it was argued, these groups have to "spread the commodity as far and wide as you can for the market you're targeting" (Detective Constable 2), and they will also need a good understanding of local demands and what they "need to satisfy the market here" (Detective Inspector 1). Because these transactions occur within a profit-oriented context, it was suggested by detectives that the adverts are tailored to attract clients rather than to reflect reality:

> that's why you'll see, what you're seeing with the lures and the adverts, and the images, you're gonna see certain things, it's going to draw people in, and they will know that because it's working, because they're making money; if they were nae making money, then they would change their business model, so that they're going to make that money. (Detective Inspector 1)

According to the perceptions of investigators, online adverts contain limited (useful) information and are signified by their lack of veracity. As one detective put it during a discussion of online adverts, "see, the fact that most adverts say that somebody is Brazilian, that's of interest, but I'm not sure it would lead us any further down the investigation route" (Detective Sergeant 1). This is an important point: just because there is information within online adverts, it does not mean that it is *useful* information. These adverts can be considered fluid rather than static:

> there's a lot of adverts out there, and I think it's fair to say that the adverts won't always get you the answer that you're looking for; the adverts can change quickly, images obviously don't always represent the girls that are being exploited, and locations will maybe give you a postcode, but especially in built-up areas ... that doesn't necessarily give you a location to work from. (Detective Inspector 3)

Another detective was asked if there was anything distinctive about an advert pertaining to a victim of trafficking from a previous investigation:

> No, not really. It was very generic, in terms of the advert, particularly that one. It was pictures of the girl involved, contact details ... Aye. (Detective Chief Inspector 1)

A central feature of online adverts, as highlighted by most participants, is the 'spuriousness' of their design: a significant amount of the information in adverts is simply there to attract clients, not to communicate the characteristics or services of women, *unless* the women actually possess the qualities deemed desirable in the local market. These marketing choices, it was argued, serve as 'hooks' or 'lures' to initially attract clients and be convincing enough to complete the transaction. Much of the information contained within online adverts is hence inaccurate, according to the perspectives of investigators. From this, it is conceivable that it may be beneficial for criminal networks to deviate from the truth up to a certain point, but being too dishonest can potentially negatively impact the business. One detective summarised it well:

> I could probably count on the one hand the number of Brazilians or Spanish that I have actually engaged with, because predominantly it has been Romanians. So are they using that as a lure? And as I said earlier on, what's advertised on the tin, and when you actually arrive there, they're not going to turn around, and go saying, "nah, I was promised a Brazilian", "I was promised an Italian", whatever else. You're there for one purpose … what I've seen when engaging with these females, is, I would say that's probably more a lure, like going fishing, to draw people in. (Detective Inspector 1)

Adverts also tend to contain pictures, but based on the experience of detectives, criminal networks frequently use stock images "which often do the rounds and probably reappear" (Detective Inspector 3) in different parts of the country. If the pictures are real, they tend not to represent the women participants made contact with at the advertised locations. Similar to how descriptive characteristics are manipulated to act as a 'honey trap', criminal networks will "advertise what they think people will want, not what they actually get" (Detective Sergeant 1). There is another dimension to this: not only may certain nationalities or other characteristics perhaps be considered more desirable in some local markets, but the discussions also suggest an element of stigma present, particularly concerning nationality. As one respondent pointed out, there is a very strong narrative and media focus on Romanian sex workers and trafficking victims, and this means that some Romanian sex workers "won't advertise that they're from Romania, people advertise they're from other places" (NGO Worker 1). Other nationalities are also stigmatised in the sex market and, for instance, one detective described a tendency amongst Chinese sex workers to advertise themselves as Japanese. Similarly, there was a widespread agreement that the advertised age seldom reflects an individual's actual age. Based on these discussions, the fabrication of details can perhaps be seen as the intersection of stigma and what is deemed desirable in the market.

If much of the information provided in adverts is inaccurate or spurious, a valid question is whether any information is important in investigative contexts. Police respondents suggested the geographical information contained within adverts can be useful in narrowing down the scope of an inquiry. Whilst it is rare to advertise a full address, postcode districts or the wider geographical areas are usually required for posting an online advert. The advertised location can also be inaccurate, but at the very least, it provides some information that a network is targeting a particular area. From the discussion with police respondents, what is potentially more useful, or at the very least, crucial to effectively utilise geographical data, is the information that allows for links to be established between adverts. There are, according to the detectives interviewed, two characteristics that can provide some evidence that adverts are linked: the phone numbers used and the account used to post the adverts. To a lesser extent, it was also mentioned that email addresses and URLs might be provided, which can also give a hint of the underlying organisation. Additionally, some pointed out that semantic similarity, especially recurring blocks of texts copy-pasted between adverts, can also suggest that adverts are linked. This, however, from the perspective of investigators, does not offer the same definitive evidence of organisation as a phone number or shared account. As one investigator put it,

> I guess, for me, the indicators that we on face value would go for, would be the phone number and the User ID, primarily. And you can then start drilling down a little bit into the movement from there. (Detective Constable 2)

From the discussions with investigators, it appears that the information contained within online adverts is not especially useful on their own: it is first when the links between accounts, phone numbers and the adverts are examined that it is possible for the police to build a picture of the scale of the network. In other words, criminal networks can be perceived as relational entities and, by extension, their online adverts can also reflect their relational nature. Therefore, the unit of analytical importance in the context of policing is the relations, or links, between adverts. The addition of geographical and longitudinal data adds value to how these data are interpreted:

> you can imagine that the [account] is ultimately the controlling influence on the adverts below. So as they come and go, you can then see the movement of potentially the same girls up and down the country, and you'll immediately then start to build a case towards the trafficking side of it, and not just the argument that it's an independent girl working in an area, and she's not under anyone else's control or coercion. (Detective Constable 2)

These findings challenge the pre-existing literature on the value of using indicators to signal the presence of exploitation. There was a perception amongst respondents—whether referring solely to online adverts or more generally in identifying trafficking offline—that indicators are of limited value:

> it is challenging and it is difficult to kind of pull out and meet the threshold at times, and understand that everyone has complicated lives, and it's not as easy as, "here's a lot of indicators. Oops, she scored 10 out of 12. Definitely trafficked"; it's not as simple as that (NGO Worker 2)

In the context of assessing an individual's situation, others also highlighted that indicators are most valuable when "lots of indicators come together" (NGO Worker 4). Some respondents noted how other police forces use matrices to catalogue indicators present in online adverts. Nevertheless, such approaches were also highlighted as challenging to use in practice due to the significant amount of work required to sift through adverts.

In an investigative context, what appears to be of interest to investigators are networks rather than the descriptive information in adverts. More broadly speaking, there is always a serious risk of conflating migrant sex worker cooperatives with criminal networks if only online adverts are observed. As was pointed out earlier, migrants might be particularly inclined to organise themselves into co-operatives due to their lack of different capital necessary for working independently. If this indeed is the case, it potentially also has implications for how to understand the online presence of networks within the sex market:

> [the police] got the categories of things, the risk factors to trafficking, that they can see by their websites, and one of them is, you know, four people use the same phone number, and that happens often because of these reasons, but that could be assumed that one person is controlling four people, often it's not the case, it's self-organising, and it's, you know, it's business, it's being savvy in business and working in a way that's working for everyone. (NGO Worker 1)

Based on this, it can be argued that the value of establishing links between adverts exceeds the value of identifying indicators potentially indicative of exploitation; nonetheless, identified networks themselves are not *evidence* of organised exploitation. Rather than perceiving certain indicators as indicative of exploitation, it is more fruitful to perceive empirically established links between adverts to indicate some form or underlying organisation. However, as pointed out by police participants, determining whether that organisation is facilitating exploitation cannot be achieved through the analysis of online adverts:

> I think from looking at most adverts that we came across in our inquiry, it's very, very difficult to identify somebody that's potentially trafficked from that, just from that advert itself. (Detective Inspector 2)

Understanding the online presence of criminal networks and other actors in the sex market is crucial, both to understand the spatio-temporal and structural features of a network more effectively and to minimise the risk of conflating independent—and predominantly—migrant sex workers with individuals who may be subjected to control and exploitation. Open-source intelligence (OSINT) generated from online escorts appears important in an investigative context, though its value ultimately depends on how well the online dimension of the sex market is interpreted and understood. The following section will more closely examine the role of OSINT within the investigative process.

Intelligence and Investigation

As was discussed in the previous sections, the police might get referrals or information on suspected sex trafficking activities and then proceed with an inquiry and, as such, be more reactive rather than proactive. According to police respondents, developing intelligence is a resource-intensive process, and it can be challenging to respond retroactively to a situation, given the transient nature of criminal networks. The added digital dimension to the sex market also necessitates investigations to evaluate open-source intelligence. While this appears to be a normal part of inquiries, it is nevertheless "very uncommon" (Detective Sergeant 1) for an investigation to be opened based solely on online intelligence, such as escort adverts. It occasionally happens that detectives or analysts would more proactively monitor online spaces to identify local intelligence, but that may be more common in police forces outwith Scotland:

> At the moment it's a few of us who do it, and it's a little bit ad-hoc ... We do days of action as such, where we'll go online, we'll spend that day looking at stuff, and then go and doing the visits. It's a bit of both really. General intelligence, checking each day, the telephone numbers, but then I'd proactively go on the websites every now and again. (Detective Constable 1, English Police Force)

More commonly, if offline intelligence is received and developed to suggest action is needed, it is first then that respondents suggested that the online presence of the suspected criminal network would be examined. Suppose there are suspicions that someone in the sex market may be under some form of control. In that case, detectives highlighted that a first step is usually to either send local community officers to the identified address or carry out support, health and wellbeing visits (SHAW visits), which involves "attending a premise … where there's known sex workers and being that conduit with the NHS and other partners to feed workers into support" (Detective Inspector 3). Depending upon the nature of the original intelligence and, particularly, if there are immediate safeguarding concerns—such as information on ongoing disturbances, shouting, or that it potentially involves a young person, this might necessitate a "police-only type of visit" (Detective Inspector 3). Otherwise, the police may continue developing that intelligence while also conducting SHAW visits. These are necessary but not unproblematic; the police and partners are likely to encounter individuals who, whilst working together, are not exploited and may not perceive interaction with the police as something positive. Alternatively, if individuals are exploited, they may not divulge any criminality due to fear of the exploiters, that they will lose what little income they have, or risk being deported. Establishing trust with sex workers and victims alike is critical, and other stakeholders also recognised the complicated nature of police interventions and that it is "a difficult job to do" (NGO Worker 2).

If a police-only or a SHAW visit gives further cause to open an inquiry, investigators suggested that it is only then that it may become important to examine the online dimension. Once the senior investigating officer (SIO) is developing an investigative strategy, detectives specialising in internet investigation may be deployed to provide a technological steer. If the investigators have images or phone numbers related to the victim, a starting point is locating them on ASWs. Detectives described how it is crucial to build an initial picture of the scale of the network:

> Can we just initially see how widely the phone number is used, and is it used against other girls, or is it just for that one girl across multiple pages. (Detective Constable 2)

According to police respondents, this would normally be a fairly manual process of identifying relevant information from ASWs and other sources through search engines. Some forces may have access to specialist technologies developed to identify patterns in escort adverts, though those are, if used, deployed at a later stage as "it doesn't always assist in narrowing down the work that we need to progress an inquiry" (Detective Inspector 3). It is also central to thoroughly review and develop incoming intelligence to minimise the risk of false-positives (i.e., mistakenly identifying an independent sex worker as a trafficking victim), and this is "why there will be investigations done usually before we get to the ASWs stage" (Detective Sergeant 1). While these technologies are often marketed as tools that can help law enforcement to even *end* sex trafficking (e.g., DeliverFund 2020), they "don't produce evidence for us at the moment" (Detective Sergeant 1). In other words, detectives pointed out that the crucial evidence required to progress an inquiry is *not* contained in online escort adverts themselves; the police need to know "who's controlling the adverts" (Detective Inspector 1). While online adverts can provide intelligence that illuminates the organisation of a network, it is the key information behind the ASWs—such as payment information and IP addresses—that is required to proceed in an investigation and for which the term 'actionable intelligence' should be reserved:

> So, physical evidence as well as online presence evidence, just to tie all these things together. So ASWs are a part of the investigation; they do provide a very valuable part of that investigation, but yeah, it's part of it, but knowing where the links are as well … But it will be the ASWs themselves and the information behind it, that will then give us the actionable intelligence. (Detective Sergeant 1)

It was highlighted by participants that while online intelligence from escort adverts can play an important role in any investigation, telecom data and the financial trail are often "the missing piece of the jigsaw" (Detective Inspector 3). Any such intelligence can then be triangulated against other forms of intelligence and evidence, such as CCTV footage, witness information, surveillance logs or other information contained within police systems. Based on this, the precise role, then, of OSINT from escort adverts is that they can provide a broad, indicative picture of the scale of networks operating in the sex market: it adds another, potentially valuable, layer to investigations. By effectively utilising this digital layer, "the better and more accurate your intelligence picture will be" (Detective Sergeant 2).

A further, more technological issue is that online intelligence, whilst useful, produces so much information that "then has to be trawled through to see whether it gives us any evidence" (Detective Sergeant 1). Detectives highlighted how the real challenge with open-source intelligence is to derive value from it:

> you go down a rabbit hole with it, and it's difficult to keep control of the large amount of data you get, it can be in different formats, you know, and actually the tools you're using are then generating the data, and then what is an analytically viable product at the end of it? 'Cause there's no point in scraping lots of flat data that you can't then index and search later. (Detective Constable 2)

More generally speaking, all information gathered online must first be processed into structured datasets prior to any meaningful analysis. However, while escort adverts provide much information, far from all of it helps distil it into an "analytically viable product". Besides, detectives also highlighted the ethical considerations associated with open-source intelligence. Indeed, scraping online escort adverts is inevitably a form of surveillance:

> You need to be careful with web scraping, I think there's a huge amount of collateral intrusion involved in just scraping data, and there's a lot of ethics involved in that as well … we certainly aren't routinely scraping data out of these sites. You know, it's not like we got a bot running in the background, scraping it every day, and it just sits in a box somewhere, that absolutely doesn't happen. (Detective Constable 2)

Subjecting independent sex workers to online monitoring is not in either the police's or the public's best interest. Online intelligence comes at a cost, and while scraping technology and advanced data analytics may help gather information, it also creates a new range of problems, as identified by police respondents. To reinforce what was discussed earlier: there is a need for highly targeted approaches applied in situations where there are perceived safeguarding issues. As some respondents pointed out, this means avoiding scraping huge volumes of data simply to create an extensive dataset for future use, but rather, to only collect adverts pertaining to a particular network under investigation. As one detective put it, "we can't monitor people's behaviour just for the sake of that there might be some crime in the background" (Detective Sergeant 3).

Increasing the surveillance and monitoring of the sex market can undoubtedly negatively affect sex workers. Proactively identifying victims online may not be the answer, even if aimed at reducing harm. This may seem a paradoxical contention, though it is crucial to establish good relationships with the sex worker community, both to better respond to their needs and concerns and avoid further criminalisation, but also because sex workers themselves can feed invaluable intelligence to the police if they have concerns that someone might be in an exploitative situation:

> I don't think proactive identification of people who don't necessarily want to be identified is the answer. I think the answer is around ensuring a supportive system for people to come forward. (NGO Worker 1)

Because a plethora of online networks operate in the sex market, many of which will display the conventional 'indicators' of sex trafficking, the resources that would go into proactively investigating and developing OSINT would be unsustainable. It is perhaps such proactive efforts that also yield the highest risks of false-positives and crossing paths with sex workers who "don't want to be identified" (NGO Worker 1), whereas efforts focused on situations where other intelligence would suggest safeguarding issues may make victims more likely to cooperate with law enforcement.

Concluding Remarks

The preceding analysis has highlighted several important issues relating to exploitation within the UK's contemporary sex markets. Whereas the most important of the findings will be discussed in more depth in chapter "Key Messages and Conclusions: Future Directions in the Computational

Criminology of Internet-Mediated Exploitation", it is still worth reiterating the key findings from this analysis at this point.

Regarding the nature of sexual labour, some participants perceived sexual labour as a form of violence against women, whereas others recognised exploitation as an inherent feature of late capitalism, particularly in unregulated markets. A limited opportunity structure and economic needs were often perceived as driving women into the sex industry. The findings also indicate that different forms of capital may be important to understand how sex markets are structured. Precarious migrants lacking the necessary capital to work independently were often perceived by respondents as being at the greatest risk of exploitation; from the perceptions of participants regarding these issues, there is a suggestion that some migrants may have to rely upon potentially untrustworthy and exploitative ties to engage in sexual labour. It was also suggested that migrants—and sex workers more widely—tend to organise themselves into cooperatives to work more safely and effectively. As such, variations in social, human and economic capital potentially serve to structure the sex market and may be associated with variable working conditions.

Based on the perspectives of respondents, victims of sex trafficking (as identified by the police or service providers) were described as often being migrants from particular geographies and often having experienced a certain degree of socio-economic deprivation prior to migration. Some were suggested to have pre-existing vulnerabilities or have been victims of other forms of abuse, such as being forced into sexual exploitation at a very young age. It was also highlighted how victims may also be reluctant to engage with law enforcement and service providers for many reasons, but perhaps most importantly, because their current situation of exploitation may be preferable to more desperate circumstances in their home countries. In this context, detectives highlighted how victims would often provide a quite different story when engaging with authorities, compared to what is eventually uncovered during the forensic analysis of communication devices. The fact that individuals may be receiving some remuneration was suggested to sometimes be enough for them to choose to remain in a controlled and exploitative situation; they may therefore be reluctant to identify themselves as victims.

In terms of recruitment, some victims were described as knowing prior to migration that they were going to engage in sexual labour, whereas others had been deceived, coming to the UK believing that they were going to do something completely different. For those who knew they would engage in sexual labour, what contributes to exploitative situations is a discrepancy between expectations and reality. Migrants might have believed they would have greater control over their working environment, or their facilitators might have charged them exorbitant fees to be able to work.

Several strategies to achieve control and compliance have been observed for those whose sexual labour is controlled by a third-party. Debts and debt bondage were often highlighted by participants, and it was suggested that some individuals might migrate to pay a previous debt, or accumulate debts to finance their migration. From the respondents' experience, violence from the exploiters would typically be a last resort if compliance cannot be achieved through other means. Threats of violence directed at the victims or their families were suggested by participants to be more common. In addition to this, it was also highlighted by participants how some criminal networks encountered were operating along ethnic lines, and at times, would have a presence in the victim's local community.

Many respondents perceived the sex market to have significantly expanded due to the emergence and widespread adoption of the internet and communication technologies. This expansion was explained by the fact that technologies increase access to sexual services and that the internet helps penetrate and extend sex markets, thus increasing the availability of sexual services. Some argued that the sex market had taken a more extreme turn, in that the norms of what is considered 'normal' or 'extreme' can be continuously negotiated in a context characterised by fierce competition. Online spaces were also perceived as occupying a paradoxical role in the sex market. They both help to make sex work safer by allowing for communication with fellow sex workers and the screening of clients, amongst other things. However, it was also argued by respondents that the anonymous nature of online spaces and encrypted communication also makes them ideal for exploitation or clients pushing the boundaries of sex workers. These dark spaces of precarity were suggested to allow criminal networks to conceal their organisation and carry on their operations in an otherwise legitimate market, despite the illegality of their business.

Criminal networks themselves were perceived as being motivated by the potential of high rewards and low risks. It was also suggested that some of these networks may also engage in other illicit activities outwith their operations in the sex market. Technologies, in this context, were highlighted as allowing networks to streamline their activities and become more efficient in the marketplace. From this perspective, larger networks may be more dependent on effectively utilising technology, such as monitoring and communicating with victims, arranging accommodation and transportation and, of course, marketing their services and penetrating new markets. Simply put, exploitation in the sex market can naturally be conducted without using technology; however, the conversations with research participants suggest that effectively harnessing technology increases a network's administrative and logistical capacities, enabling more sophisticated control mechanisms while simultaneously allowing them to remain at the periphery of conventional policing.

Due to the perceived sophistication of criminal networks operating in the sex market, and that it was also frequently highlighted that victims themselves may feel ambivalent about their situation, investigating sex trafficking is both difficult and resource-intensive. The police have limited resources and must effectively prioritise incoming intelligence and decide what can be developed into an inquiry. Safeguarding concerns are always central to decision-making and inevitably direct the course of action. Sometimes, this means the appropriate action is to open an investigation, whereas other times, it may be better to signpost to services. However, what potentially makes this very challenging is that what constitutes 'safeguarding concerns' from the perspective of the police may be vastly different to how sex workers understand the situation.

Because criminal networks, non-criminal networks and independent sex workers all inhabit the same online spaces, it becomes crucial to understand how their respective presence is manifested online. There was a wider agreement that the use of indicators to signal the presence of criminal networks can be problematic, primarily due to the more often than not spurious information provided in online adverts. These are designed solely to attract clients rather than a commitment to reflecting the offline reality of sex workers or the services provided. It is the relational nature of these digital traces that was highlighted as making them valuable in a policing context; in other words, a sole advert might not be able to tell us much, but a large-scale, transient network operating across vast geographies for a more extended period might suggest a certain degree of underlying organisation.

According to police respondents, investigating the online dimension of sex trafficking is necessary due to the increasing technologisation of the sex market. However, it is rare for open-source intelligence to be the starting point of an inquiry; rather, the online dimension will be investigated when (more reliable) intelligence from other sources would suggest safeguarding issues. At this point, OSINT can be an important addition in guiding the SIO to the next course of action. Nevertheless, it is important to note that the evidence that will eventually make it possible to proceed in an investigation is usually found beyond OSINT and the sites hosting escort adverts. The value of OSINT in this context is that it can provide a broader, indicative picture of the scale and organisation of criminal networks in the sex market, thus offering another layer of information to ongoing investigations.

While OSINT is useful in understanding the scale and geographies of networks, it was highlighted that effectively collecting and analysing online data requires specialists and high technical capabilities. Besides this, there are also clear ethical considerations, as monitoring the sex market is a form of surveillance to which independent sex workers will also be subjected. As such, proactive investigations into the online dimension of the sex market may not be the best course of action, since it would be untenable due to the resources it would require to develop that intelligence, but also, that it can negatively impact the relations between sex workers and the police.

Whereas the preceding analysis has contributed with important insights into exploitation within sex markets, and the role of technology therein, it is also based on a very limited sample and situated in a very particular epistemological context. All respondents were either currently serving police officers, or involved in advocating for, or providing support to, migrants, sex workers and trafficking victims. As such, the insights generated on the issues examined in this analysis may, epistemologically speaking, be quite far detached from the lived realities of migration, sexual labour or exploitation. This is especially important since the policing of the sex market can cause significant harm to sex workers, and the accounts relating to the present analysis only provide a very partial and fragmented perspective on some highly complex social phenomena. The findings from this chapter, as such, need to be interpreted in light of these epistemological shortcomings and in the context of the existing inequalities between law enforcement and those who are active in the sex market. A clear priority of future research should thus be to investigate these issues from the perspective of those with lived experience.

References

Braun V, Clarke V (2006) Using Thematic Analysis in Psychology. Qual Res Psychol 3(2):77–101. https://doi.org/10.1191/1478088706qp063oa

DeliverFund (2020) Where We Are. https://deliverfund.org/how-deliverfund-is-fighting-human-trafficking-in-america/

Ellison G (2017) Criminalizing the Payment for Sex in Northern Ireland: Sketching the Contours of a Moral Panic. Br J Criminol 57(1):194–214. https://doi.org/10.1093/bjc/azv107

Igbinomwanhia OG (2021) Human Trafficking and Poverty in South-south Nigeria. PhD Thesis, University of Stirling.

Complexity, Similarity and Tie Formation in Advert Networks

As was alluded to from the qualitative analysis in the previous chapter, there appears to be a variety of networks of varying complexity present within the online sex market. To date, however, we do not have much of an understanding of the structures of these networks. This has, nevertheless, not prevented other researchers from suggesting that we can use the information found in online escort adverts to identify sex trafficking (Skidmore et al. 2018; Antonopoulos et al. 2020; L'Hoiry et al. 2024). Some forms of online networks tend to mirror offline networks (Subrahmanyam et al. 2008). For instance, we would normally assume social media profiles on social networking sites to represent an actual individual, and that the ties between them—especially in localised contexts—represent some form of an offline relationship. This relationship between the observed online representation and the offline context is likely to be very different in this research context than in others, since the units of analysis are escort adverts created to market specific services. Here, the empirical ties are either shared phone numbers or user accounts, and it is impossible to elucidate exactly how many individuals may be involved and their offline relationships.

R. Kjellgren, *Internet-Mediated Exploitation in the Scottish Online Sex Market*,
Transnational Crime, Crime Control and Security,
https://doi.org/10.1007/978-3-032-09275-5_8

In this chapter, a blend of computational methods and social network analysis is combined to challenge the epistemologically naive assumption that 'indicators' found in escort adverts are useful signals of potential trafficking. Instead, the focus is shifted from the presence or absence of certain indicators, to instead consider the relational characteristics of online adverts. Indeed, we might expect some marketing choices to be predictive of the empirical ties, and that certain underlying marketing and network mobility processes contribute to tie formation. These processes may look different depending on the structure of the network itself. In other words, we may expect a certain degree of homogeneity in advert networks more likely to represent independent sex workers, and perhaps more heterogeneity in networks with more complex digital footprints. This chapter aims to illuminate these types of processes, as opposed to more simplistic views of the sex market, which equate any indication of organisation to *organised* exploitation.

This chapter will go on to present and discuss the methods used for this analysis, as well as provide some background to the research context and questions, and how to interpret the network statistics. The analysis draws upon the complexity scale mentioned in chapter "Methods in Practice: Designing an Effective Workflow in Computational Criminology" (section "Stage 8: Operationalising Network Complexity") to compare networks. The analysis will begin by examining how indicators commonly used in trafficking research are inefficient and lead to a false sense of confidence, whilst ignoring the wider complexity of the sex market. Following this, the analysis proceeds with an examination of advert similarity, both in terms of the attributes, as measured by the E-I index, and textual descriptions, which are measured by cosine similarity. Bivariate patterns between observed networks and important advert attributes through the application of quadratic assignment procedures (QAP) are then examined. The final analysis consists of multivariate quadratic assignment procedure models (MRQAP), which consider the joint influence of predictor variables upon tie formation in more complex networks. The chapter concludes with a discussion concerning the significance of the identified patterns.

Methods

Indicator Analysis

The first part of this analysis evaluates the presence of indicators often assumed, though not empirically substantiated, to be indicative of trafficking, in a longitudinal collection of 213,693 online adverts, or to be more precise, advert records (see chapter "Methods in Practice: Designing an Effective Workflow in Computational Criminology", section "Stage 3: Data Management", for a more thorough discussion of differences). The reason for relying on advert records (i.e., adverts live at different time points of the study period), as opposed to unique adverts (i.e., records grouped into unique advert identifiers), is because the primary interest is whether or not an indicator was present at the time of data collection. A subset of items from the *Sex Trafficking Identification Matrix* (STIM), developed by L'Hoiry et al. (2024), was explored. To be more precise, there were only 12 indicators that could feasibly be applied to the current dataset, since some variables (or images) required to fully use the STIM were not present in the dataset. The analysis relied on using regular expressions to identify keywords in free-text, or otherwise used data that were already structured and suitable for quantitative analysis. The number of indicators present in each advert was then calculated, and the rates of indicators explored in more detail. All adverts with a maximum score—that is, all 12 indicators present—were extracted from the collection, and the three networks posting these high-scoring adverts were compared against networks of similar, or greater, size.

The descriptive analysis is relatively simple, particularly with regard to textual data in adverts, relying on regular expressions of the keywords mentioned in the STIM, as opposed to more sophisticated forms of machine learning or language models, which undoubtedly would have provided a much more comprehensive and satisfying picture. Nevertheless, the purpose of this analysis is to illustrate the shortcomings of using indicators in this context, and it thus serves as a starting point for more thoughtful empirical investigations of the sex market.

Relational Data and Methodological Considerations

Since this chapter is primarily focused on the dyadic relationships between online adverts rather than the adverts themselves, a selection of methods associated with social network analysis was deemed appropriate. The primary unit of analysis was unique adverts (or, more precisely, the *relations* between unique adverts) rather than advert records themselves. This was described in more detail in chapter "Methods in Practice: Designing an Effective Workflow in Computational Criminology"; advert records represent escort adverts at a specific point in time, and these are nested in a unique advert identifier. This advert identifier gives a more plausible representation of an actual individual, rather than the advert records, since one person is likely to post several adverts on different occasions. This is particularly important for this analysis, since relying on advert records would introduce bias to the networks and emphasise the relational processes relating to the posting patterns occurring on ASW 1. Whilst we cannot know the offline configurations of these online networks, unique adverts are arguably more likely to represent notional persons or personas; even if that is not the case, it will nevertheless reduce some of the bias associated with advert records and posting patterns. As such, advert identifiers represented the nodes in networks, and the links between them consisted of phone numbers or user accounts. With the empirical networks assigned a complexity score, a series of statistical analyses were conducted to identify differences between networks based on their complexity. All models or statistics were calculated for each network, and the results were thereafter subjected to an aggregated analysis, shifting the focus from individual networks to broader processes in the online sex market.

Because network complexity was operationalised based on adverts posted over a prolonged period, the complexity scores assigned to networks are strongly related to time. In other words, networks can become more complex over time because they leave an increasing number of digital traces. As such, if the assignment of complexity scores had focused on a specific point in time, the networks under study would look very different. A decision was made to focus the analysis on the networks present across the entire time period, as opposed to specific time points, to better understand *how complex* networks could become. Future research could, however, benefit from incorporating the element of time into the statistical modelling of online networks in this context.

Group Embedding and Homo/Hetero-Philous Processes: E-I Index

The analysis began with an examination of the external-internal index (E-I index), which is a measure developed by Krackhardt and Stern (1988) to understand group embedding in networks. This is sometimes referred to as a homophily index, since it measures the tendencies of homophily and heterophily, or in other words, the propensity to form or not to form ties to others with similar attributes. The E-I index was applied at a network level (compared to subgroup or node level) and, in this context, it measures the extent to which nodes in a network are connected, based on various attributes (Hanneman and Riddle 2011). The E-I index is calculated by:

$$\frac{EL - IL}{EL + IL}$$

where the internal links are subtracted from the external links and divided by the total number of links. The E-I index ranges between -1.0 (all the subgroup's links are internal) and +1.0 (all the subgroup's links are external). In this research context, a positive value represents a tendency for adverts with different values on the attribute in question to be connected (out-group or external links), whereas a negative value suggests a tendency for adverts to be connected to adverts with the same values (in-group or internal links). The E-I index was calculated for the following variables: age group, British ethnicity (dichotomous), ethnic group, region, local authority, A Levels (anal sex), OWO (oral sex without protection), PSE (pornstar experience), WS ('water sports'; acts involving urine), all extreme services (the presence of all aforementioned service variables) and GFE (girlfriend experience). As such, 11 E-I indexes were calculated for each network. All networks with two or more unique adverts (or adverts identifiers; ADIDs) were used in this part of the analysis ($N = 7939$). This means that single adverts that were reposted over and over again were excluded, and the analysis is therefore focused on slightly more complex networks. The results were then compared across the network complexity scale; in this case, it was operationalised into quintiles, with the fifth quintile containing the most complex networks, and the first the least complex. Because of the criteria (and indeed necessity) of networks containing two or more ADIDs, the E-I index comparison was limited to networks from quintiles 3–5; all networks in quintiles 1–2 consisted of networks with only one ADID. To aid the comparison between complexity quintiles, both concerning the E-I index and other statistics, one-way analysis of variance (ANOVA) models were fitted to assess statistically significant differences. To estimate the effect size of the associations between network complexity and the outcome measures, the Eta-squared (η^2) statistic was calculated, which is a measure of the proportion of variance explained in the outcome variable.

Advert Textual Similarity: Cosine Distance

Whilst the E-I index measures network cohesion, and homophilous and heterophilous processes based on observed ties and categorical attributes, a different method had to be considered to measure textual similarity between adverts and networks. Considering that a significant feature of online adverts is the textual descriptions written by the poster, it is crucial to examine similarities and differences in textual marketing strategies. To achieve this, the cosine similarity was calculated to estimate the textual similarity between adverts. Prior to calculating this, the textual data were processed to exclude common English stop words, punctuation and other non-informative symbols. In brief, the cosine similarity is a statistic for measuring how similar two documents are whilst adjusting for their size, which makes it an appropriate measure in this context. This is achieved by representing the collection of documents in a term-frequency matrix, where each column is a unique term, each row a unique document and the cell values the term frequencies. The algorithm calculates a similarity score ranging from 0.0 (no similarity) to 1.0 (perfect similarity) for each pairwise combination of documents (Han et al. 2012). This can be computationally demanding, since the number of pairwise combinations in an undirected network increases exponentially with the number of cases n:

$$\frac{n(n-1)}{2}$$

In this research, this meant there were 6,781,407,570 possible combinations to consider. As such, the cosine similarity was applied in two different ways: (1) the similarity was calculated for all possible combinations *within* a given network; and (2) for all possible combinations *between* networks. The latter was achieved by combining the textual data from all adverts within a network into one document, representing that particular network. The comparison between networks thus involved 15,010 × (15,010 - 1) ÷ 2 = 112,642,545 unique combinations. For purposes of comparison, the average within and between similarity scores were examined. One-way ANOVAs were then used to examine differences between the means.

Predictors of Tie Formation: QAP and MRQAP

Quadratic assignment procedure (QAP), and its multivariate counterpart, MRQAP, were used to examine the predictors of tie formation in the empirical networks. These are two methods from the social network analysis paradigm specifically designed for the modelling of dyadic data (Dekker et al. 2007). Because the primary units of analysis in this chapter are the dyadic relationships between adverts rather than adverts themselves, common forms of modelling like Ordinary Least Squares (OLS) regression are inappropriate due to the inherent dependence of observations (Campana and Varese 2013). Krackhardt (1988) proposed MRQAP to account for these issues of autocorrelation by regressing the Y matrix (empirical network) on the X matrices (in this case, the ties formed based on X variable attributes). In its essence, the algorithm repeatedly generates random permutations of the original network, performs multiple analyses to create an empirical sampling distribution, and then calculates beta coefficients through the application of OLS. The standard errors are thus estimated based on the comparison between the coefficients of the empirical networks and those of the randomly permutated networks and the sampling distribution (Krackhardt 1988; Dekker et al. 2007; Campana and Varese 2013). In this case, 1000 permutations were used to estimate both QAP correlations and MRQAP models. The independent variables used were age groups, extreme services, local authority and ethnicity.

It should be noted that different methods could be used for modelling the dyadic data. One increasingly popular alternative is exponential random graph models (ERGMs), which are better suited to operationalise relational theories, and to model a wide variety of endogenous dependencies (Cranmer et al. 2017). As such, the options for model specification are more extensive with ERGMs, compared to QAP and MRQAP, but they are more difficult to apply in practice, especially if fitted on networks characterised by a very high or very low density of connections (Cranmer et al. 2017). Whilst more limited, QAP and MRQAP are more parsimonious alternatives to ERGMs, and were deemed appropriate given that this research is exploratory and, moreover, that the aim of this particular analysis is relational hypothesis testing, as opposed to (statistically) disentangling complex relational processes.

Again, because of how computationally intensive it was to estimate these models with all empirical networks combined into one graph, a decision was made to conduct QAPs and MRQAPs for individual networks and then analyse the aggregated results. The QAP correlations were derived for all networks with ten or more ADIDs (2140 networks). However, because of how the statistical tests were calculated by the algorithm, p-values could not be calculated for perfect correlations.[1] As such, the aggregated analysis of QAP correlations only involved 1395 networks, for which the p-value was successfully calculated.[2] Because simpler

[1] The QAP and MRQAP algorithms were run in R (v. 4.1.3), using the statnet package (v. 2019.6): https://statnet.org/.

[2] Note that this means that one or more QAP correlations were derived for 1395 networks, not that the p-value was correctly calculated for all networks across all variables.

networks tend to have more similar characteristics, and therefore more likely to yield perfect correlations, these are underrepresented in the analysis. Additionally, the criteria of only analysing networks with ten or more ADIDs skewed the analysis towards more complex networks (these are the networks of primary research interest).

The MRQAP focused on all the networks for which all QAP correlations were correctly identified (N = 325). Similar to the issues in calculating p-values for QAP correlations, some models would struggle to identify and converge when there were high degrees of multicollinearity, and predictors that caused perfect prediction were automatically dropped from the models. After running MRQAP models for all networks, correctly identified models were separated, and the final analysis involved a second round of modelling of 257 networks. This final sample produced a more reasonable portrayal of the structure of more complex networks. Because ties were undirected and not valued, logistic MRQAP models were fitted, and odds ratios were calculated to aid interpretation. In addition, adjusted pseudo R-squared, Bayesian information criterion, and the total fraction of correct predictions were also presented to examine model fitness.

Research Context and Questions

Before presenting the findings from the analysis, it is worth briefly highlighting how the analysis relates to the research questions. The methods used in this chapter have never been applied in the context of online escort adverts, and some elaboration is necessary. The core questions in this section relate to how networks are structured and how any identifiable network structures potentially relate to vulnerability or exploitation.

In light of the findings presented in the previous chapter, it may be plausible that different types of networks are structured differently; we could imagine that online networks representing either one independent sex worker or a collective of sex workers are largely homogeneous and homophilous, in terms of their advertised characteristics. If that indeed is the case, and there is maybe one person responsible for posting all adverts, we would also anticipate that adverts are fairly similar, and that characteristics such as ethnicity and locality are central in how the observed networks are structured. In comparison, a more complex network, which potentially could involve a number of different people posting the adverts, or simply involving a lot more sex workers, could plausibly lead to online networks that are more diverse and heterogeneous. By examining the E-I index, we can understand how similar adverts are in relation to their marketing strategies. The textual similarity may also suggest that either one or more persons are responsible for posting the adverts, and on a network level, it also informs us of how unique textual marketing strategies are between networks. The quadratic assignment procedure models allow us to examine the extent to which an advert exhibiting a certain characteristic is likely to be connected to another advert with the same characteristic. Taken together, these methods allow for a deeper understanding of how networks are structured, and this is important in considering whether some structures are, hypothetically speaking, likely to be associated with vulnerability or exploitation.

Tables 1, 2 and 3 show hypothetical examples of how to interpret the network statistics. In these examples, networks 1 and 2 are quite distinct, likely representing two very different offline networks. With regard to the E-I index, network 1 is homogeneous—all adverts share the same ethnic category. Network 2, in contrast, displays a tendency for adverts of varying ethnicity to be connected. The story from the QAP is very similar; ethnicity is perfectly predictive of the empirical ties of network 1, and the correlation for network 2 would suggest ethnicity to have a moderate effect upon the structure of the network, but that there likely are other, potentially more important variables structuring the network. The cosine similarity is fairly straightforward to interpret; all adverts are close to perfectly similar in network 1, implying that the same advert is being

Table 1 Example of the E-I index

Network	Ethnicity EI index	Interpretation
1	-1.00	All of the ties between adverts share the same ethnicity.
2	0.62	There is a positive tendency toward external tie formation; adverts are likely to be connected to adverts exhibiting different ethnicities.

Table 2 Example of QAP correlation

Network	Ethnicity QAP correlation	Interpretation
1	1.00	Ethnicity is (perfectly) predictive of ties within the network.
2	0.37	There is a moderate relationship between ethnicity and the empirical ties within the network.

Table 3 Example of cosine similarity

Network	Within similarity	Between similarity	Interpretation
1	0.98	0.07	Adverts are extremely similar within the network, but the text is dissimilar to the text of other networks.
2	0.43	0.67	Adverts are somewhat similar within the network, but the text is fairly similar to the text of other networks.

reposted albeit, with minor textual changes. There is considerably more textual diversity in network 2, potentially suggesting that one or more people are writing the text for the adverts, contributing to greater textual diversity within the network. In terms of the between-network textual similarity, a value of 0.07 would suggest that network 1's adverts are quite unique when compared to all the other networks. The opposite is true for network 2, where there is a tendency for the network's textual descriptions to be similar to that of other networks, potentially indicating more generic forms of textual marketing strategies.

Together, the different methods provide a rich story of the two hypothetical networks. This story is substantively important: the stability in marketing strategies and the homogeneous nature of the adverts associated with network 1 suggest that the network may be indicative of an independent sex worker who manages all the adverts. In contrast, the patterns in network 2 tell a different story. The diversity in marketing strategies and tendency to heterophily could imply that one or more persons are posting the adverts, or that the underlying offline network itself is quite diverse. As such, this has different implications for vulnerability towards exploitation, and this chapter will continue to elaborate upon this. The analysis itself is somewhat more complex than the examples presented in the examples; the statistics are interpreted in the same way, but the analysis focuses on the patterns of multiple networks.

The Perils of Indicators

It has been highlighted in previous chapters how 'indicators' are highly ambiguous—and largely uninformative—in the context of identifying exploitation in internet-mediated sex markets. The following analysis illustrates how some indicators, which are commonly highlighted as indicative of sex trafficking, may in fact not be very useful, since their presence is often much more widespread than is assumed by research that is not using computational methods (Skidmore et al. 2018; Antonopoulos et al. 2020; L'Hoiry et al. 2024). In their work, L'Hoiry et al. (2024) present 28 different indicators used in their *Sex Trafficking Identification Matrix* (STIM). In addition to being of questionable validity, there is not yet any quantitative evidence demonstrating the discriminatory power of the indicators in identifying trafficking. As such, the potential for false positives—identifying sex workers as trafficking victims, or false negatives—failing to identify trafficking victims—remains unknown. Another severe limitation of using tools like the STIM is that it relies on manually scanning adverts for information and ticking boxes—something which is particularly problematic in this context since such approaches are incapable of appreciating how any one particular advert relates to *all* other adverts on the ASW in question. It is precisely for these reasons that computational criminology is of increasing importance.

The following analysis is based on a subset of indicators from the STIM, which could feasibly be used and applied at scale to the current data. In total, 12 indicators from the STIM were chosen for this exercise, and rates of identified indicators are presented in Table 4. It can be observed that most indicators are relatively common: 79% of adverts offer 10 or more services, 60% advertise duo services, 90% do not advertise as being British, 73% advertise A-Levels or OWO (i.e., 'extreme') services, 55% are listed as being under 25, and 30% use words argued by

Table 4 Rates of a subset of indicators from the STIM present within online adverts

Description	n Adverts	Total Adverts	% Adverts
If over 18, subject no older than 24 years old	116,382	213,693	54.5%
Subject's nationality/ethnicity matches local marketplace	193,123	213,693	90.4%
Use of 's/he'/'they'/'we' instead of 'I'	11,641	213,693	5.4%
Same contact number in different ads	181,922	213,693	85.1%
Same poster/user ID across multiple ads	190,566	213,693	89.2%
Same/similar text as other ads for different subjects	51,478	213,693	24.1%
References to being new: 'new in town'/'just arrived'/'new for you'	20,582	213,693	9.6%
References to youth: 'young and cute'/'sweet'/'fresh'/'candy'	64,177	213,693	30.0%
Long list of services offered in ad e.g.,: 10 or more services	168,144	213,693	78.7%
Specific services: bareback/anal/OWO (oral without a condom)	155,274	213,693	72.7%
Multiple subjects available e.g.,: 'duo services'	126,664	213,693	59.3%
Availability in multiple locations	154,081	213,693	72.1%

others to reference youth. The only indicators which can possibly be described as rare are the use of plural language (implying more than one sex worker), or references to being 'new in town'. Both of these indicators were evaluated using very simple regular expressions and are likely underestimates of the true prevalence. Even so, it is also fully conceivable that these specific marketing strategies would be used by sex worker cooperatives touring together.

The distribution of adverts, as shown in Fig. 1, is somewhat skewed to the left but otherwise roughly follows a normal distribution, and the co-occurrence of a handful of indicators appears to be the norm. Only 7 adverts scored a maximum of 12 indicators present. The seven adverts were posted by three different networks, which will be examined in more detail.

The 3 networks identified by the co-occurrence of 12 indicators had all posted 200 or more adverts within the study period, with the most common advertised ethnicities being Latina Non-British or Mixed Non-British. In Fig. 2, the three identified networks are compared with all

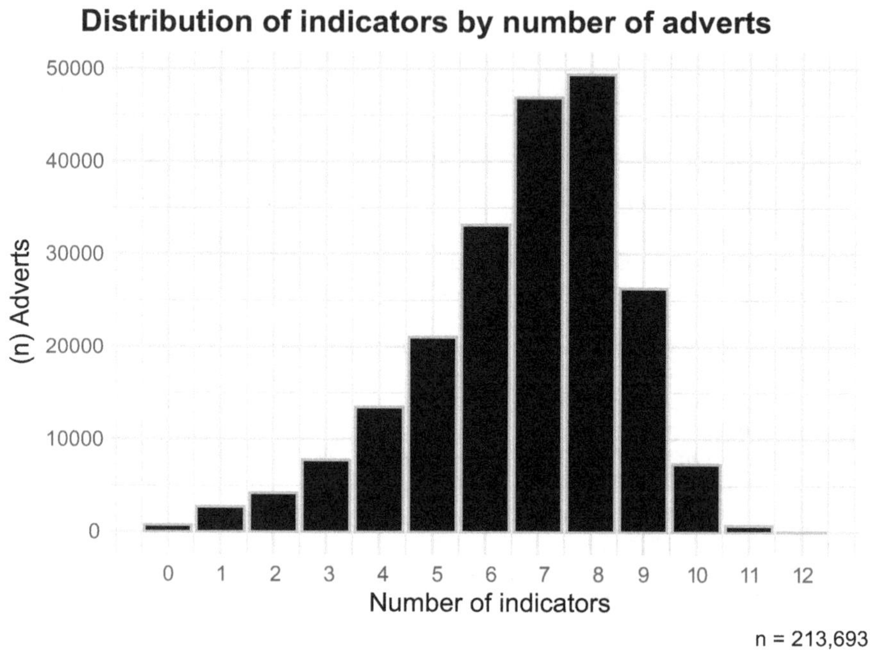

Fig. 1 The distribution of indicators by number of adverts

other networks in the dataset, which had posted 200 or more adverts (n = 136 networks). The points in the graphs represent distinct networks (the three indicator networks in black, others in grey). Two things are immediately clear. First, the three networks identified through the indicator approach are by no means unique—there are well over a hundred networks that are either similar or more complex. Second, whether we examine the number of user accounts or phone numbers used by the networks, the number of adverts posted, number of locations where adverts are posted in, or the geographical dispersion, the story is very similar: the three networks identified by indicators are far from being the largest, most complex networks operating in the sex market.

The perils of using indicators are that they may result in a false sense of confidence, or certainty, in that the approach effectively captures patterns that are meaningful and, importantly, that it fails to grasp the wider context in which the patterns occur. In other words, the examination and

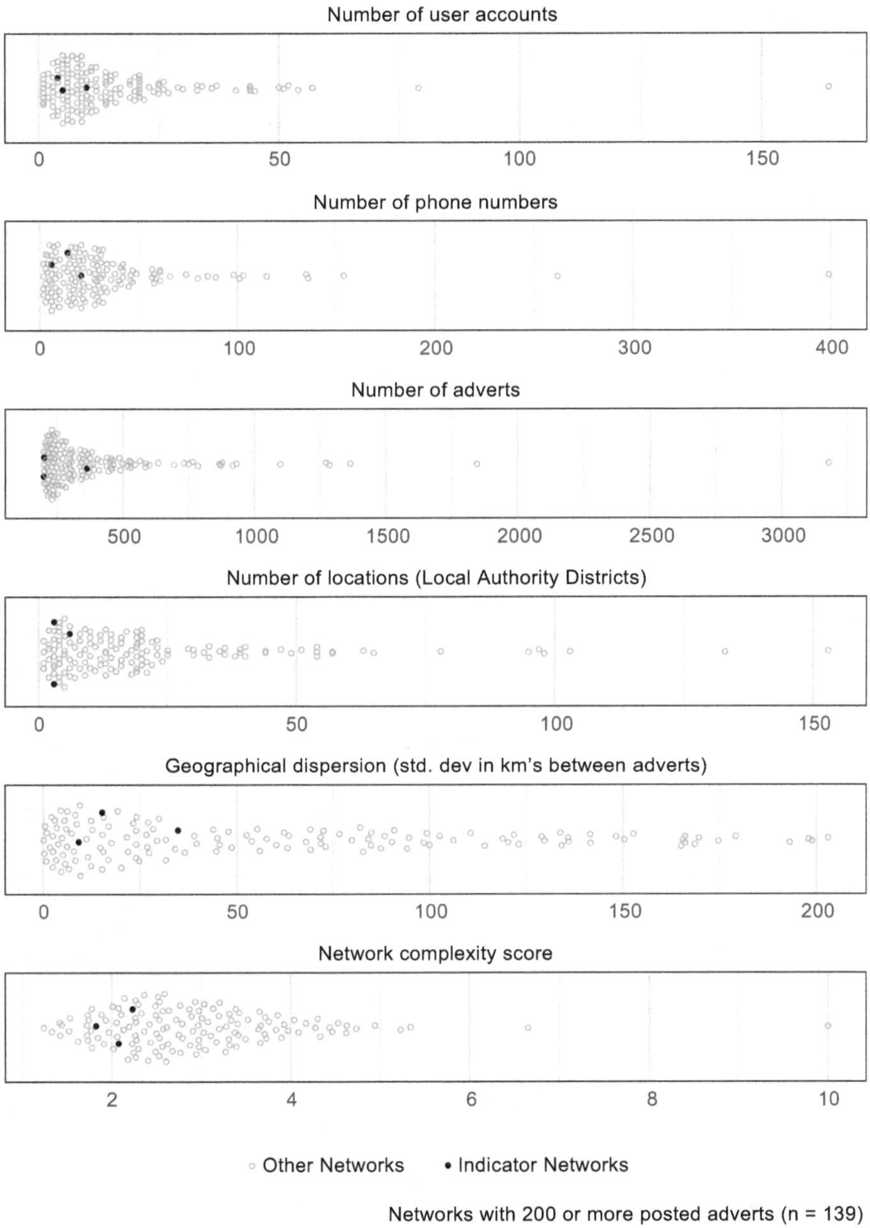

Fig. 2 Comparison of networks identified from indicators (n = 3) and networks with 200 or more posted adverts (n = 136)

evaluation of *one* online escort advert is of very limited utility; it is first when every single advert can be compared to all other adverts on the ASW that wider patterns can be appreciated. Even so, just because patterns can be identified, this does not mean that they are of significance or associated with exploitation and sex trafficking. Rather than focusing on single adverts, the remaining analyses of this chapter will focus on the relational qualities of adverts and how they are organised into different types of networks.

Group Embeddedness and Advert Similarity

The E-I indexes for 11 different variables across 7939 networks are shown in Fig. 3. The graphs show the average E-I indexes with 95% confidence intervals[3] (y-axis) and the underlying distribution of networks. In this case, the E-I indexes are shown by network complexity quintiles 3–5 (x-axis). The graphs also show the underlying density distribution of the E-I indexes. The dashed line at the value of 0.0 separates the distribution of networks in terms of their propensity to be either more or less homophilous. A value below the dashed line thus suggests a tendency towards internal tie formation (more homophilous), whereas a positive value signifies a tendency for external tie formation (more heterophilous). In order to interpret the graphs, consider the point estimate is located, and

[3] The reason for using confidence intervals is related to how the data were collected; as was highlighted in *Stage 2: Quantitative Data Collection*, it is likely that some adverts which were posted on ASW 1 was not captured successfully in the scraping process. As a result, there is a possibility that some networks which were in fact operating in the period of data collection were not captured in the final dataset. As such, the use of average estimates with 95% confidence intervals provide an appropriate measure of uncertainty, since the networks used in this analysis can be perceived as a sample of the true (and unknown) population, or the actual networks on ASW 1, in the period of the study. Similarly, the p-values from the various models are important for the same reason: a quantification of uncertainty in relation to the observed relationships, and the likelihood that the observed relationship occurred by chance, if there in fact was no relationship in the true population of networks on ASW 1. In the context of QAP and MRQAP, the interpretation of p-values require some clarification, as it tell us about the likelihood that the observed relationship between X and Y matrices are due to chance, as compared to randomly permutated networks (as opposed to the total population of networks). When the results of multiple models are presented (e.g., Figs. 8 and 10), it allow us to observe trends in significance, or in other words, the extent to which the observed relationships are unlikely to be a result of chance. See Dekker et al. (2007) for a more extended discussion on permutation tests in QAP and MRQAP.

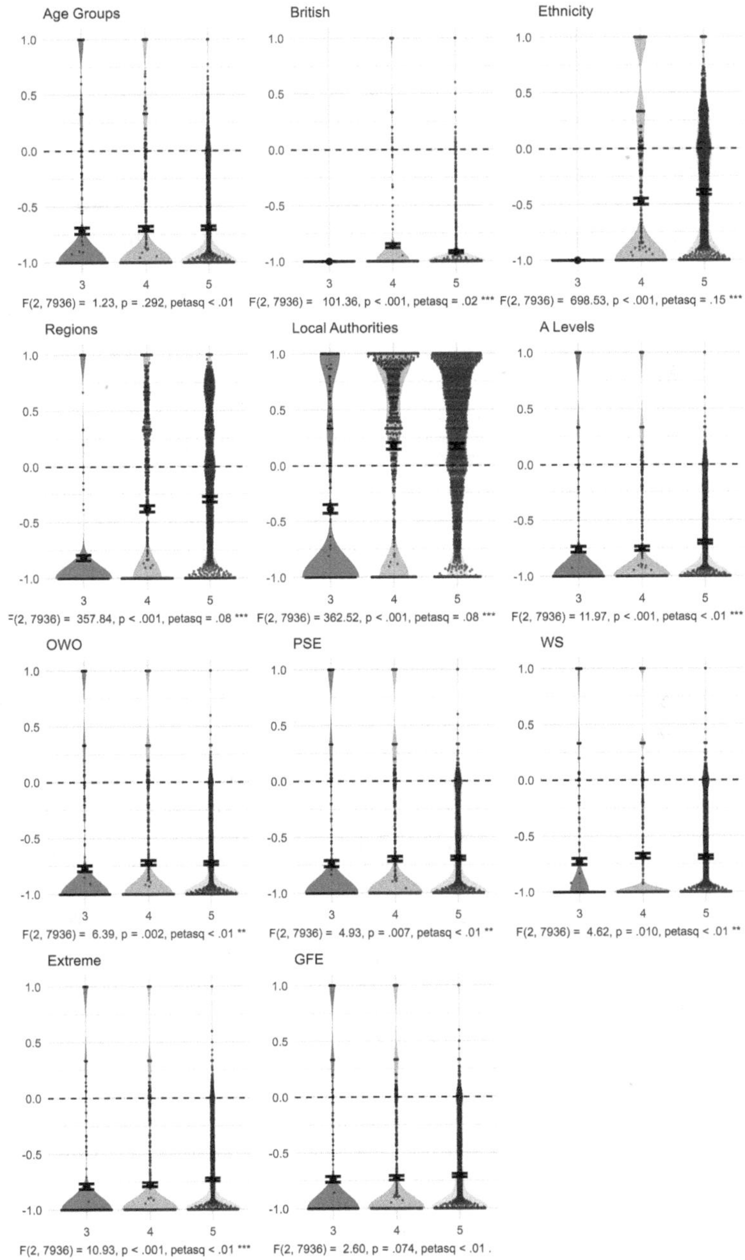

Fig. 3 E-I indexes for different characteristics by network complexity quintiles (3, 4, 5)

this can be examined in relation to the wider network distribution, in terms of skewness.[4]

To begin, there are significant differences in the E-I indexes between network complexity quintiles for all variables, except for GFE and Age Groups. The most noticeable differences can be observed between quintiles 4–5 and 3; in many cases, however, there are only marginal differences between complexity quintiles. In other words, group embeddedness appears to be quite similar across more complex networks, and we would expect clearer differences if quintiles 1 and 2 were included in the analysis.[5] The relationship between group embeddedness and network complexity is strongest for ethnicity ($\eta^2 = 0.15$), in which external group connections increase with network complexity. Region and local authority also seem somewhat important in this context. The association is equal in magnitude for regions ($\eta^2 = 0.08$) and local authorities ($\eta^2 = 0.08$). However, the mean E-I indexes are quite a bit higher for local authorities than for regions, and positive for quintiles 4–5 in relation to local authorities. Put differently, there is a stronger tendency for external ties for local authorities than for regions, and we would expect to see adverts in more complex networks connected to adverts in different local authorities. In more precise terms, we expect the likelihood of two adverts in the same network, but in different regions, being connected to be lower than it is for two adverts of the same network but in different local authorities. After all, several local authorities (especially in densely populated cities) may be very close in a geographical sense, whereas regions encompass larger geographical spaces.

Besides ethnicity, region and local authority, network complexity only explains a very small proportion of variance in the E-I indexes of the other variables. The mean E-I indexes are consistently below zero, implying a tendency for adverts to be connected to adverts with similar values

---

[4] The graphs are a combination of error bars, quasi-random beeswarm plots and violin plots. Each dot, which is more easily visible in some of the graphs shown later in this chapter, represents a unique network, and the coloured shading highlights the distribution, whereas the point estimate and error bars tend to show the average or median.

[5] The same analysis was repeated but with adverts, rather than advert identifiers, as the primary unit of analysis. Differences were indeed stronger, but it is arguably more valid to use advert identifiers because they are more likely to correspond to individuals than adverts themselves. See section "Stage 2: Quantitative Data Collection" for a more thorough discussion.

on the respective variables. However, even if the effect of network complexity is weak, the pattern still suggests it is more common for simpler networks to be more homophilous, which is consistent with the idea that these networks are most likely to represent independent sex workers or smaller collectives of sex workers. There is an increased tendency for external tie formation within more complex networks, which, again, reinforces the notion that more complex networks tend to be more diverse.

In relation to ethnicity, two interesting observations can be made. When ethnicity is dichotomised as British versus Non-British, there is an overwhelmingly strong tendency for the network to consist of internal ties, meaning that ties between Non-British and British ethnicities are unlikely. However, there is a more nuanced relationship when ethnicity is in its original form consisting of 12 categories. Here, the likelihood of two adverts listing different ethnicities being connected appears to increase with network complexity. The tendency towards ethnic heterophily is weak to moderate at best, but nevertheless much stronger in comparison to the more homogeneous tendencies observed when ethnicity is binary. The Implications of this are that simpler networks, which are partially defined by their tendency to list fewer ethnicities, are less likely—even if multiple ethnicities are present within the network—to have ties between adverts of varying ethnicities. Conversely, there is a tendency for more complex networks to primarily be structured around internal ties, though the presence of external ties increases with complexity.

Overall, the effect of network complexity in explaining the variance in the respective E-I indexes is modest at best, and that would be in the case of region, local authority and ethnicity. There is, nevertheless, a certain degree of variability in the tendency of group embeddedness concerning the variables examined. The results do, however, suggest shared characteristics to be central to the structure of the network, but it is not necessarily a network's complexity that best explains these processes.

Whereas quantitative variables can give us an indication of advert similarity, it is also important to consider the role of textual similarity. A significant component of online adverts is the free-text descriptions, which allow the network to build its brand and market its services. Because adverts are posted for the same purpose, we would expect a certain degree of similarity since they will all be concerned with descriptions pertaining to the same topic. Nevertheless, it is also plausible that every sex worker could have a unique way of describing themselves and their services, thus reducing the similarity to other adverts. In contrast, it is also possible that some sex workers and networks, particularly those with limited English skills, might take inspiration from or copy the content of other adverts, potentially increasing the similarity between otherwise unconnected adverts. Each of these possibilities would serve to alter the semantic similarity between adverts.

The average cosine similarity between adverts *within* networks (N = 7939) is shown in Fig. 4. Again, because it was only applied to networks with more than one advert identifier, only quintiles 3–5 are present. Similar to the previous graphs, it shows the average scores and 95% confidence intervals by network complexity quintiles, and each circle represents one network and how they are distributed. There is a weak but

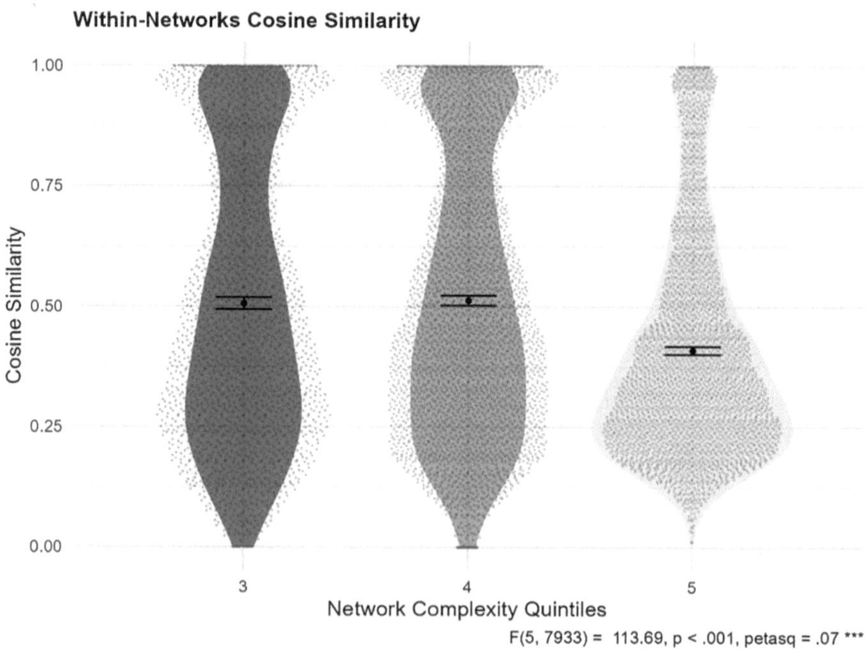

Fig. 4 Within-networks cosine similarity

statistically significant relationship between network complexity and the average within-network cosine scores ($\eta^2 = 0.07$).[6] Whilst the mean scores are similar for quintiles 3 and 4, the scores are significantly lower for quintile 5. In other words, the textual descriptions of the adverts tend to become more dissimilar the more complex the network.

The relationship between advert similarity and network complexity is well in line with what we might expect. Simpler networks are more likely to represent independent, or at the very least, few sex workers. As such, we would expect the adverts posted by the same person also to be highly similar. If we posit network complexity to correlate with the number of persons involved with the network, we would also expect advert similarity to decrease, as several persons may be writing and posting the adverts. Additionally, a lesser degree of similarity in a larger network may also imply that different descriptions are required to portray a more diverse sex worker population in the network.

Of course, we are not only interested in how adverts within a network compare to each other, but how similar the textual content is *between* networks. Here, the unit of analysis is shifted from a unique advert to a unique network *template*, which consists of the texts collated from all adverts in a given network. The between-networks textual similarity is shown in Fig. 5, again showing the distribution of the average between-network similarity by network complexity quintiles. First, it should be noted that the relationship for between-network similarity is quite a bit stronger ($\eta^2 = 0.29$) than it is for within-network similarity ($\eta^2 = 0.07$). However, the actual average cosine scores tend to be higher within networks than between them.

A clear positive relationship can be observed, in which the mean similarity increases as network complexity increases. In more substantive terms, this means that the textual marketing strategies of simpler networks tend to be unique when compared to other networks. Conversely, the more complex the network, the more likely we are to find its textual descriptions more similar to that of other networks. We have to be careful

[6] The relationship between network complexity and within-network similarity was substantially stronger when the same analysis was carried out on an advert record level, in which it was quite clearly evident that simpler networks tended to have extremely similar adverts.

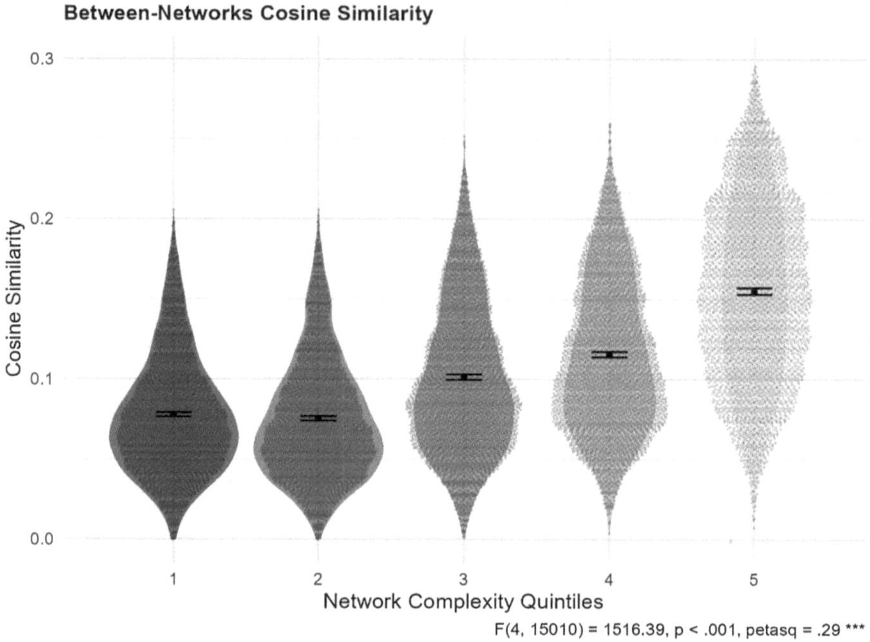

Fig. 5 Between-networks cosine similarity

in assessing these relationships, however. As was previously discussed in relation to within-network similarity for complex networks, the necessity to use a broader vocabulary to represent a diversity of sex workers could naturally lead complex networks to be increasingly similar to each other. Another possibility is that plagiarism is involved. There could conceivably be two reasons for this: first, one network may simply copy-paste or modify the text of other adverts to suit their purposes, which perhaps is particularly likely if someone possesses limited English skills. Second, it is also possible that the textual correlations genuinely represent content written by the same person(s). This could happen if the adverts from two seemingly independent networks are posted by the same person(s), but because they may not share phone numbers and user accounts, they would not be formally identified as a distinct network. It is, of course, very difficult to make an accurate assessment without having access to any data that could confirm this. Yet another possibility is that some networks are 'mimics': networks consisting of fake adverts that are simply there to scam potential sex buyers, and that these might copy-paste the content of other adverts to appear legitimate.[7]

The same relationships, albeit with complexity expressed as a continuous variable, are shown in Fig. 6. The graphs are scatterplots with network complexity as their X variable and the mean cosine similarity as the Y variable. The line represents the non-linear trend (calculated with the locally estimated scatterplot smoothing function), and the shaded area represents the confidence intervals. With regard to between-networks cosine similarity, there is a moderately strong correlation between network complexity and mean cosine similarity ($r = 0.55$, $p < 0.001$). As for within-networks similarity, the correlation is weaker ($r = 0.24$, $p < 0.001$). It is quite clear how between-network similarity increases as networks become increasingly complex, and conversely, how within-network similarity decreases with complexity.

Whereas the average between-networks similarity has been highlighted, it is also important to examine the highest between-networks similarities. Figure 7 shows a graph of all the networks with one or more edges with a cosine similarity of 0.8 or higher (N = 2582). The graph was generated with the Fruchterman Reingold algorithm and shows all edges with a cosine similarity score greater than or equal to 0.80 (edges = 100,604, nodes = 2582). The nodes are coloured by the network complexity quintile they belong to, and the edges are weighted by the magnitude of the cosine similarity (ranging from 0.8 to 1.0). It is evident at first glance that there is a multitude of networks with a high degree of similarity to one another. The E-I index of 0.08 indicates a very weak, positive tendency of networks to be semantically connected to networks belonging to different complexity quintiles. There is a dense cluster of several networks that are indeed very similar to one another. The networks consist of 395 distinct components, with the largest component including a total of 1399 networks, all with a cosine similarity of 0.8 or greater. Networks in the

[7] This is always a possibility when working with online data pertaining to various markets. The most complex and peculiar networks were researched in more depth, often involving web searches for other digital footprints such as online escort reviews. In many cases, this added credibility to the identified networks, but there is always an element of uncertainty when research involves online data.

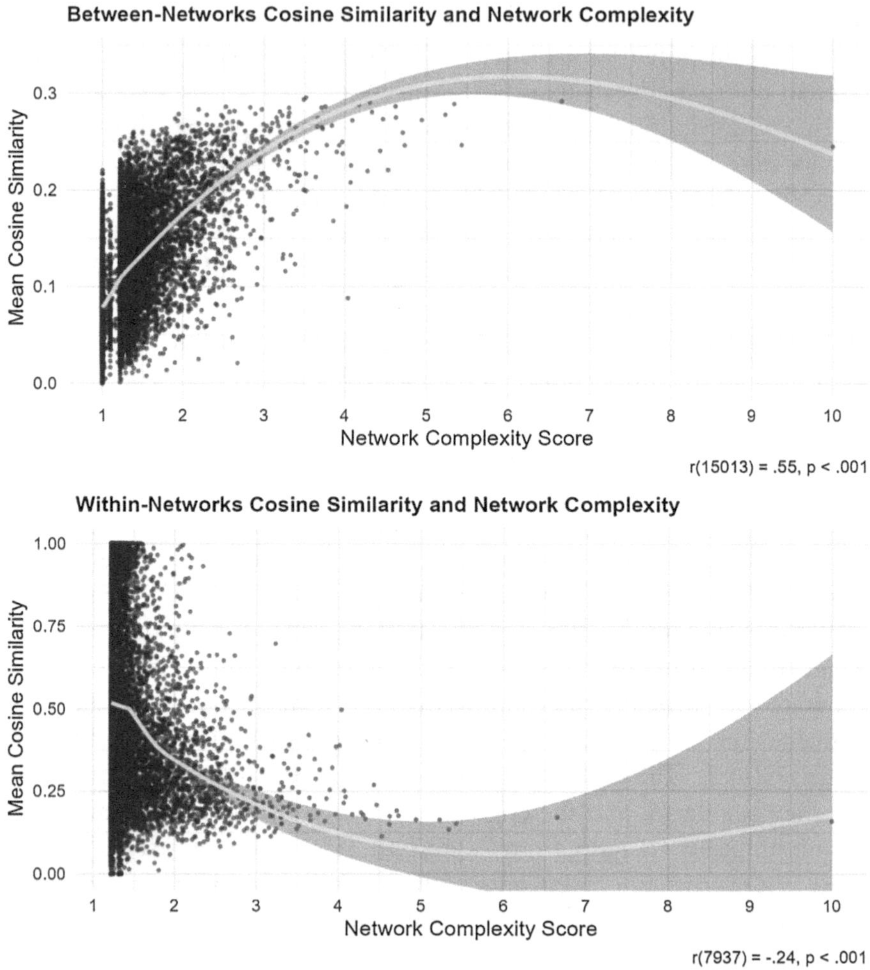

Fig. 6 Network similarity and complexity scores

fifth complexity quintile comprise most networks in this dense component. This implies the possibility that the textual marketing strategies of many networks may be very generic and, therefore, similar to one another. It could also indicate that some of the connected networks belong to the same overarching network. This could be the case if a network creates new user accounts and only uses new phone numbers, while recycling the old textual content used previously.

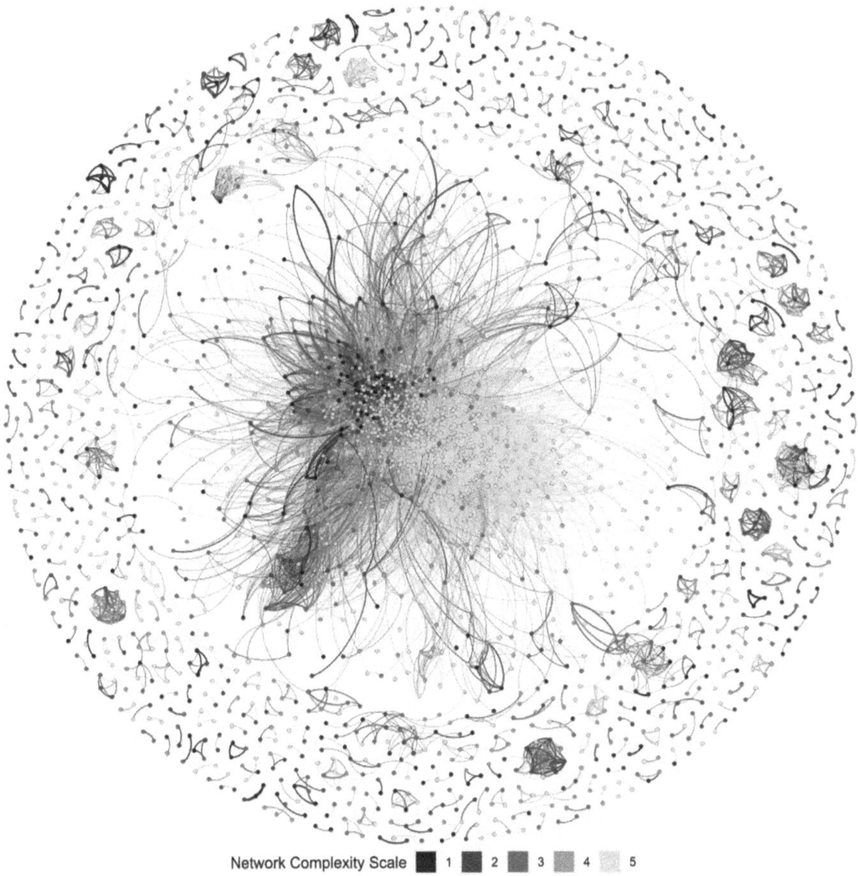

Fig. 7 Similarity and connections between networks

Besides the giant component of similar networks, it also appears fairly common for a network to be similar to one or two other networks, in terms of their textual content. Whether these connections are meaningful or not is difficult to know. Some of them could plausibly indicate networks are connected but simply uses different phone numbers or user accounts, or they could alternatively be similar because they genuinely use similar language to describe similar topics.

Modelling Tie Formation

The previous examination of the E-I indexes suggested a tendency for adverts to be connected to adverts with similar characteristics. The following analysis examines the patterns of correlations between the empirical networks and the variables of age group, extreme services, local authority and ethnicity. For each part of the analysis, one model was fitted per network. The first part consists of bivariate QAP models of all networks with ten or more unique adverts (N = 2140). Out of these, 1395 bivariate models were successfully fitted.[8] From these, 325 bivariate models converged across all independent variables. MRQAP models were thus fitted on these 325 models, and 257 successfully converged. Some very poorly fitted models were excluded from the analysis to create a better representation of the average tendencies within networks. As such, the final MRQAP comparison included a sample of 243 models.

The distribution of QAP correlations is shown in Fig. 8. As can be observed, insignificant correlations are largely normally distributed across all independent variables. In terms of the significant correlations, all distributions are skewed right. Note, however, that these distributions exclude perfect correlations; most of these would be simple networks, and the effects would therefore be stronger than they appear in the graph. Nevertheless, the average correlation coefficients for the different independent variables are very similar. The average (significant) correlations range from 0.25 for local authority to 0.31 for extreme services. Whilst local authority has the smallest effect size, it did have the highest number of converged models – 1266, followed by 1045 for ethnicity, 747 for age group, and 679 for extreme services. Overall, the results point to a moderate tendency of adverts to be connected based on the examined attributes, and it does not appear to be any greater variation between the four attributes. Importantly, the patterns suggest considerable variability in the effect of the various attributes between networks; from negligible but statistically significant to almost perfectly correlated and statistically significant.

[8] Models with perfect predictions were automatically excluded, i.e., instances where all dyadic relationships on the X variable would contain the same value.

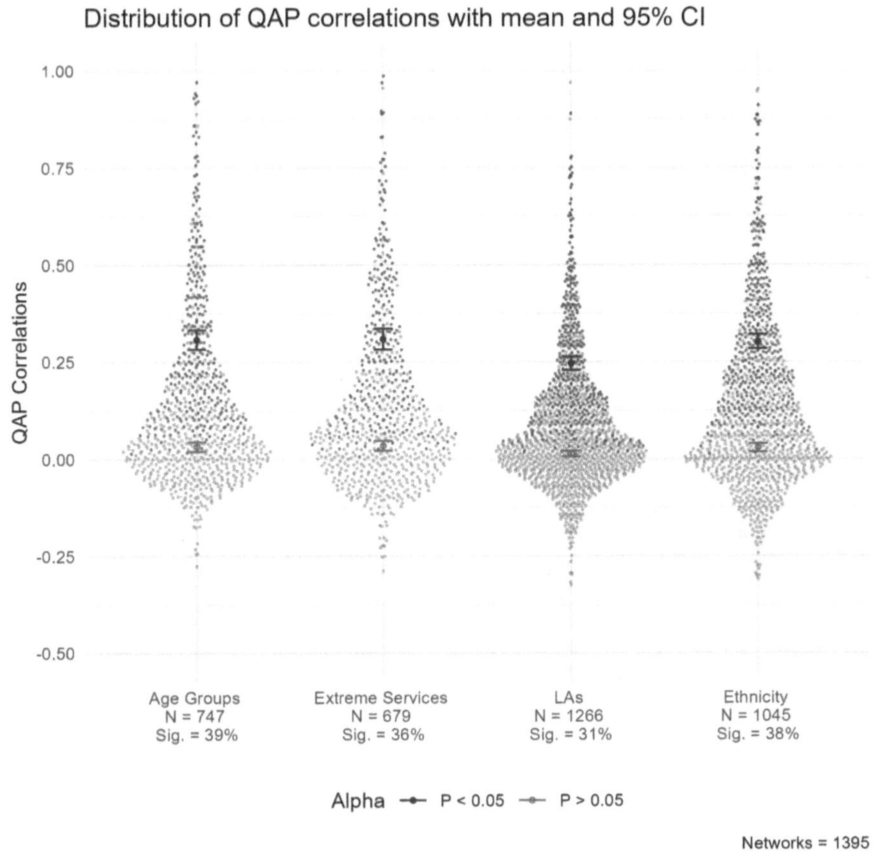

Fig. 8 Distribution of QAP correlations

Because of the variability between networks in the effects of the different variables, a possible interacting variable could be network complexity. The correlations between QAP correlations and network complexity can be observed for each of the independent variables in Fig. 9. Networks with a complexity score greater than nine were excluded (only one network, in this case), because of their leverage and to capture a more accurate representation of the broader patterning of these relationships. From the Pearson's *r*, it is evident that there are negative and significant correlations for all variables. The weakest correlation is for local authority and

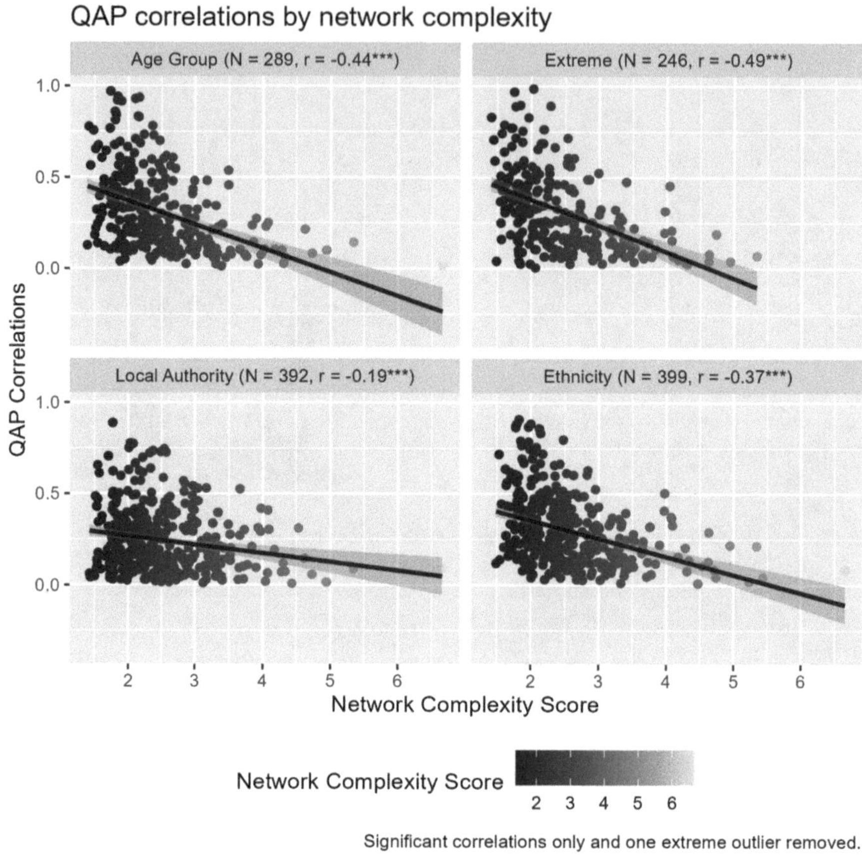

Fig. 9 QAP correlations by network complexity

network complexity (r = −0.19), and the correlation is strongest for extreme services (r = −0.49). This reinforces the notion that the effect that the various variables have upon tie formation is related to network complexity. In this case, adverts in simpler networks have a greater tendency to be connected than they do in more complex networks.

Following on from the initial analysis, a multivariate analysis is appropriate. The beta estimates from all 243 models are shown in Fig. 10, which shows the average effect of each variable on the empirical networks. The colour of the nodes shows whether or not the coefficient was

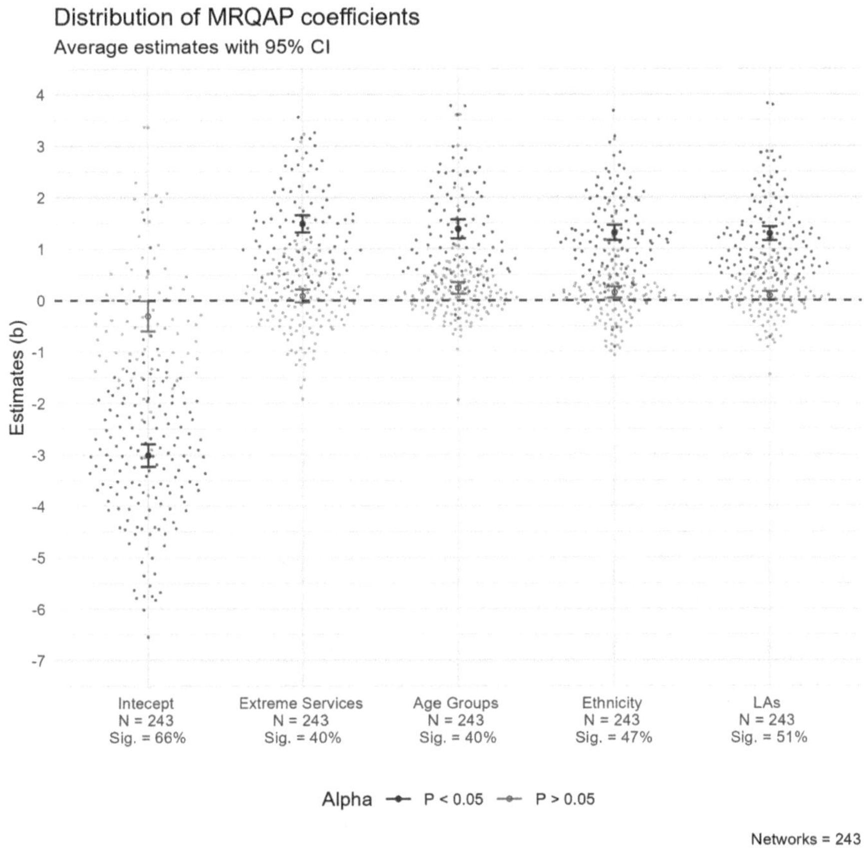

Fig. 10 MRQAP average estimates

significant. All independent variables show, on average, positive effects upon predicting tie formation. The average point estimates are very similar, ranging from 1.29 (local authority) to 1.48 (extreme services). Most estimates suggesting a negative effect of the independent variables are insignificant, though there are exceptions; for instance, in three networks, ethnicity is negatively associated with tie formation.

The odds ratios for significant estimates only are shown in Table 5. The percentages show the rate of significant predictors as the per cent of the

Table 5 Odds ratios for MRQAP models

Parameter	N Sig.	% Sig.	Mean (OR)	SD (OR)	Median (OR)	Range (OR)
Intercept	161	66%	0.18	0.64	0.05	0.01–5.89
Extreme Services	96	40%	6.40	6.44	4.05	1.24–35.40
Age Group	96	40%	6.39	8.03	3.33	0.71–43.90
Ethnicity	114	47%	5.20	5.36	3.39	0.41–40.10
Local Authority	124	51%	5.20	6.42	3.30	0.49–46.10

Table 6 Co-occurrence of significant predictors

	Extreme services	Age group	Ethnicity	Local authority
Extreme services		18.9	21.4	23.5
Age group	18.9		19.8	23.5
Ethnicity	21.4	19.8		28.8
Local authority	23.5	23.5	28.8	

total number of converged models. 'Extreme services' is the only variable with a consistently positive effect in all networks, and the odds ratios range from 1.24 to 35.40. In other words, the effect of extreme services is mildly positive to extremely strong, depending upon the network in question. It also has the strongest average effect, though with considerable variability (mean = 6.40; SD = 6.44). The average effect of age group is similar in magnitude (mean = 6.39), though with somewhat more variability (SD = 8.03). This variable also has a negative effect in some networks. Since the distribution of odds ratios across all independent variables are quite skewed, the median of the average effects might provide more plausible estimates. According to the median, the effects are fairly similar across all variables, ranging from 3.30 for local authority to 4.05 for extreme services. The variables most frequently statistically significant across models were local authority and ethnicity.

In addition to the effect sizes, it is also important to examine the co-occurrence of significant predictors. Table 6 shows a matrix of the independent variables, and each cell shows the percentage of models that had significant effects across the pairwise combinations. Local authority and ethnicity had the strongest tendency (29%) to both have significant effects across all models. Whilst all other combinations had fairly similar

Table 7 Fit statistics for MRQAP models

Statistic	Mean	SD	Median	Range
Adj. pseudo-R^2	0.24	0.13	0.23	0.00–0.48
BIC	9714.00	17784.00	2303.00	132–92457
Correct predictions	0.73	0.09	0.73	0.51–0.93

rates of co-occurrence, age group and extreme services stand out with a particularly low rate of co-occurrence (19%). It appears that it would be somewhat more plausible to find that local authority and ethnicity play a greater role in structuring the networks than the other combinations of variables.

Table 7 shows model fit statistics for all the fitted models. The mean and median adjusted pseudo-R^2 suggest that the converged models fit the data fairly well. There is a wide range of R^2 values, however, indicating that some models might be quite poor. It is difficult to compare model parsimony and deviance since the models were not nested; nevertheless, the distributions of BIC values are heavily skewed, perhaps suggesting some fairly parsimonious models and some models which are quite problematic. A better indication of model fitness is potentially the total fraction of correct predictions. According to this, the average model would correctly predict 73% of empirical dyads based on the independent variables. The range and distribution suggest the models perform fairly well according to this criterion, though some models did not perform better than what might be expected from chance alone.

The MRQAP models included a fairly broad range of complexity scores. As such, it is important to assess the relationship between the model fit statistics and network complexity. These relationships are shown in Fig. 11. There is a moderately strong relationship between adjusted pseudo-R^2 ($r = 0.63$, $p < 0.001$) and network complexity. The relationship is similar in magnitude for the total fraction of correct predictions ($r = 0.62$, $p < 0.001$) and network complexity. In other words, the more complex a network, the better the model fit. With regard to BIC, there is a weaker relationship ($r = 0.35$, $p < 0.001$); a couple of less complex networks tend to have extremely high deviance, which slightly offsets the relationship.

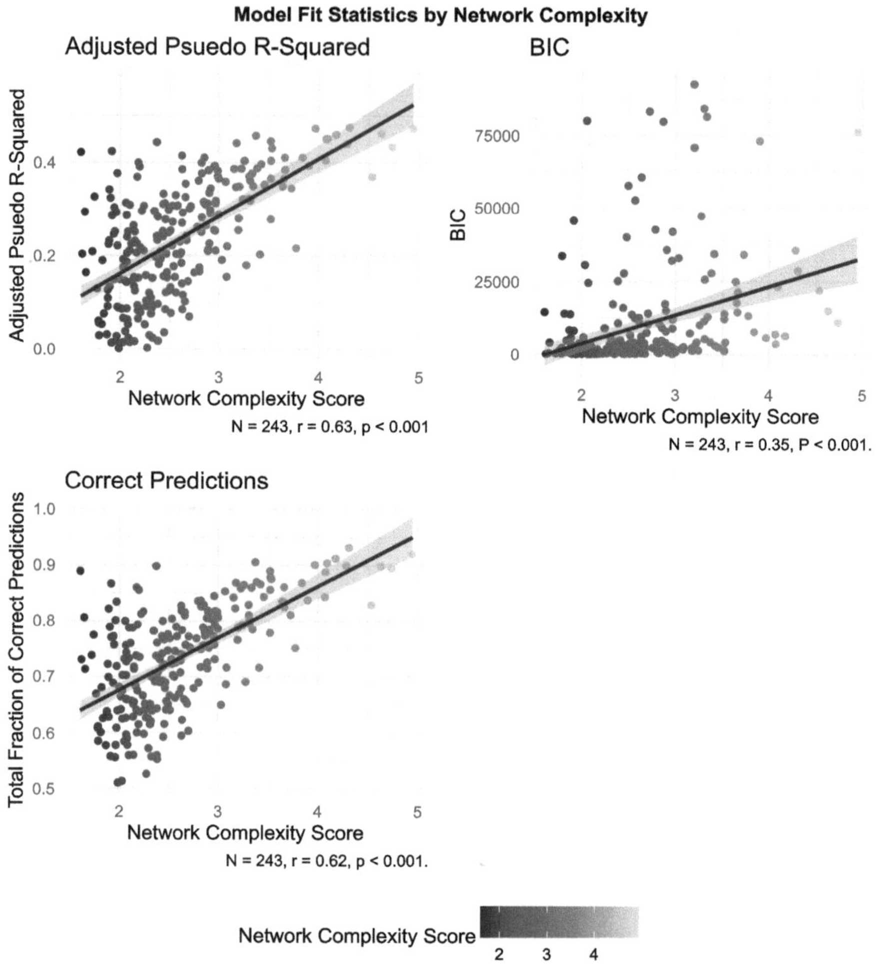

Fig. 11 MRQAP model fit statistics by network complexity

Overall, the models suggest that the examined variables predict tie formation in the examined networks. However, as has also been shown, there is considerable variability from network to network. Whilst there are some strong central tendencies in the variables' contribution to predicting ties in the empirical networks, the effects vary from negligible to extremely strong, depending upon the network in question. This suggests the possibility that the presence of ties between adverts is linked to various underlying social processes, which cannot be observed from this data alone. Because the observed ties are based on phone numbers or user accounts, there is a suggestion that the poster of one advert may post another advert similar to the first one. This, of course, is largely what we expect—especially so in the context of independent sex workers. However, in the case of more complex networks, it rather appears that networks are clustered along characteristics such as the local authority they are posted in, and that subsequent adverts likely include a wider variety of characteristics.

Conclusions

Throughout this chapter, it has been demonstrated how the use of indicators applied to online escort adverts provides relatively little insight into the complexity of networks operating in the sex market. The STIM, intended to be used by law enforcement practitioners to manually evaluate online adverts, produces very limited information, and it is very challenging to imagine how such tools can successfully distinguish between trafficking victims and sex workers, not to mention identifying any form of meaningful patterns pertaining to vulnerability or exploitation. Even when part of the process is automated, as was done in this analysis, the STIM only identified 3 out of 129 networks that had posted 200 or more adverts during the study period, which brings its validity, reliability and utility into question.

The subsequent analysis moved beyond the idea of sex markets being made up of individual, online adverts, and instead shifted the focus to the relational qualities of advert networks. From this, it was demonstrated how a variety of factors predict the formation of ties between adverts. This suggests there are underlying social processes which may affect the likelihood of adverts being connected, and consequently, these processes may look different depending on a network's complexity. Generally speaking, there is a tendency for adverts in a network to be connected to adverts with similar characteristics. What largely alters this tendency is the complexity of a network. Simpler networks tend to be largely homophilous. There appear to be stronger tendencies for more diverse connections in more complex networks, which, again, support the hypothesis that complex networks may involve a wider variety of people in the offline organisation.

Of the variables selected, the most important appears to be region and local authority, in which network complexity had the greatest effect. As we might expect, simpler networks tend to show homophilous tendencies with regard to these variables, which likely reflects the mobility patterns associated with independent sex workers. More complex networks tend to have more widespread geographical footprints, which is likely why we also see a greater tendency for adverts in varying geographies to be connected.

Besides the tendency of certain variables to structure the composition of a network, the textual components of adverts also tend to be more or less similar depending upon the complexity of a network. The relationship between network complexity and advert similarity looks different depending on whether we measure similarity within or between networks. Adverts in simpler networks tend to be highly similar, whereas more complex networks have more textually diverse marketing strategies. On a network level, the text of simpler networks tends to be unique, whereas the text of complex networks is increasingly similar to that of other networks. There are in fact numerous networks, of varying complexity, that are—semantically speaking—closely related. A possible explanation for this is that the texts generated by complex networks reflect a diversity of individuals, possibly written by different persons, leading to a multitude of different textual marketing strategies. Complex networks may therefore become more heterogeneous in their marketing, thus causing semantic overlaps with other, particularly larger, networks. Simpler networks possibly reflect a unique form of advert homogeneity, in which more detail and effort are put into the adverts, as opposed to more generic content generated by networks controlling a substantially larger number of adverts.

From the modelling of the networks, it was also shown how certain variables increase the odds of ties existing between two adverts and, furthermore, how the effect of those variables also operated differently across different networks. While broader patterns suggest that ethnicity, age, geography and the propensity to advertise multiple extreme services all increase the odds of tie formation, the precise effect of each variable varies from network to network. More broadly speaking, it is clear that adverts connected by either phone numbers or user accounts also tend to share other attributes and textual components. What is also clear is that the extent of this similarity is non-random and largely mediated by network complexity.

References

Antonopoulos GA, Baratto G, Di Nicola A, Diba P, Martini E, Papanicolaou G, Terenghi F (2020) Technology in Human Smuggling and Trafficking: Case Studies from Italy and the United Kingdom, 1st edn. Springer, Cham

Campana P, Varese F (2013) Cooperation in Criminal Organizations: Kinship and Violence as Credible Commitments. Ration Soc 25(3):263–289. https://doi.org/10.1177/1043463113481202

Cranmer SJ, Leifeld P, McClurg SD, Rolfe M (2017) Navigating the Range of Statistical Tools for Inferential Network Analysis. Am J Polit Sci 61(1):237–251. https://doi.org/10.1111/ajps.12263

Dekker D, Krackhardt D, Snijders TAB (2007) Sensitivity of MRQAP Tests to Collinearity and Autocorrelation Conditions. Psychometrika 72(4):563–581. https://doi.org/10.1007/s11336-007-9016-1

Han J, Kamber M, Pei J (2012) Data mining: Concepts and Techniques, 3rd edn. Elsevier, Burlington

Hanneman RA, Riddle M (2011) Concepts and Measures for Basic Network Analysis. In: The SAGE Handbook of Social Network Analysis. SAGE, London, pp 340–369

Krackhardt D (1988) Predicting with Networks: Nonparametric Multiple Regression Analysis of Dyadic Data. Soc Netw 10(4):359–381. https://doi.org/10.1016/0378-8733(88)90004-4

Krackhardt D, Stern RN (1988) Informal Networks and Organizational Crises: An Experimental Simulation. Soc Psychol Q 51(2):123–140. https://doi.org/10.2307/2786835

L'Hoiry X, Moretti A, Antonopoulos GA (2024) Identifying Sex Trafficking in Adult Services Websites: An Exploratory Study with a British Police Force. Trends Organ Crim 27(1):34–55. https://doi.org/10.1007/s12117-021-09414-1

Skidmore M, Garner S, Desroches C, Saggu N (2018) The Threat of Exploitation in the Adult Sex Market: A Pilot Study of Online Sex Worker Advertisements. Policing 12(2):210–218. https://doi.org/10.1093/police/pax007

Subrahmanyam K, Reich SM, Waechter N, Espinoza G (2008) Online and Offline Social Networks: Use of Social Networking Sites by Emerging Adults. J Appl Dev Psychol 29(6):420–433. https://doi.org/10.1016/j.appdev.2008.07.003

Network Influences on Extreme Service Advertisement

Introduction

This chapter sets out to understand the online context and extent to which 'extreme' services are advertised. In this context, it refers to the four variables used in the previous chapter (and discussed in more detail in chapter "Methods in Practice: Designing an Effective Workflow in Computational Criminology", section "Stage 10: Multilevel Modelling"): A Levels (anal sex), OWO (oral sex without protection), PSE (pornstar experience) and WS ('water sports', which refers to acts involving urine). In the broader literature on policing the online sex market, it has previously been suggested that 'extreme' or 'risky' services could indicate the adverts being posted by potential trafficking or criminal networks (Skidmore et al. 2018; L'Hoiry et al. 2024). Whilst there is no agreement on how to precisely delineate extreme from non-extreme services, what is usually referred to as extreme services in this context are potentially harmful services, or services which can be considered deviating from more common or normative services. Examples of this are unprotected sex, anal sex and acts involving faeces or urine. However, as eloquently pointed out by others—with more nuanced understandings of the sex market—it

R. Kjellgren, *Internet-Mediated Exploitation in the Scottish Online Sex Market*,
Transnational Crime, Crime Control and Security,
https://doi.org/10.1007/978-3-032-09275-5_9

is not *uncommon* for sex workers to explicitly advertise services that they do not intend to offer, for the simple reason that it is an important marketing strategy to do so (Holt et al. 2021). In other words, highlighting a wide variety of services in adverts increases visibility and the chances of being included in more searches.

From the qualitative analysis of this research (chapter "Exploitation and the Policing of Contemporary Sex Markets in Scotland"), it was evident that there were diverging views on extreme services as an indicator of potentially vulnerable sex workers or more exploitative working conditions. Indeed, some police respondents argued that advertising that 'everything goes' could indicate that someone else is controlling the working environment and trying to maximise the profit margins. As pointed out by an NGO worker, what is to be considered 'extreme' will vary between sex workers, and it is not our position as non-sex workers to label services as extreme or not.

In this chapter, multilevel models will be fitted to disentangle the relationships between extreme services and other marketing strategies, as well as the structural properties of the networks themselves. If extreme services as a marketing strategy indeed indicate vulnerability, it would be expected that other marketing strategies potentially indicating vulnerability would be associated with this. For instance, age can be considered a factor in vulnerability, in that less experienced sex workers may possess less social and human capital, and therefore be more reliant on potentially untrustworthy managers and third parties; we would therefore expect that extreme services will be associated with age (Englund et al. 2008). Migrant sex workers are potentially more vulnerable than British sex workers since they may also lack access to location-specific capital, citizenship or a secure legal status (Mai 2009). If so, it would be expected that non-migrant British sex workers would be less likely than other ethnic groups to advertise extreme services.

An extension of these points is that there are possible interaction effects in operation, and the role of ethnicity and age in explaining the advertisement of extreme services may be contingent upon network complexity. In other words, it would be plausible that increased age is associated with a decreased propensity to advertise extreme services; however, it may well be that the effect of age is less important in larger networks, where the norm is to advertise such services. In a similar vein, a migrant sex worker who is already capable of working independently may not be at an increased risk of vulnerability. However, ethnicity could conceivably be associated with extreme services in networks with a propensity to advertise extreme services. As such, network complexity may alter some of the relationships we expect to observe.

If indeed criminal networks are operating in the online spaces of the sex market and, particularly if exploitation is involved, it would be expected that they try to maximise profit margins at the expense of the wellbeing and safety of victims. There are three distinct scenarios in which we expect larger networks to operate throughout the sex market: (1) migrant sex worker collectives working together to increase their safety, and perhaps engaging in a more distinctive division of labour and role specialisation; (2) larger agencies advertising on behalf of sex workers; and (3) criminal networks facilitating the exploitation of sex workers. Migrant sex workers and potential victims of criminal networks are arguably more vulnerable than sex workers employed at an agency, and we would expect higher rates of extreme services to be advertised in the former two groups. As such, there is one particular hypothesis that is the focus of this chapter:

H_0: There is no relationship between network structure and the propensity to advertise extreme services.

H_{alt}: Network structure predicts the advertising of extreme services.

The null hypothesis proposes there is no relationship between a network's structure and the outcomes, which in this case would be the propensity to advertise certain services. If the null hypothesis can be rejected, we would expect network structure to predict advert-level outcomes, such as the propensity to advertise—or not to advertise—specific services. Network structure, in this case, is represented by the complexity scale originally developed in Kjellgren (2023, 2025) and described in chapter "Methods in Practice: Designing an Effective Workflow in Computational Criminology", and based on the findings of previous chapters, there is reason to believe that network complexity may be central in mediating advert-level outcomes. The remainder of this chapter will explain how this hypothesis will be tested and, subsequently, proceed to present the results from multilevel models aimed at testing the hypothesis.

Method

There are some significant challenges in examining these hypothesised relationships. The structure of the data requires careful consideration of how to best operationalise the variables. The data are naturally clustered; advert records are nested in unique adverts to account for changes over time, and unique adverts are naturally clustered in networks. The aims of this chapter necessitate a focus on variability between adverts *within* networks, and *between* networks themselves. As such, multilevel modelling was deemed the most appropriate approach, with the longitudinal dimension being of less importance for the specific aims of this analysis.

Multilevel models (MLMs) are a special type of statistical model that accounts for hierarchical data in which we assume that the clustering of observations is important for explaining the variability in the dependent variable (Robson and Pevalin 2015). This certainly is the case in this research in which regular multiple regression models—with escort adverts as a unit of analysis—would violate the assumptions of non-independence amongst observations, since all adverts are clustered in networks, and therefore likely to share a number of characteristics. Ignoring this clustering would lead to biased estimates, and in particular, incorrectly estimated error terms, since there will be a level of correlation between observations. Moreover, there is a strong theoretical justification for using multilevel models in this context, since it is likely that most of the variance will be associated with the higher-level units; in other words, it is expected that adverts in a network will be homogeneous in terms of their characteristics, but that there will be considerable variation between networks. Since multilevel models estimate error variance across all analytical levels, these models are particularly useful in this context, as they allow for an examination of how the clustering of adverts relates to the outcomes.

Different variations in clustering the data were examined through multilevel modelling.[1] Perhaps the most intuitive way to model the data would have been to cluster advert records within networks. Doing so would prove difficult because of small variations between advert records in some networks. For example, a network could consist of 10 advert records that were identical in all respects and posted under the same advert identifier (i.e., an old advert being changed rather than a new advert being posted), save some changes in the services offered; in another network, there may be a thousand advert records posted under 100 different advert identifiers. Because of this, the data were aggregated, and the level 1 unit of analyses was shifted from advert records to advert identifiers (i.e., unique adverts). This, of course, meant that all variables had to be transformed into averages or probabilistic categorical variables. For instance, if nine out of ten adverts (in an advert identifier) had the age listed as 25, and one advert listed the age as 30, the mean age within that advert identifier was coded as 25.5 years.[2] For dummy variables, the percentage of advert records within a unique advert with the value of 1 was first calculated, and if that value was greater than 50%, the unique advert was recoded as 1. Similarly, for categorical variables with more than two categories, the mode was used to identify the most meaningful category. These operations inevitably lead to a reduction in nuance and increased uncertainty, though they did produce more parsimonious models.

In the initial stages of the analysis, different model specifications were used. Originally, before a decision was made to operationalise the data on the advert identifier, the idea was to use mixed effects logit models. The shift to advert identifiers, as explained previously, meant that the original dichotomous variables were transformed into continuous variables. An attempt was made to convert the continuous outcome variables into probabilistic binary variables, in order to fit mixed effects logit models. These preliminary logit models were compared to linear mixed effects models, with the outcome variables in their continuous functional form.

[1] Stata 17 was used for all MLMs.

[2] Different arithmetic operations were used on continuous variables; in the case of age, models were also fitted with median and mode age. Another plausible operationalisation would have been the highest reported age. There was little variation between the different operationalisations and average age was substantially appropriate.

Given that these models were not nested (due to the outcome variables being in different functional forms), common model fit statistics (e.g., Bayesian Information Criterion, log-likelihood) could not be compared between the models. Instead, the sign and significance of the explanatory variables were used to compare the different models. The results of this exercise indicated that the linear models were a better fit to the data than the logit models, primarily because some of the random intercept logit models failed to converge.[3] As the original outcome variables were continuous (the percentage of advert records within an advert identifier advertising a particular service), and that the sign and significance of the explanatory variables were similar across the linear and logit models, a decision was made to use linear models for the final sets of models, since all models converged successfully with a linear model specification.

Table 1 provides an example of how the dataset was structured, using the ethnicity variable as an example. The rationale for defining advert identifiers as the level 1 unit is not solely based on statistical reasons. Advert identifiers, or unique adverts, are arguably more likely to represent notional persons than advert records. Advert records are contingent upon how and when someone posts and reposts adverts, and subsequently, the occasions in which the records were collected. The first three rows represent three unique advert records, clustered in one shared advert identifier which is nested in one network. In this scenario, the ethnicity

Table 1 Multilevel dataset structure

Advert record (N = 6)	Level 1: advert identifier (N = 4)	Level 2: network identifier (K = 2)
1 (White British)	1 (White British)	1
2 (White British)	1 (White British)	1
3 (White Non-British)	1 (White British)	1
4 (Black British)	2 (Black British)	2
5 (Latina British)	3 (Latina British)	2
6 (Asian Non-British)	4 (Asian Non-British)	2

[3] Stata 17 was used, using the 'melogit' and 'xtlogit' commands. The models that failed to converge were the A Levels model and offering Any Extreme Service.

actually changes in the last observation, so when the data are aggregated to level 1—advert identifier level—the modal ethnicity becomes White British. This could indicate an independent sex worker, or in other words, one notional person, reposting the same adverts but then changing the ethnicity at some point.[4] In the second scenario, three unique advert records are nested in three unique advert identifiers, belonging to the same network. In this case, recoding ethnicity is more straightforward, as there are no discrepancies within the advert identifiers. Whilst we do not know how many individuals the adverts represent, the data structure would suggest a potential that the network consists of three notional persons, or personas. These epistemological considerations have implications for how the models are best fitted; normally in social science research, ethnicity would be modelled as a fixed effect, since it is unlikely that people change their ethnicity. In this context, however, we expect a certain degree of change in ethnicity—both as a result of one individual creating different personas and because we do not know how many individuals are represented within the advert; ethnicity is therefore likely to be variable. As such, ethnicity was added as a random effect in some models.

In addition to the statistical modelling of the data, descriptive analysis was first used to evaluate the distributions of key variables. Random effects models were fitted using a combination of fixed and random effects. These were estimated using the maximum likelihood estimation in Stata 17. Advert identifiers were thus the level 1 unit of analysis (N = 121,993), and they were nested in the empirical networks described in chapter "Methods in Practice: Designing an Effective Workflow in Computational Criminology" (K = 15,015, $\bar{k} = 8.1$).[5] Variable selection was informed by their theoretical value and hypothesised contributions. The modelling strategy first involved null models with and without random intercepts, and likelihood ratio tests were conducted to confirm the viability of using random effects. In each of the models estimated, the

[4] As was noted in previous chapters, there are many reasons that sex workers may elect to utilise a variety of different online marketing strategies. This change could reflect such a strategy or it could simply be a reporting error.

[5] Network 124, which was the largest network in the dataset, was dropped from this analysis because of its high degree of leverage and being a quite atypical network, in terms of its extreme complexity. This network is used as a case study analysis in Kjellgren (2025).

intraclass correlation was examined to evaluate how much of the variance could be attributed to differences between networks. Explanatory variables and random slopes were added, and likelihood ratio tests were again used to ensure that each new term added made a significant contribution to the reduction of deviance. The log-likelihood was compared across models to evaluate model fit, and the Bayesian information criterion (BIC) was used to examine model parsimony. Using R-squared to summarise the explained variance in the dependent variable is not straightforward in multilevel models (Robson and Pevalin 2015). The use of R-squared in this context has been subjected to considerable debate; however, for the purposes of this analysis, Snijders and Bosker's (1994) calculation of R-squared was implemented and cautiously used as an indication of model fitness.

To better interpret the models, marginal effects were calculated based on substantially informative values of relevant variables, and the best linear unbiased predictions (BLUPs) of the models were examined. Since multiple nominal variables were used in the models (e.g., ethnicity and region), the calculations were conducted as follows: the predicted value for each case was calculated, based on the case's observed values of the covariates included in the models and at the values specified for the independent variable of interest (network complexity scale, network complexity quintiles, and network services scale), and the average of the predicted values was then calculated and plotted.

Descriptive Statistics and Bivariate Analysis

Before proceeding to present the model results, the distributions of, and relationships between, key variables will be examined. Table 2 shows all continuous variables used in the analysis. From a glance, it is apparent that many of these variables are heavily skewed, and their suitability for modelling leaves much to be desired. In relation to the outcome variables, it can be concluded that these services are relatively common; the proportion of adverts listing unprotected oral sex is almost exactly the same as those offering the girlfriend experience. One exception here is A Levels, which on average is offered by 41% of adverts. The most heavily

Table 2 Summary statistics for continuous variables

	N	Mean	Median	SD	Min	Max	Skewness	Kurtosis
OWO	121,993	73.80	100	43.47	0	100	-1.08	2.20
A Levels	121,993	41.22	0	48.76	0	100	0.36	1.16
PSE	121,993	63.73	100	47.71	0	100	-0.57	1.34
WS	121,993	60.37	100	48.53	0	100	-0.42	1.19
Dining	121,993	73.73	100	43.75	0	100	-1.08	2.18
GFE	121,993	73.92	100	43.44	0	100	-1.09	2.21
Extreme Scale	121,993	6.21	10	4.43	0	10	-0.49	1.44
Network Services	121,993	29.65	7.04	37.49	0	100	0.90	2.18
Age	121,993	25.06	24	5.05	18	60	2.46	11.53
VIP	121,993	1.31	0	10.28	0	100	8.61	78.86
Featured	121,993	3.45	0	16.89	0	100	5.11	28.22
Highlight	121,993	1.75	0	11.73	0	100	7.39	58.70
Network Complexity Scale	121,993	2.13	1.887	0.96	1	6.65	1.52	5.90
Network Mode	121,993	5.83	0	20.35	0	100	3.82	16.52
Days Active	121,993	440.86	450	264.36	0	3269	2.68	18.45

skewed variables are the extra features that can be paid for to increase advert visibility ('VIP', 'Highlight' and 'Featured'); it seems very rare to actually do so. As might be expected, the mean and median of the network complexity scale seem to indicate that most networks tend to be relatively simple.

Regarding the categorical variables in Tables 3, 4 and 5, it can be observed that there are quite large differences between the various categories. In relation to ethnicity, adverts including White British are a clear minority compared to some of the larger categories such as White Non-British, Latina Non-British and Other Non-British. It should be borne in mind, however, that because the original form on the website reflects the self-selection of both national identity and ethnicity, caution must be exercised in interpreting this variable. In other words, this variable reflects ethnicity as a marketing strategy, which will be used to increase visibility and overcome or appeal to racialised and hypersexualised stereotypes, and so on.

Table 3 All ethnicities

Ethnicity	N	Per cent
1. White British	5462	4.48
2. Asian British	438	0.36
3. Latina British	164	0.13
4. Black British	1070	0.88
5. Mixed British	917	0.75
6. Other British	965	0.79
7. White Non-British	30,678	25.15
8. Asian Non-British	7394	6.06
9. Latina Non-British	36,882	30.23
10. Black Non-British	2093	1.72
11. Mixed Non-British	11,689	9.58
12. Other Non-British	24,241	19.87
Total	121,993	100.00

Table 4 Ethnicity: British and Non-British

British	N	Per cent
0. Non-British	112,927	92.57
1. British	9066	7.43
Total	121,993	100.00

Table 5 Region

Region	N	Percent
1. London	22,987	18.84
2. Northern Ireland	2027	1.66
3. South East	12,795	10.49
4. East of England	12,410	10.17
5. East Midlands	7878	6.46
6. Yorkshire and The Humber	10,487	8.6
7. North West	15,000	12.3
8. West Midlands	13,454	11.03
9. Scotland	8784	7.2
10. Wales	2039	1.67
11. South West	8557	7.01
12. North East	5575	4.57
Total	121,993	100.00

Table 6 Continuous variables by network complexity quintiles

	1	2	3	4	5	Total	Eta-squared
OWO	55.83	61.23	63.09	69.15	76.63	73.80	0.12***
A Levels	36.19	41.15	32.41	38.83	42.61	41.22	0.06***
PSE	38.47	44.82	48.26	52.32	68.72	63.73	0.18***
WS	39.99	42.40	44.61	51.48	64.71	60.37	0.16***
Dining	60.70	64.64	64.33	66.97	76.58	73.73	0.11***
GFE	58.98	64.44	65.56	70.35	76.13	73.92	0.10***
Extreme Scale	3.92	4.36	4.64	5.19	6.67	6.21	0.19***
Network Services	19.71	22.61	18.75	23.74	32.29	29.65	0.12***
Age	28.64	28.56	27.60	26.91	24.25	25.06	0.28***
VIP	4.26	0.00	1.82	1.94	1.09	1.31	0.06***
Featured	6.95	0.00	4.44	3.53	3.35	3.45	0.05***
Highlight	5.18	0.00	2.42	2.40	1.51	1.75	0.06***
Network Mode	4.75	4.24	5.14	7.45	5.67	5.83	0.04***
Days Active	460.81	125.97	348.60	384.24	469.44	440.86	0.24***

N = 121,993. Mean scores by network complexity scale quintiles, with results from one-way ANOVA's and the Eta statistic. Legend: *$p < 0.05$; **$p < 0.01$; ***$p < 0.001$

Some of the smaller categories could arguably be combined into broader categories; however, a decision was made to make the analysis as nuanced as possible, given the importance of ethnicity and nationality in this context. Instead, a British dummy variable is used in some models to improve model parsimony. Nevertheless, only 7% of the adverts are posted as British. With regard to region, London contains the largest proportion of adverts. Northern Ireland and Wales are quite underrepresented, and it is plausible that other escort sites may be more popular in those regions.

Table 6 shows the means of the continuous dependent and independent variables used in the analysis, broken down by the quintiles of the network complexity scale. To get an indication of the relationships between the variables, one-way ANOVAs were conducted, and the Eta-squared statistic was calculated to quantify the magnitude of these relationships. It should be noted, however, that this does not account for the nested structure of the data; this will be explored in more detail in the random effects models.

With regard to all variables representing various services, there tends to be a positive trend between them and network complexity; on average, the presence of these services tends to increase with network complexity. It should be noted, however, that this is not only true for the more extreme services, but also for GFE and Dining. This implies that it may be a more generalised marketing strategy with complex networks to simply advertise all services as available. Interestingly, A Levels diverges from this, and there is not a similarly clear linear pattern. The age pattern is also quite clear, and on average, age decreases the more complex the network is. Some weaker associations can be found for network mode and the various extra paid-for advert features. They are all statistically significant, but this is also not surprising given the sample size, and the magnitude of those associations suggests they are of minor importance. The number of days a network has been active shows an interesting pattern, in which the highest averages are found within quintiles 1 and 5. This could potentially highlight two different aspects of time: (1) simpler networks, which may be more likely to represent independent sex workers, appear to have been active for a longer period of time, possibly linked to the brand-building process associated with independent sexual labour; and (2) linear increases in complexity score for the remaining quintiles may suggest they are complex networks *in the making*, meaning that whilst they may appear less complex, they could in fact develop into highly complex networks in the future.

There is a moderate association between ethnicity and network complexity (Table 7). Most adverts tend to be found within the higher quintiles (complex networks post more adverts than simple networks), though it can quite clearly be observed that the proportion of British ethnicities is higher than Non-British ethnicities in the lower quintiles. There is a much stronger association between ethnicity and network complexity (Table 8) when a dichotomous variable is used instead (Gamma = -0.63). Indeed, for British adverts, the proportion in the fifth quintile is 37%, compared to 77% for non-British adverts.

The relationship between region and network complexity is relatively weak (Table 9). More complex networks appear more commonly in the North East, South West, Yorkshire and the Humber, and East of England, whereas simpler networks are somewhat more common in London.

On the whole, it is clear that network complexity is associated with a variety of different variables, not least the extreme services variables.

Table 7 Ethnicity by network complexity quintiles

Ethnicity	1	2	3	4	5	Total
1. White British	10.16	11.66	17.08	30.01	31.09	100.00
2. Asian British	15.07	10.96	9.59	19.18	45.21	100.00
3. Latina British	6.10	6.10	4.27	3.66	79.88	100.00
4. Black British	7.57	7.20	10.09	28.88	46.26	100.00
5. Mixed British	10.69	11.01	16.14	22.90	39.26	100.00
6. Other British	11.09	12.85	11.19	17.62	47.25	100.00
7. White Non-British	2.17	1.69	6.93	13.50	75.71	100.00
8. Asian Non-British	4.15	3.29	10.41	24.01	58.14	100.00
9. Latina Non-British	1.08	1.33	5.09	12.79	79.70	100.00
10. Black Non-British	5.69	5.54	10.22	23.70	54.85	100.00
11. Mixed Non-British	1.71	1.43	3.29	9.28	84.28	100.00
12. Other Non-British	1.63	1.95	4.93	10.97	80.53	100.00
Total	2.46	2.46	6.49	14.18	74.41	100.00

Ethnicity by network complexity, showing row percentages. Gamma = 0.25, $\chi^2(44, N = 121{,}993) = 12694.44$, $p < .001$

Table 8 British by network complexity quintiles

Ethnicity	1	2	3	4	5	Total
0. Non-British	1.85	1.78	5.81	13.16	77.41	100.00
1. British	10.11	11.00	14.96	26.85	37.08	100.00
Total	2.46	2.46	6.49	14.18	74.41	100.00

British by network complexity, showing row percentages. Gamma = -0.65, $\chi^2(4, N = 121{,}993) = 9254.29$, $p < .001$

However, a similar propensity of higher rates of adverts offering GFE and Dining would suggest that it is perhaps not the case that they are more likely to simply offer extreme services, but that they in fact are more likely to advertise all services possibly available. The following statistical models will further examine this pattern.

Random Effects Models

The first series of models fitted were null models with random intercepts. Here, 121,993 adverts were clustered into 15,015 networks, and the number of adverts within networks ranged from 1 to 1282, with an average of 8.1. With respect to these models, as shown in Table 10, the

Table 9 Region by network complexity quintiles

Region	1	2	3	4	5	Total
1. London	3.53	3.52	10.69	13.76	68.50	100.00
2. Northern Ireland	3.06	2.52	10.06	15.93	68.43	100.00
3. South East	2.27	2.24	5.24	18.41	71.84	100.00
4. East of England	1.90	1.63	4.00	14.35	78.12	100.00
5. East Midlands	2.68	2.67	5.41	14.66	74.59	100.00
6. Yorkshire and The Humber	2.27	2.34	5.27	11.71	78.41	100.00
7. North West	2.29	2.37	6.61	15.99	72.75	100.00
8. West Midlands	2.27	2.48	5.77	13.31	76.16	100.00
9. Scotland	2.03	2.02	6.83	12.22	76.91	100.00
10. Wales	2.80	3.33	7.95	18.15	67.78	100.00
11. South West	1.97	2.03	3.89	12.74	79.36	100.00
12. North East	1.85	1.63	4.38	10.13	82.01	100.00
Total	2.46	2.46	6.49	14.18	74.41	100.00

Region by network complexity, showing row percentages. Gamma = 0.10, $\chi^2(44, N = 121{,}993) = 1995.55$, $p < .001$

Table 10 Linear random intercept null models

Variable (model)	OWO	A Levels	PSE	WS	Dining	GFE
Intercept	65.09***	39.00***	49.32***	48.42***	65.91***	67.15***
Random Effects						
ICC	0.69	0.64	0.68	0.67	0.68	0.66
Level 1 Variance	685.73 (2.97)	876.50 (3.78)	787.76 (3.40)	813.60 (3.51)	701.12 (3.03)	734.46 (3.18)
Level 2 Variance	1505.33 (21.83)	1552.89	1686.40 (24.24)	1661.14 (24.04)	1459.22 (21.34)	1409.60 (20.96)
Statistics						
N	121,993	121,993	121,993	121,993	121,993	121,993
Log-likelihood	-586,057	-599,769	-594,367	-596,054	-587,092	-589,448
BIC	1,172,149	1,199,573	1,188,769	1,192,143	1,174,220	1,178,932

$^*p < 0.05$; $^{**}p < 0.01$; $^{***}p < 0.001$. Standard errors in parentheses

intra-cluster correlations (ICCs) and variance components suggest strong network effects. The results from log-likelihood ratio tests suggest random intercept models to be a significantly better fit than single-level regression models. Indeed, there is evidence of a significant degree of variation between networks in relation to all six outcome variables. Importantly, the variance between networks is greater than the variance between adverts within networks. This means that we would expect a degree of advert similarity within networks and, conversely, greater differences between networks. In these models, which do not control any advert-level factors, approximately 64–69% of the variation in the respective outcome variables can be explained by differences between networks.

The null models confirm a need for accounting for the nested structure of the data. Figure 1 allows for a closer examination of the network-level random intercepts. These are estimated from linear random intercept models with control variables, but without the introduction of random slopes (these are shown in Table 11, along with all covariates). Again, a significant degree of variation can be observed between the networks. The range of these intercepts suggests strong network effects, and it can also be seen how some services appear more commonly throughout networks. For instance, OWO, GFE and Dining appear to be advertised more frequently, whereas A Levels, WS and PSE seemingly occur less frequently.

The same linear mixed effects models are shown in Table 11, with the addition of random slopes (or random coefficients) for age. With regard to the models' fixed effects, some quite interesting patterns can be observed. When controlling for other variables, age has negative effects across all the models, with only relatively minor differences in magnitude. The effects of paid-for extra features of adverts are very small, and the low, or lack of, significance—despite the large sample size—suggests these variables are not substantially important. Ethnicity has relatively strong effects when holding other variables constant. Broadly speaking, the effects follow a similar pattern across the models: the majority of ethnicities, when compared to adverts listing White British as the ethnicity, have negative effects on the propensity to offer the various services. There are variations in magnitude; for instance, Asian British and Asian Non-British adverts have comparatively larger coefficients in relation to White British adverts. A notable exception is Latina British adverts, in which there are positive coefficients for A Levels but negative for GFE; however, there is much uncertainty here, given that this category contains relatively few cases. Similar to ethnicity, region also has an independent effect on the dependent variables. With London as the reference category, some relatively minor effects can be observed when the other regions are compared to London. There are, however, some notably large differences

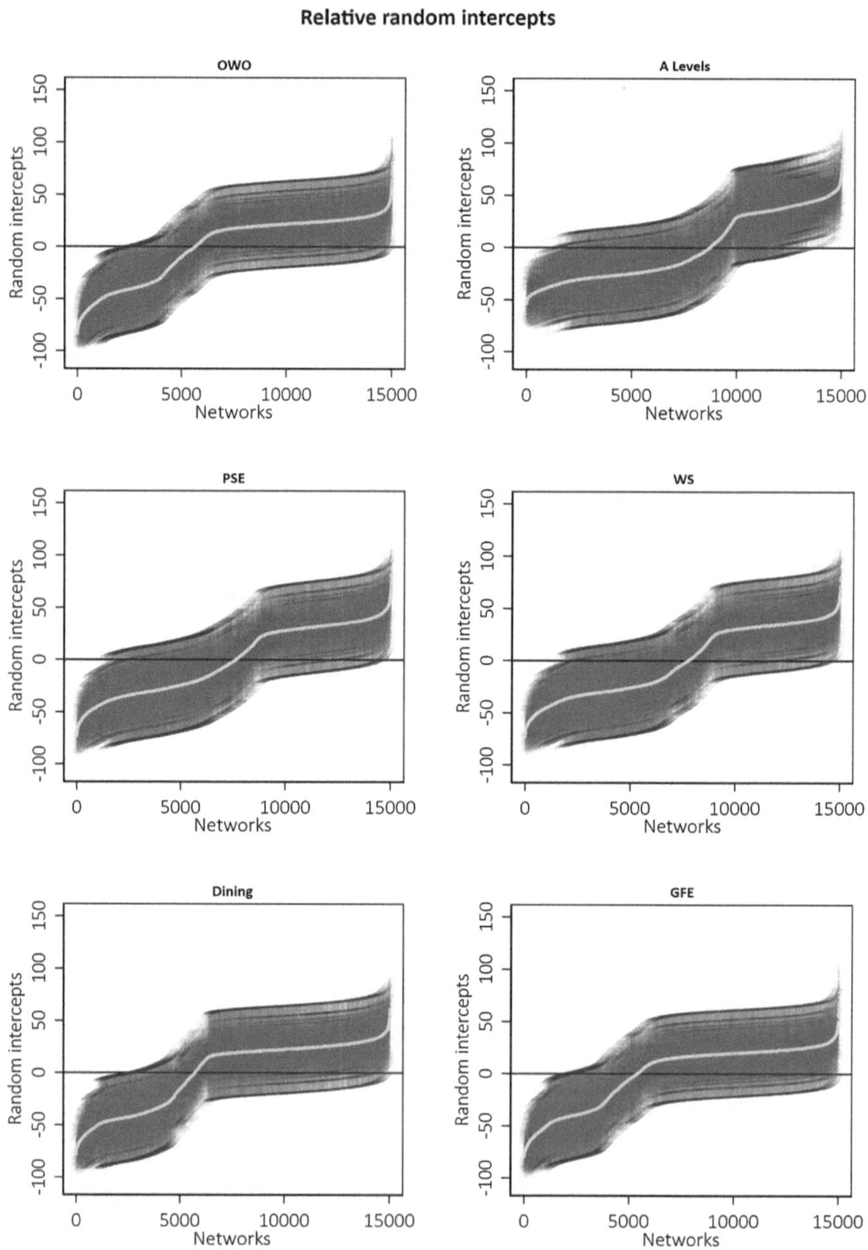

Fig. 1 Relative random intercepts from linear random intercepts models

Table 11 Linear mixed effects models with all covariates

Variable	OWO	A Levels	PSE	WS	Dining	GFE
Age	-0.89***	-0.67***	-1.27***	-1.11***	-0.95***	-0.85***
VIP	0.05***	0.07***	0.03**	0.03**	-0.01	0.06***
Featured	-0.01*	0.03***	-0.02**	0.01*	-0.03***	0.01
Highlight	0.07***	0.07***	0.07***	0.07***	0.02	0.07***
Ethnicity (White British)						
Asian British	-16.95***	-11.80***	-19.60***	-16.38***	-16.02***	-9.57***
Latina British	-1.26	9.79***	2.45	-3.68	-2.07	-8.73***
Black British	-11.49***	-13.40***	-13.22***	-10.72***	-6.46***	-6.81***
Mixed British	-10.67***	-5.68***	-4.54**	-6.29***	-3.42*	-7.30***
Other British	-6.97***	0.15	-0.57	-3.72*	-0.34	-4.10**
White Non-British	-12.10***	-5.75***	-8.00***	-8.59***	-4.16***	-12.97***
Asian Non-British	-18.96***	-16.50***	-19.78***	-17.25***	-20.75***	-20.13***
Latina Non-British	-10.40***	-3.19***	-4.54***	-5.88***	-2.90***	-10.92***
Black Non-British	-13.56***	-8.98***	-12.89***	-13.57***	-6.54***	-12.73***
Mixed Non-British	-9.63***	-3.95***	-5.42***	-7.07***	-1.87*	-13.27***
Other Non-British	-13.54***	-7.38***	-9.34***	-10.12***	-7.18***	-14.98***
Region (London)						
Northern Ireland	-32.03***	-26.02***	-25.09***	-26.00***	-2.29	-28.90***
South East	1.13**	-0.41	2.02***	1.39**	0.98*	0.98*
East of England	1.02*	0.19	1.65***	1.39**	0.60	1.04*
East Midlands	-3.58***	-4.57***	-1.45*	-1.58*	-2.33***	-4.32***
Yorkshire/Humber	-1.95***	-2.38***	0.24	-0.34	0.05	-3.38***
North West	0.80	-1.60**	0.08	0.00	-1.31*	-2.47***
West Midlands	-0.43	-1.27*	0.97	0.86	-0.20	-1.93***
Scotland	0.09	0.62	1.98**	1.29	-0.41	-0.24

(*continued*)

Table 11 (continued)

Variable	OWO	A Levels	PSE	WS	Dining	GFE
Wales	-0.08	1.96*	1.07	0.02	-1.21	0.22
South West	-0.82	-0.79	0.55	-0.04	-0.67	-0.60
North East	2.04**	2.83***	3.97***	4.30***	2.64***	1.77*
Network Complexity (1)						
2	1.39	-1.88	-0.49	-1.49	-0.17	1.80
3	6.45***	-5.61***	4.16***	2.60*	0.55	5.30***
4	10.78***	1.22	9.50***	8.37***	3.37**	9.92***
5	14.87***	3.50**	18.12***	17.28***	8.55***	12.33***
Network Mode	-0.60***	-0.33***	-0.44***	-0.44***	0.02	-0.62***
Days Active	-0.01***	-0.02***	-0.02***	-0.01***	-0.01***	-0.01***
Intercept	69.15***	44.93***	49.63***	50.46***	69.54***	73.25***
Random Effects						
ICC	0.64	0.62	0.64	0.64	0.64	0.59
Variance (Age)	9.89 (0.40)	9.70 (0.40)	7.81 (0.36)	10.60 (0.43)	8.18 (0.37)	7.98 (0.37)
Level 1 Variance	631.47 (2.78)	817.83 (3.58)	740.73 (3.25)	754.37 (3.32)	661.37 (2.91)	692.07 (3.04)
Level 2 Variance	1100.73 (18.81)	1338.50 (22.38)	1301.76 (21.71)	1334.52 (22.25)	1172.40 (19.78)	1006.99 (17.64)
Statistics						
N	121,993	121,993	121,993	121,993	121,993	121,993
R2 (Level 1)	0.12	0.07	0.13	0.10	0.07	0.12
R2 (Level 2)	0.14	0.08	0.15	0.11	0.08	0.14
Log-likelihood	-582,069	-596,883	-591,116	-592,693	-584,592	-586,312
BIC	1,164,572	1,194,198	1,182,665	1,185,819	1,169,618	1,173,056

$^*p < 0.05$; $^{**}p < 0.01$; $^{***}p < 0.001$. Continuous explanatory variables are centred at their mean

when Northern Ireland is compared to London: the propensity of offering specific services is much lower in Northern Ireland when compared to London. This could indicate that London has a much more diverse sex market than Northern Ireland.

One of the level 2 variables—network complexity—has a positive effect across all models. In this particular case, it is operationalised as an ordinal categorical variable consisting of quintiles. When comparing the higher quintiles (i.e., most complex) to the lowest quintile, there are, with few exceptions, incremental increases in the coefficients. This can most notably be observed in the PSE and WS models, where the effect seems particularly strong. The effect is weakest in the A Levels model. Interestingly, the differences in effect sizes are quite strong when the PSE and WS models are compared to the GFE and Dining models. This is consistent with the hypothesis that more complex networks may be more likely than simpler networks to offer extreme vis-à-vis non-extreme services.

Network mode, which is measured on the second level, also has a significant and negative effect on the propensity to offer the different services, with the exception of the Dining model. The effect sizes are quite modest, and additionally, if agencies indeed served as a protective barrier against more extreme services, it would be expected that the pattern would be reversed in the GFE model, which contrasts with the possibly more extreme PSE. However, it may also be the case that agencies simply are less inclined towards specifying what services are offered. Whilst the effect sizes are fairly small, the days a network has been active reduce the rates in which the various services are offered—especially so for A Levels and PSE. This is consistent with the idea that experience may reduce vulnerability.

Overall, the patterns suggest strong network effects when controlling for other factors likely to be associated with the propensity to advertise the various services. Whilst advert-level variables certainly predict the advertisement of different services, network complexity still appears to have the strongest independent effect. This reinforces the notion that network structure may more plausibly suggest the presence of vulnerability or exploitation, rather than advert-level indicators.

To more closely examine the effects of network complexity on the various services, the marginal effects from the models are shown in Figs. 2 and 3. The marginal effects shown in Fig. 2 are from the models in Table 11, with the predicted values shown by network complexity quintiles. The models in Fig. 3 are exactly the same, except for a linear functional form of the network complexity scale rather than quintiles. With regard to the predictions based on complexity quintiles, what is particularly interesting is that the predicted values are quite high for OWO, dining and GFE, irrespective of network complexity. Similarly, there is little evidence of a meaningful pattern concerning A Levels. Conversely, the strongest pattern can be observed for the PSE and WS models, in which the differences in predicted values are particularly clear when the fifth quintile is compared to the first or second quintile.

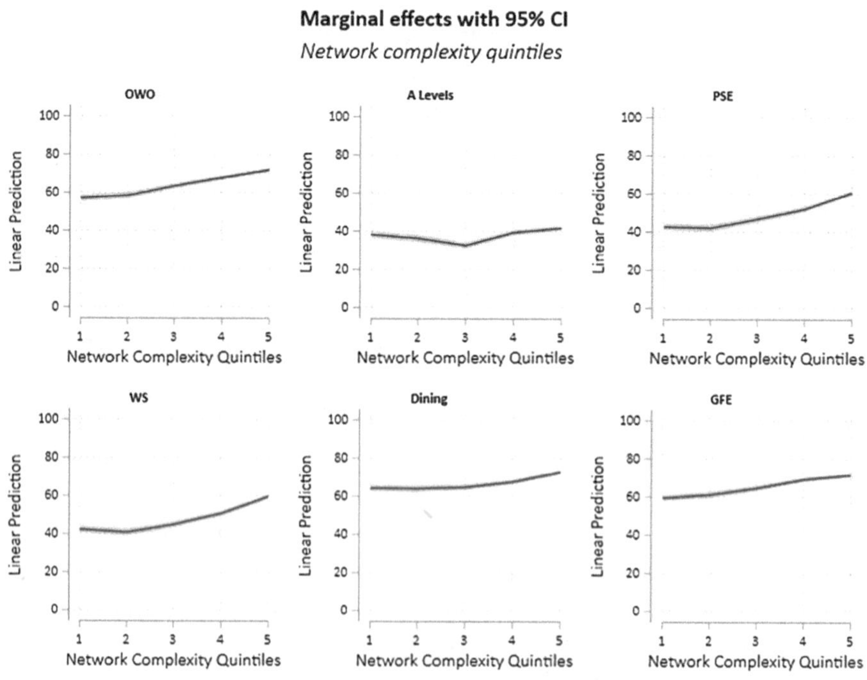

Fig. 2 Marginal effects from mixed effects models with network quintiles

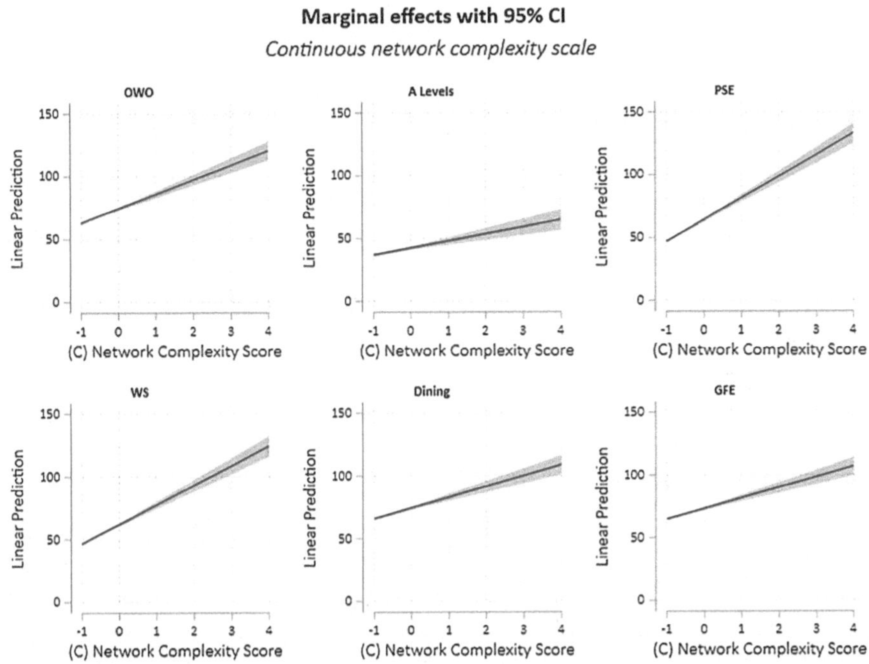

Fig. 3 Marginal effects from mixed effects models with continuous complexity scores

Arguably, the quintiles provide a better description of the empirical networks at hand, though the models with the continuous complexity scale are important for two reasons; the scale is continuous in nature, and it is of substantive importance to understand how the full range of specific values is related to the different outcomes. As can be observed, the contrasts between the different complexity scores become much clearer with complexity in a continuous functional form. A slightly different pattern is also evident in which network complexity appears more strongly related to the propensity to advertise the different services. In fact, the predictions for some of the highest complexity scores are outside of the possible range of values (i.e., 100%).

The most important finding from these models is that there are strong network effects in operation, and that we would expect to find more variability between networks rather than within them. Even more interesting is that the complexity of a network is important in estimating the prevalence of the various services modelled. Age appears particularly important in this context, and the effect of age also varies between networks. The effects of the other explanatory variables included in the models are modest at best, and this again reinforces the importance of network structure. However, it appears that some slightly different processes may be in operation regarding some services, specifically contributing to the propensity to offer PSE and WS. As such, the next round of modelling includes a combined measurement of these two services as the outcome variable.

From the results shown in Table 12, with the combined measure of extreme services as a continuous outcome variable, it can be seen that there is a significant degree of variance on both levels and across all models. Similar to the previous models, approximately 67–70% of the variance is at the second level; in other words, the network effects are stronger, but this is also because some level 1 covariates were excluded from these models. The fixed effects follow a similar pattern across all models: the propensity to advertise extreme services increases with network complexity when controlling for age, network mode, days active and ethnicity. The effects of age, network mode and days active are consistently negative across all models. British adverts are, with covariates held constant, somewhat more likely to offer extreme services when compared to Non-British adverts; this effect, however, is only statistically significant in the (full) random intercepts model. When ethnicity is modelled as a random coefficient, the fixed effect ceases to be significant. As evidenced by the significant variance for the random slope, the effect of advertising as British varies from network to network. There is a moderate and statistically significant correlation between the best linear unbiased prediction (i.e., the predictions derived from the random coefficient estimates) and network complexity (Pearson's $r = 0.24$, $p < 0.001$). On average, the effect of advertising as British increases the propensity to advertise extreme services in more complex networks, whereas the opposite is true for simpler networks.

The final model in Table 12 includes an interaction between network complexity and age; this was outlined in the introduction of the chapter as potentially important in explaining patterns of vulnerability. The

Table 12 Linear mixed effects models: extreme services scale (PSE and WS)

Variable	Null	Simple	Full	Random Slopes	Interactions
Network Complexity Scale		1.74***	1.77***	1.69***	1.66***
Network Mode			-0.04***	-0.04***	-0.04***
Days Active			-0.002***	-0.002***	-0.002***
Age			-0.09***	-0.09***	-0.09***
Ethnicity (Non-British)					
British			0.46***	-0.02	0.04
Network Complexity Scale * Age					0.02***
Intercept	4.88***	6.34***	6.25***	6.28***	6.28***
Random Effects					
ICC	0.70	0.70	0.67	0.67	0.67
Variance (Ethnicity)	–	–	–	7.14 (0.70)	7.10 (0.70)
Level 1 Variance	6.35 (0.03)	6.36 (0.03)	6.34 (0.03)	6.27 (0.03)	6.27 (0.03)
Level 2 Variance	15.07 (0.21)	14.54 (0.21)	12.71 (0.19)	12.77 (0.21)	12.71 (0.21)
Statistics					
N	121,993	121,993	121,993	121,993	121,993
R2 (Level 1)	–	0.02	0.11	0.11	0.11
R2 (Level 2)	–	0.03	0.13	0.13	0.13
Log-likelihood	-300,983	-300,776	-299,872	-299,486	-299,472
BIC	602,000	601,600	599,837	599,088	599,073

*$p < 0.05$; **$p < 0.01$; ***$p < 0.001$. Standard errors in parentheses

interaction is positive and significant, albeit relatively small in magnitude. Figure 4 shows the predicted values based on network complexity and age to further illuminate this interaction. The predicted values are rather high, and in fact, networks with a complexity score higher than five are predicted to have values that exceed the maximum range of the extreme services scale. The effect of age for networks with a complexity value of five is almost non-existent, whereas a negative effect is evident for networks lower on the complexity scale, and particularly strong for the simplest types of networks. In plain terms, this means that we expect the advertisement of extreme services to become increasingly rare with increasing age if a sex worker is working independently or as part of

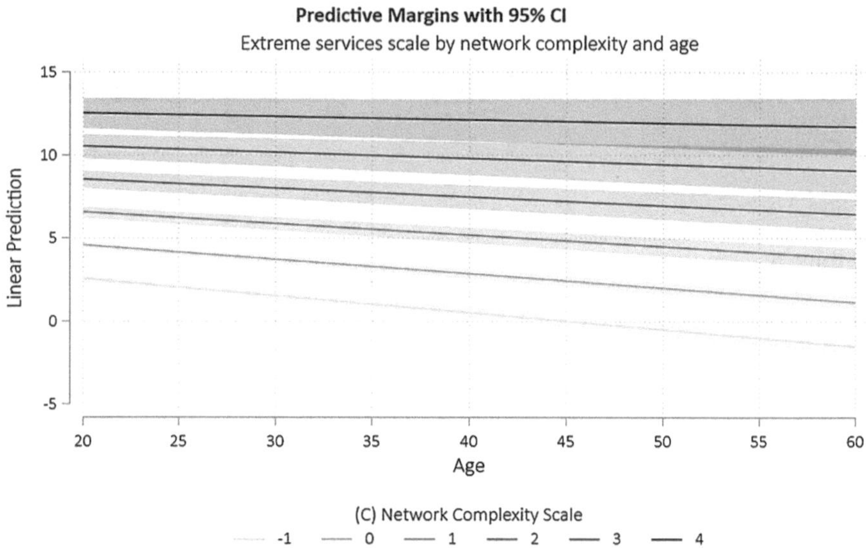

Fig. 4 Marginal effects of network complexity and age upon extreme services

smaller networks. In complex networks, however, we expect extreme services to be advertised irrespective of the advertised age. The confidence intervals suggest a fair degree more uncertainty for the more complex networks; this is expected as there is a lot fewer complex than simple networks, and some caution is therefore necessary in interpreting the significance of these effects.

These models have shown quite distinct patterns in the advertisement of PSE and WS. The services offered tend to vary based on characteristics such as advertised age and ethnicity; the effects of these, in turn, seem to vary based on the structure of the network they belong to. In other words, the processes occurring at a network level appear much more important than the advert's characteristics themselves in estimating the prevalence of certain services. Whilst it has been established that the propensity to offer some of the services that can be considered more extreme varies between networks, it is less clear whether this stems from a proclivity to specifically advertise those services, or if more complex networks simply tend to advertise *all* possible services available on ASW 1. The final series of models will attempt to shed some more light on this.

To examine this relationship, a continuous level 2 variable measuring the percentage of adverts within a network that offers all services except WS and PSE was used as a control variable. Two random intercept models are presented in Table 13, with the second including an interaction between network complexity and the services variable. In both models, 52–53% of the variance occurs within the network level, and a minor reduction in the level 2 variance is evident with the introduction of the interaction term. The fixed effects of both models follow a similar pattern as in earlier models; network complexity and advertising as British increases the extent to which extreme services are offered, and age, days active and network mode reduce it.

The network-level services variable is a significant predictor of the extent to which extreme services are advertised. In other words, the higher the rate of adverts within a network advertising all services, save PSE and WS, the higher the rate of actually advertising those two services is

Table 13 Linear random intercepts models: extreme scale

Variable	Full	Interactions
Network Services	0.06***	0.05***
Network Complexity Scale	1.05***	1.10***
Days Active	-0.001***	-0.001***
Network Mode	-0.03***	-0.03***
Age	-0.07***	-0.07***
Ethnicity (Non-British)		
British	0.50***	0.51***
Network Complexity Scale * Network Services		-0.01***
Intercept	6.12***	6.18***
Random Effects		
ICC	0.53	0.52
Level 1 Variance	6.32 (0.03)	6.32 (0.03)
Level 2 Variance	7.01 (0.11)	6.96 (0.11)
Statistics		
N	121,993	121,993
R2 (Level 1)	0.38	0.38
R2 (Level 2)	0.43	0.43
Log-likelihood	-296,343	-296,308
BIC	592,792	592,733

*$p < 0.05$; **$p < 0.01$; ***$p < 0.001$. Standard errors in parentheses

expected to be. The interaction between network complexity and network services is negative and significant. The marginal effects of this interaction are plotted in Fig. 5 to aid interpretation. Here, the predicted values are based on the percentage of adverts in a network offering all services for networks with complexity scores of one, three and six (i.e., low, medium and high complexity). With regard to these predicted values, there is most certainty for predictions based on networks with a value of one. There is a moderately strong, positive linear pattern: networks with 0% of adverts offering all services (excluding PSE and WS) are predicted to seldom offer WS and/or PSE. If, on the contrary, 100% of adverts within such a network offer all other services, they are predicted, with a small margin of error, also to offer PSE and WS in those adverts. The pattern is very similar for networks with a complexity score of three, albeit, the linear trend is not as strong, and there is a higher degree of uncertainty in the predicted values.

In relation to the most complex networks, with a score of six, there is actually a reversed and slight negative trend evident. Even if no adverts in

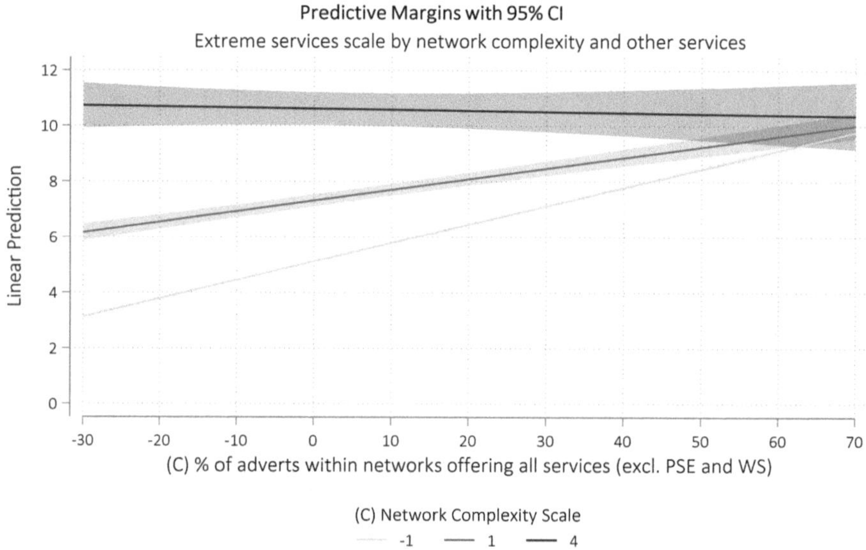

Fig. 5 Marginal effects of network complexity and other services upon extreme services

the network are offering all services, adverts are still predicted to include PSE and WS. As the percentages of adverts in a network offering all services increases, we would expect a slight decrease in the propensity to offer PSE and WS; however, it should be noted that there is a large degree of uncertainty regarding these predictions, and the point estimates are consistently above the max value of 10 (i.e., all adverts are offering PSE and WS). These findings are, nevertheless, important because they demonstrate two things: (1) more complex networks are more likely than simpler networks to advertise PSE and WS, irrespective of the extent to which they simply advertise all possible services; and (2) simpler networks do offer PSE and WS, albeit to a lesser extent, and if they do, they are more likely to do so as part of a marketing strategy of offering all available services.

Conclusions

A range of factors has been demonstrated to be associated with the propensity to advertise more extreme services, and network complexity often mediates these relationships. Both the bivariate analysis and subsequent multivariate models provided evidence that network structure predicts advert-level outcomes, allowing for the rejection of the null hypothesis. It was demonstrated that network structure not only contributes to advertising specific services, but that more complex networks are significantly more likely to advertise extreme services.

The bivariate analysis consistently showed how, depending on network complexity, there is significant variation across a range of other variables. Some of the stronger associations were for variables which potentially allude to some form of underlying vulnerability, such as more extreme services and the advertised age. Region appears less important in this context, though there was some evidence of regional variation which possibly highlights a preference for some networks to advertise in some regions rather than others (for instance, London rather than Northern Ireland). Similarly, it could indicate that some markets characterised by fierce competition have become increasingly extreme and diversified. It could, of course, be the case that sex workers are posting adverts outwith the vicinity of their own postcodes and rather appeal to markets that arguably get more visibility online, such as densely populated urban areas. Such mechanisms can of course not be captured through the analysis of online data alone, since they pertain to offline processes.

Ethnicity plays a complex role in the sex market. We expect migrants to make up a significant portion of the off-street sex market, and we also have reason to think that some ethnicities may be particularly vulnerable to exploitation due to both processes of racialisation and the exclusion associated with a more precarious legal status. We would, as a result, also expect ethnicity to stratify the online sex market. To a certain extent, it does, though its precise role is possibly obfuscated by the role that ethnicity and nationality also play as marketing strategies. From a bivariate perspective, the relationship between the dichotomous variable of advertising as British or Non-British and network complexity is stronger than the relationship between complexity and the more nuanced operationalisation of ethnicity. Overall, and contrary to what we intuitively would expect, the rate of extreme services is on average higher for adverts listing British ethnicities than for non-British ethnicities. However, this is in part because the effect of advertising as British as a form of marketing strategy varies significantly from network to network. This effect is stronger in complex networks, and for simpler networks, the effects are, on average, negative and lower the rate of extreme services. It is conceivable, though not possible to demonstrate with the current data, that (1) non-British migrants are more likely to be organised into larger networks, (2) British nationals are more likely to work independently and be represented online as simple networks and truthfully use their 'Britishness' as a marketing strategy, (3) complex networks consisting of migrants use 'Britishness' as a false marketing strategy, and (4) the stratifying effects of ethnicity that we can observe in online escort adverts are a result of these processes.

From the analysis, it is evident that the role of network complexity in mediating the propensity to advertise extreme services largely depends on the particular service in question. The role of complexity was less important in relation to some services which may be considered more extreme, such as OWO and A Levels, whereas it was more important for WS and PSE. However, the importance of network-level effects in this context was evident across all models. Indeed, processes operating on the network level appear much more important than the characteristics in adverts when assessing extreme services. Furthermore, the variability between networks appears much more important than the variability within networks and between adverts. This is an important finding since it suggests that assessing patterns of vulnerability and exploitation in escort adverts is more appropriate on a network rather than advert level.

To return to the original research question—the extent to which it is possible to identify patterns of vulnerability and exploitation—it can, with a fair degree of certainty, be concluded that *if* we consider some subtypes of services as indicative of vulnerability, there are indeed patterns evident, which largely can be attributed to the structure of the networks the adverts are embedded in. Naturally, the extent to which some services are 'extreme' and tap into an underlying dimension of vulnerability and exploitation is more questionable. It seems, however, that more complex networks, after controlling for other factors, are more likely to advertise *all* services and therefore by extension, also more likely to advertise extreme services. This reverberates with what was previously discussed in chapter "Exploitation and the Policing of Contemporary Sex Markets in Scotland", in which law enforcement respondents hypothesised that advertising that "everything goes", or that all services can be negotiated, would be a favourable marketing strategy for criminal networks. This, of course, needs to be viewed in light of the finding that simpler networks, which are perhaps more likely to represent independent sex workers, also advertise extreme services or simply all services available, albeit, they do so to a lesser extent than more complex networks. An interesting example of this relates to the age-complexity interaction, in which it was shown how network structure mediates the relationship between age and the propensity to advertise extreme services. This potentially suggests two things. First, being in more complex networks increases the likelihood that extreme services are offered. Second, individuals in complex networks are less likely to cease offering extreme services as their age increases. The opposite appears true for less complex networks, where age clearly decreases the advertisement of extreme services.

The more conceptual implications of these patterns are that they plausibly tap into a latent, unmeasured dimension of vulnerability, but more precisely, the underlying organisation of the network posting the adverts. Advertising all services, including extreme services is perhaps not much of an indication of vulnerability in simpler networks. Conversely, larger digital footprints are likely to correspond to an increasingly complex offline network. In such networks, we might anticipate a larger number of brokers, managers or middlemen, and with the presence of such actors, the risk of exploitation plausibly increases. It should not be implied that this latent dimension is a proxy for sex trafficking; rather, it merely reinforces the notion that where a third-party is involved in facilitating sexual services, there is a non-deterministic yet increased possibility that exploitation, irrespective of where that falls along the continuum, is also present.

References

Englund C, Viuhko M, Jokinen A, Aromaa K, Resetnikova A, Markina A, Söderström U, Nilsen M (2008) The Organisation of Human Trafficking: A Study of Criminal Involvement in Sexual Exploitation in Sweden, Finland and Estonia. Swedish National Council for Crime Prevention, Stockholm

Holt V, Kenway E, Berry A (2021) Sex Workers as Collateral Damage, Once Again: A Critique of the New 'Sex Trafficking Identification Matrix' Tool. SWARM. https://www.swarmcollective.org/sex-workers-as-collateral-damage-once-again-a-critique-of-the-new-sex-trafficking-identification-matrix-tool/. Accessed 24 Aug 2025.

Kjellgren R (2023) "Dark Spaces of Precarity": Networks and Complexity in the Off-street Sex Market. PhD Thesis, University of Stirling.

Kjellgren R (2025) The Geographies and Complexities of Online Networks in the Off-street Sex Market. Criminol Crim Just 25(1):81–103. https://doi.org/10.1177/17488958241245287

L'Hoiry X, Moretti A, Antonopoulos GA (2024) Identifying Sex Trafficking in Adult Services Websites: An Exploratory Study with a British Police Force. Trends Organ Crim 27(1):34–55. https://doi.org/10.1007/s12117-021-09414-1

Mai N (2009) Migrant Workers in the UK Sex Industry: Full Research Report. Economic Social and Research Council, Swindon

Robson K, Pevalin D (2015) Multilevel Modeling in Plain Language, 1st edn. SAGE Publications Ltd., London

Skidmore M, Garner S, Desroches C, Saggu N (2018) The Threat of Exploitation in the Adult Sex Market: A Pilot Study of Online Sex Worker Advertisements. Policing 12(2):210–218. https://doi.org/10.1093/police/pax007

Snijders T, Bosker R (1994) Modeled Variance in Two-Level Models. Sociol Method Res 22(3):342–363. https://doi.org/10.1177/0049124194022003004

Key Messages and Conclusions: Future Directions in the Computational Criminology of Internet-Mediated Exploitation

Research Questions and Context

This research was concerned with understanding the organisation of the sex market, the role of online technologies in this context and, more specifically, how criminal networks use technology to facilitate their operations. In addition, it also sought to examine the extent to which it is possible to identify networks and patterns of vulnerability and exploitation from online data. Previous research has noted the important role that the internet and technology play in the sex market (Sanders et al. 2018); yet, there is a scarcity of robust research relating to how criminal networks *actually* use technology to facilitate their operations (Kjellgren 2022), and especially so in the UK context. Certainly, there have been attempts to develop indicators and matrices to identify exploitation (e.g., Skidmore et al. 2018; L'Hoiry et al. 2024), or the use of virtual ethnography to study trafficking (Antonopoulos et al. 2020). However, these tend to suffer from limited understandings of exploitation and revitalise cultural myths of the 'ideal' victims that are quite far detached from the empirical realities of sex trafficking (Christie 1986; Doezema 1999; Albanese et al. 2022; Kjellgren 2022). Similarly, the few studies that move beyond qualitative assessments (e.g., Giommoni and Ikwu 2024)

R. Kjellgren, *Internet-Mediated Exploitation in the Scottish Online Sex Market*, Transnational Crime, Crime Control and Security,
https://doi.org/10.1007/978-3-032-09275-5_10

are based on indicators unable to distinguish between organised sexual labour vis-à-vis organised exploitation.

It is certainly challenging to research exploitation and the sex market through the analysis of digital traces. A significant challenge of this research was integrating critical theoretical understandings of sexual labour, exploitation and the epistemological qualities of online data, with methods capable of quantifying patterns occurring within the off-street sex market. This research is unique in that it combines a variety of traditional sociological methods, such as qualitative interviewing, social network analysis and regression modelling, with more novel forms of methods, including web scraping, quantitative text analysis and multivariate quadratic assignment procedure. Given the current knowledge gap relating to how technology is used to facilitate exploitation, and the extent to which we can examine patterns related to it, this research sought to address the following research questions:

1. How are online technologies used within the off-street sex market?
2. How do criminal networks and OCGs use online technologies to facilitate their operations, specifically with regard to advertising victims and connecting with sex buyers?
3. To what extent is it possible to identify networks operating within the off-street sex market, and patterns of vulnerability and exploitation, from online data?
4. To what extent could any identifiable patterns and network structures be useful for law enforcement and partner agencies?

A mixed-methods research design was deemed appropriate, which involved semi-structured interviews with practitioners, and the development of a quantitative workflow, capable of automatically collecting and cleaning the data, and identifying distinct online networks. The actual patterns within the data were identified through statistical modelling and social network analysis, and thereafter interrogated and triangulated against the qualitative findings.

Socio-Ecological Synthesis

Socio-ecological models are based upon the premise that behaviours and social phenomena are influenced by factors operating at different, interacting levels. Indeed, in their analysis of violence as a public health problem, Dahlberg and Krug (2006) proposed four analytical levels: individual, relationship, community and societal. The individual level is comprised of an individual's personal history, biology, demographic factors (e.g., age and gender), which, in the context of the current research, may contribute to victimisation, such as substance use or a previous trauma. The second level—relationships—has been the primary focus of the current case study. This includes relationships with friends, family, colleagues or people who may seek to exploit someone for financial gain. The third level is concerned with factors operating in the community, which may include employers, schools and neighbourhoods (Dahlberg and Krug 2006). Finally, the societal level encapsulates the social structures and policies which shape the experiences of individuals, for instance, patriarchal gender norms or restrictive immigration policies. The significance of this model is that it recognises that there tend to be multiple factors causing or contributing to complex behaviours, and that interactions across different levels shape social phenomena and the lives of individuals. In some ways, exploitation is a perfect example of such complex interactions, and a socio-ecological model provides a framework for exploring, researching, responding to and preventing social harm. Because of how socio-ecological models have successfully been applied to reduce violence, other research has explored their applicability to exploitation and human trafficking (Sanchez and Pacquiao 2018; Barner et al. 2018; Such et al. 2020; Barlow et al. 2022). In the following sections, the synthesised findings from the case study will be framed in light of such a socio-ecological model of exploitation. In particular, the role of different forms of capital and technologies, operating at the four levels and mediating the risks of exploitation, will be explored.

Key Findings

There is little doubt that online technologies have played a major part in reconfiguring the sex market. From the perspectives of the respondents, there was a collective understanding that the introduction of these technologies has led to an expansion and diversification of the sex market. Importantly, these developments have also seemingly had paradoxical effects: according to the views of respondents, technology generally creates safer and improved working environments for sex workers, but it also provides the perfect conditions for exploitation to take place. These 'dark spaces of precarity', it was argued, allow for anonymity and invisibility, and there are few safeguarding mechanisms in place; those seeking to exploit sex workers can do so more easily.

Based on the synthesis of previous research and the qualitative data generated from the semi-structured interviews, technology can be perceived as providing the overarching infrastructure of the off-street sex market, and criminal networks in these spaces will—precisely like sex workers—use technology to their advantage. According to the perspective of respondents, and more broadly, from previous research, technology allows for greater flexibility in the modus operandi and increases the number of possible permutations in the crime script. More precisely, technology appears to enhance the logistical and administrative capacities of networks. Based on the experiences of the respondents of this research, there is likely to be an element of technology across all the stages of sex trafficking, though it is certainly more prominent during some stages than others. Online technologies may be a feature of the recruitment process, but informal social networks are still seemingly central. Arranging and facilitating travel is potentially less risky since technologies reduce the need for a physical and controlling presence throughout the process. More importantly, the findings from this research suggest that technology offers new means of monitoring and controlling victims, and allows a network to advertise victims and connect with sex buyers whilst remaining at the periphery of routine police activities. Indeed, the findings suggest that through the use of technology, it may be significantly easier for a criminal network to be more transient in its operations; a network can more easily penetrate local markets and maintain a consistent presence in different localities, while the core of the network may direct the activities from somewhere completely different. In its essence, technology may allow criminal networks to streamline their business models, and plausibly make it simpler to facilitate large-scale exploitation since it is easier to conceal the scale of an operation.

In terms of the extent to which we can identify networks and patterns of vulnerability and exploitation, the findings suggest two things. First, whilst neither vulnerability nor exploitation can be directly assessed from online data alone, and certainly not from focusing specifically on the content of adverts, it is possible to estimate a network's complexity. Second, the evaluation of risk is likely to be much more successful if observations are based on the relational characteristics of online adverts. The construction of the *network complexity scale* illustrated how it is possible to estimate a network's complexity based on its empirical characteristics. The identified networks from this research, which were discussed with investigators, were also demonstrated to correspond well to what investigators had experienced during online investigations into human trafficking. It is not implied that more complex networks can be equated with the presence of vulnerability, exploitation or trafficking; rather, using more robust methods and theoretically informed models of the sex market provides a significantly better starting point to evaluate risks within networks.

Finally, the identified patterns and network structures are useful for law enforcement and partner agencies in some very specific ways. The findings suggest that the OSINT developed from this research will be of much value in providing investigations into sex trafficking with a digital overlay. OSINT is especially useful in developing investigative strategies and understanding the online presence of a network being investigated. As such, the primary value of OSINT is when it is triangulated against more robust forms of intelligence and evidence, which credibly can suggest the presence of exploitation. Therefore, OSINT will best be used as part of highly targeted approaches to credible threats of exploitation, rather than as part of systematic monitoring, which otherwise would increase the surveillance of independent sex workers, and the risk of generating false positives. Acting overtly on false positives would likely contribute to a deterioration of the relationships between sex workers and the police, and in the worst case, cause harm to sex workers.

Technology and the Off-Street Sex Market

In terms of our understanding of the off-street sex market, this research has made two important contributions. First, it has, contrary to the suggestion that technology simply increases exploitation (Hughes 2002; Farley et al. 2014; McKinley 2017), highlighted the paradoxical developments resulting from the introduction of online technologies to the sex market. Moreover, it also theorised the role of economic, human and social capital in mediating the risk of exploitation, and in doing so, offered plausible suggestions as to why there is a tendency for organisation within the sex market. Second, building upon this capital model of exploitation, it has also provided quantitative evidence that suggests that the sex market is likely to perhaps be more organised than previously imagined, and that the observed networks fall along a continuum of complexity. Technology, as such, can be perceived as operating on the fourth ecological level by creating an infrastructure, which sex workers may utilise to their advantage, but which may simultaneously also be beneficial to those seeking to exploit them. In this way, technology mediates how individuals—both exploiters and victims—negotiate risk and relationships.

Diversification, Expansion and Paradoxical Changes

In relation to the societal ecological level, the qualitative findings suggest that technology has facilitated a shift from street-based sex work to an expanding off-street sex market. As such, the suggestion that the internet and technology are central to contemporary sexual labour reverberates with what others have observed (Finn and Stalans 2016; Sanders et al. 2016, 2018). The infrastructure provided by the internet was highlighted by research respondents as both contributing to this expansion and increasing the diversity of the sex market.

One of the more substantively important findings from the qualitative analysis of this research relates to the observation that technology potentially has led to dual and paradoxical impacts on the sex market, by both increasing safety and creating online spaces characterised by precarity. It was noted in this research how technology has important implications for sex worker safety, in that it allows for the screening of clients, interaction and support from other sex workers and, more generally, a shift from the dangers associated with street-based sex work. This is highly similar to what has previously been noted (Cunningham et al. 2018; Sanders et al. 2018; Campbell et al. 2019). Paradoxically, as noted elsewhere (Crocker et al. 2017; Scoular et al. 2019), these low-visibility environments, characterised by anonymity and little safeguarding, may also be conducive to exploitation and other threats. Whilst the overarching technological infrastructure enabling internet-mediated sex work and exploitation can be perceived as operating on the societal level, it directly affects how individuals navigate the sex market, and the communities they are embedded in, which, in turn, mediate processes linked to safety and risks of exploitation.

According to the qualitative findings, stigma potentially fuels violence in the sex market, and its intersection with precarious online spaces is a cause for concern. Contrary to currently proposed changes to legislation, such as criminalising online spaces by making it illegal to advertise sexual services online, the findings from this research suggest that such measures are counterproductive and deeply problematic. This could conceivably increase the stigma attached to sexual labour, push sex workers back to the streets and displace online advertising to even more precarious online spaces like the dark web. From the qualitative interviews with investigators, it is clear that this would make it significantly more difficult for law enforcement to gather intelligence and effectively utilise the digital traces of criminal networks. In socio-ecological terms, the findings suggest that further criminalisation of online spaces, as a societal level intervention, is likely to do much more harm to sex workers, and also reduce the capacity of identifying and preventing exploitation in the first place.

The Capital Model of Exploitation

Previous research has suggested that organisation, or the presence of networks in the sex market, is a clear indicator of sex trafficking (Antonopoulos et al. 2020; L'Hoiry et al. 2024). However, both the qualitative and quantitative findings from this research suggest that there is a broader tendency towards organised sexual labour, and potentially, that variations in economic, human and social capital mediate this process. Drawing on the findings from chapter "Exploitation and the Policing of Contemporary Sex Markets in Scotland", which included a discussion of the importance of human and social capital in this context, the following paragraphs will elaborate upon what will be referred to as the capital model of exploitation. This can be perceived as an extension of the socio-ecological framework, since it considers how different forms of capital mediate the social processes associated with the four ecological levels described earlier.

First, in relation to individual and relationship level factors, as suggested by the qualitative findings, even though victims may have pre-existing vulnerabilities, and that deception may play a part in recruitment, many who go on to be exploited were aware that they were migrating for sexual labour. This is well in line with what has previously been observed (Doezema 1999). Second, if victims encountered by the police or support organisations consider themselves as victims, it is far from guaranteed that they would specifically consider themselves victims of *sexual* exploitation; indeed, based on the experiences of research participants, some victims will consider themselves as having been sexually exploited, and others may perceive their exploitation as economic or labour exploitation, or a combination of several forms of exploitation. This is an important insight, which has also previously been observed by others (e.g., O'Connell Davidson 2006). A related and important finding, which has also been noted elsewhere (Bjelland 2016), is that some individuals may prefer to remain in an exploitative situation—even if it is characterised by intimidation, threats and violence—because the alternative may simply be even worse. The complex interplay of factors operating at different ecological levels is evident here: individuals may, prior to victimisation, have been in a situation characterised by a lack of opportunities and patriarchal gender orders (societal level), then deceived and recruited into sex work (relationship level), completely detached from social networks and increasingly dependent upon the facilitator (community level), experienced a deterioration in mental health (individual level), and even if threats or violence become feature of their situation (relationship level), a lack of capital required to negotiate their situation may be absent (individual, relationship and community), and a precarious migration status may mean no recourse to public funds (societal level).

With all of these findings taken together, there is a suggestion that decision-making processes are central in the context of exploitation, contrary to other accounts that portray victims solely at the mercy of other forces outwith their control (e.g., Farley et al. 2014; McKinley 2017). There certainly are situations where the capacity to exercise agency is minimal, but by not recognising that victims have agency, we become further detached from the empirical reality of exploitation. The findings from the qualitative analysis suggest different forms of capital to be central in mediating decision-making processes, both in contributing to the overall capacity to exercise agency, but also more indirectly by mediating the risk factors of exploitation, operating on different ecological levels.

The decision to engage in sexual labour, including migration for sexual labour, was perceived by research respondents as often being motivated by a lack of economic capital; the financial incentives associated with the sex market can be substantial, and especially so for migrants from weaker economies. Human capital, in this context primarily characterised by language skills, knowledge and experience concerning local sex markets, including the expectations and informal rules regulating interactions and transactions, was perceived by respondents as incredibly important and affects the ability to work safely and autonomously. The qualitative findings suggest that social capital is perhaps most important in this context, as this affects the opportunities and support networks available to sex workers and migrants. Taken together, migrant sex workers may be more likely than non-migrant sex workers to lack human capital, and social capital may be limited to their country of origin, or possibly include weaker and more untrustworthy connections in the destination country.

With limited human and social capital, it may in fact be very difficult for sex workers to work independently, and the insights from the qualitative analysis suggest a particularly strong tendency for migrants to be organised into networks. As such, if the lack of economic capital acts as an instigator to migrate for sexual labour, the lack of human capital potentially makes sex workers more reliant upon social capital. Based on the qualitative findings, there is a suggestion that the reliance on social capital can of course both have positive and negative effects; working with trusted acquaintances and friends can serve as an effective barrier against exploitation, whereas a reliance on more untrustworthy ties may increase the risk of exploitation. With risk factors for exploitation, such as a hostile immigration system, present on the societal level, supportive relationships and community integration are especially important. This research highlighted how an increasingly hostile immigration system increases the vulnerability of migrants and, consequently, the need to rely on untrustworthy third-parties—smugglers, brokers and facilitators—which may render exploitation more likely. These findings also support previous research suggesting that smugglers and brokers facilitating sexual labour are in powerful positions, which can result in exploitative situations (Lainez 2017).

The Continuum of Organisation

A very important finding emerging from both the qualitative and quantitative chapters, with implications for both policing and our understanding of the sex market, is that a continuum of organisation can be observed within the internet-mediated sex market. These findings challenge previous research, which suggests that any evidence of organisation is a strong indicator of internet-mediated sex trafficking (e.g., Antonopoulos et al. 2020; L'Hoiry et al. 2024). The contributions from this research suggest that law enforcement will likely encounter networks within the sex market which are *unlikely* to amount to the threshold of sex trafficking. What the aforementioned authors have highlighted as indicative of trafficking—such as poor English, similar phraseology and shared phone numbers—are probably more likely to be indicative of migrant networks than the organised crime groups they are purported to represent. In light of what was discussed in the previous section, it should be expected to find adverts with similar phraseology and shared phone numbers; after all, the qualitative findings suggest it is likely that the person in the network with the highest level of English will be posting the adverts or answering the phones, simply because they are in the best position to do so. This is not to suggest there is not a presence of organised crime within the off-street sex market; indeed, the qualitative findings suggest the presence of such groups. Different organised crime groups were suggested by respondents to be present in the off-street sex market and structured more broadly around ethnic lines. At times, poly-criminality and crossovers between different criminal markets, and co-operation and competition between different organised crime groups, had also been observed by respondents, and argued to be features of contemporary organised crime within the sex market.

The quantitative findings from this research reinforce the notion that a plurality of networks is present within the off-street sex market. The results from the quantitative analysis suggest a continuum of organisation across the observed networks, and based on the qualitative findings from the semi-structured interviews, we should also expect a continuum of organisation within criminal networks as well. From these interviews, respondents described how exploitation had been observed to include as little as one perpetrator, to large-scale networks spanning the whole of the UK. The quantitative analysis reinforced the notion that the digital traces of networks also span a wide continuum. As such, the notion that certain indicators "could be used to detect and even predict human trafficking" (L'Hoiry et al. 2024, p. 38) is misguided at best: we can, with a high degree of certainty, observe digital traces *implying* variable levels of offline organisation, but far from all observable networks in the sex market will represent trafficking. In other words, equating indications of organisation as a proxy for sex trafficking is a poor substitute for more robust assessments.

Technology and the Crime Script

Technology can be perceived as providing a societal level infrastructure which can be utilised by criminal networks to facilitate exploitation. Whereas other research has noted the role that technology plays in sex trafficking (Di Nicola et al. 2017), few studies have actually elaborated upon precisely how it affects the *process* of committing sex trafficking. Similarly, technology is often portrayed as a requirement for sex trafficking (e.g., DeliverFund XE "DeliverFund" 2020), with little elaboration of *when* and *to what extent* it actually is important in the facilitation of this crime. The findings from this research, whilst limited in scope and situated within a UK context, indicate that technology plays a variable role. In the next sections, key findings from this case study are compared to the previous research and discussed in light of Cornish's (1994) crime script analysis, which was initially discussed in chapter "Criminal Networks, Opportunity Structures and the Process of Exploitation", section "Unpacking the Sex Trafficking Crime Script". Essentially, technology is potentially important for criminal networks trying to facilitate large-scale exploitation in the off-street sex market, and it is important precisely because it increases the number of permutations within the crime script.

Recruitment and Deception

Previous research has highlighted the use of technology in the recruitment process (Di Nicola et al. 2017). This research found very modest evidence suggesting technology and social media play any role whatsoever in the recruitment process. However, it should be noted that those who had encountered victims as part of investigations, or supported victims in other capacities, often had very limited knowledge of the precise context in which recruitment occurred, because it most likely occurred outside of the UK. Similar to what was noted by Englund et al. (2008), there was evidence to suggest recruitment to primarily be facilitated through informal social networks; technology may of course be part of facilitating the communication, but pre-existing offline connections appear more important. There was also evidence to suggest potential crossovers between child sexual exploitation and adult sex trafficking; investigators described how underage victims had been sexually exploited by organised crime groups in their home country prior to being trafficked as adults for exploitation in the UK's off-street sex market. Even though a technological infrastructure is present within society, it still appears that, in terms of recruitment, the greatest risk factor is relationships and social networks, and whether or not interactions appear online or offline may be of secondary importance in this particular context.

The most likely recruitment strategy used by criminal networks, according to the perspective of respondents, was to involve elements of deception; some women knew they were migrating to engage in sexual labour, whereas others thought they were coming to the UK for other types of work. False promises of non-existent job opportunities, or in case they knew they would be working in the sex market, misleading expectations of the nature or remuneration of their labour, appear to be the most prominent strategies. These findings reverberate with what has been observed elsewhere: women who know that they are migrating for sexual labour may nevertheless have very little knowledge regarding the conditions they will be working in (Kempadoo 2004; Agustín 2006; Chimienti 2009; Plambech 2017).

The findings from this research also suggest that homophily potentially mediates the recruitment process, thereby increasing the likelihood that victims and offenders may be from the same geographical region and share the same ethnicity. This aligns with what has previously been observed (Zimmermann et al. 2006; Englund et al. 2008; Wijkman and Kleemans 2019). Technology, according to the findings from this research, may not be crucial to recruiting victims. It is likely, however, that technology increases the opportunities associated with recruitment, even though informal social networks may be more important in this context. Additionally, part of the communication can be facilitated through technology even if the connection was not established online in the first place. As such, while technology is not required to execute the recruitment stage of the crime script, it nonetheless affords criminal networks novel opportunities to initiate and maintain communication.

Transience and Mobility

In terms of the initial transportation between the country of origin and the UK, relatively little was uncovered as part of this research. Part of the reason for this, which others have noted (Di Nicola et al. 2017), is that transportation is likely to occur legally in many cases, and victims are likely to cooperate and travel willingly. However, the findings provided a clearer picture with regard to the transportation that is likely to occur within the UK, as part of the exploitation phase.

Indeed, some of the key findings from this research suggest that transience and fluidity are crucial to the success of criminal networks in the sex market, and technology is critically important in facilitating more transient operations. There are different layers to this, and as others have noted, online technologies make it easier to control and monitor victims without the necessity of a physical, controlling presence (Englund et al. 2008; Volodko et al. 2019). For instance, this research found evidence from the qualitative interviews that threats were often made through the use of mobile phones, and some victims were required to be in constant communication with their exploiters. Besides the role that technology plays in controlling victims, technology was described by respondents as being used by criminal networks to engage in a variety of activities, from booking and arranging transportation and accommodation to online banking.

The most crucial aspect of technology, according to the experiences of the research participants, relates to how it provides access to the off-street sex market through the posting of online escort adverts. Indeed, previous research has suggested the online marketing of sexual services to be central to contemporary sex trafficking (Europol 2011, 2020; Latonero 2011, 2012; Walby et al. 2016; Crocker et al. 2017), and the findings from this case study support those claims, even if limited in scope and based on a modest sample. According to the current research, one of the principal functions of technology is that criminal networks have the potential to more effectively penetrate local markets. Indeed, the qualitative findings suggest that networks with substantial logistical and administrative capacity can also continuously maintain their presence throughout multiple localities, utilise a more nuanced division of labour or centralised 'call centres', and thus rotate victims in circuits across the UK.

Most importantly, the findings from the qualitative analysis suggest that if a criminal network in the UK is engaging in sex trafficking, or more precisely, the *commercial* exploitation of adult women, and if they aspire to do this on a larger scale, technology will be pivotal and used in numerous ways—but of most significance, it will be used to gain access to the off-street sex market. Contrary to the argument made by others (Hughes 2004; Farley et al. 2014; McKinley 2017)—that technology has led to an explosion in sex trafficking—technology is better perceived as having reconfigured the crime script, allowing criminal networks to operate more fluidly and on a larger scale. We do not simply have the quantitative evidence to make causal claims about how technology has increased the scale of sex trafficking; the findings from this case study, however, suggest that technology may increase opportunities, or the available permutations, within the sex trafficking crime script. There is a potential that technology will be used at every stage of sex trafficking, though its significance is likely to be variable from network to network, and it will certainly be most prominent in the context of market penetration.

Epistemology and Online Escort Adverts

Previous research involving online escort adverts often suggests that the characteristics within them can be used to evaluate the potential presence of sex trafficking or organised crime (e.g., Ibanez and Suthers 2014; Alvari et al. 2017; Li et al. 2018). The findings from this case study would, on the contrary, suggest it is highly problematic to use indicators to evaluate the presence of sex trafficking. This largely comes down to the fact that the indicators used do not possess the discriminatory power required to differentiate between sex trafficking and other forms of organised labour within the sex market, but also because escort adverts are highly epistemologically ambiguous. Giommoni (2024, p. 10) expertly captured this point:

> relying solely on the information provided in the advertisements, such as writing patterns, services offered, movements, prices, etc., will never be sufficient to determine with scientific validity whether someone is being exploited.

This research is consistent with Giommoni's (2024) conclusions, and the findings from this case study would rather suggest it is more appropriate to shift the discussion to consider the extent to which patterns of vulnerability can be observed, but even that is challenging due to the limited and uncertain information available within adverts.

The Nature of Adverts

Whereas some authors tend to conceive of the information provided in online adverts as mirroring an independent, offline reality (e.g., Whitney et al. 2018; Antonopoulos et al. 2020), the findings from this research suggest a more critical appreciation of adverts is appropriate. Indeed, it is particularly important to recognise that adverts are produced in a market context: their sole purpose is to attract clients in a market characterised by heterogeneity and fierce competition. Adverts, as such, and from the perspective of research participants, were found to be generic and likely tailored to appease particular market demands, whether that is in terms of the images used, the advertised nationality, ethnicity, age or the particular services said to be offered. This qualitative finding is further supported by the quantitative text analysis conducted in chapter "Complexity, Similarity and Tie Formation in Advert Networks", which showed that advert similarity correlates with the scale and complexity of networks. An important observation from the qualitative interviews is that adverts part of sex trafficking investigations were also highlighted as not being different—in any meaningful way—from other online adverts, which were not part of investigations.[1] This challenges many of the assumptions of other

[1] This is a very important observation, and what would significantly have increased the overall validity of this assertion were if online adverts that had been part of the investigations could be compared directly against a sample of adverts which had not been part of investigations. Future research should seek the inclusion of a source of 'ground truth' (e.g., online adverts where exploitation has previously been confirmed) to add rigour to research into the trafficking-technology nexus. This

research (e.g., Konrad et al. 2017; Antonopoulos et al. 2020; L'Hoiry et al. 2024), which suggests the information provided in adverts can be used to evaluate the presence of sex trafficking. In fact, one of the most important findings emerging from the current research is that the structure of online advert networks is exceptionally more informative than the actual content within online adverts.

Advert Networks

Other research has highlighted that networks can be observed through the analysis of online escort adverts (Latonero 2011, 2012; Li et al. 2018), yet no other research has—to date—offered the same level of detail and nuance concerning empirical online networks in the sex market as provided in this case study. A key finding emerging from the qualitative analysis is that the characteristics within online adverts are not particularly useful in investigative contexts; what is useful, based on the perspectives of respondents part of this research, are the phone numbers, user accounts and geographical locations of the adverts, as this allows investigators to appreciate the relational qualities of adverts. The importance of networks in investigative contexts, or the relations between online escort adverts, should not be understated.

Patterns of Vulnerability and Exploitation

Whilst the findings from this research suggest that indicators are incapable of accurately distinguishing between sex workers and trafficking victims in online escort adverts, the question of the extent to which we can identify patterns related to vulnerability and exploitation requires some further elaboration. The results from the current research suggest the presence of exploitation is unlikely to be correctly and accurately inferred from the analysis of online escort adverts; the details required to inform such a judgement are simply not available in this source of data. Even

---

was always an aspiration of this research project, but police officers were not in a position to share such data at the time of this research.

though there was broad agreement amongst investigators that the identified networks presented in the course of interviews corresponded well to what they had observed in their investigations (as highlighted in chapter "Exploitation and the Policing of Contemporary Sex Markets in Scotland"), this does not *prove* that exploitation was present in the identified patterns. In light of the capital model of exploitation discussed earlier, estimating *vulnerability towards exploitation*, rather than *exploitation* itself, may be a more sensible approach.

Indeed, other research has previously suggested that the presence of facilitators, brokers or middle-men involved in a network can both have positive effects—in terms of increasing safety and allowing for more opportunities—but also in contributing to the risk of exploitation (Morselli et al. 2014; Lainez 2017). This idea is closely related to the capital model of exploitation, namely, that lower levels of capital necessitate relying on people with higher levels of capital to facilitate their labour. This logic dictates that the risk of exploitation potentially correlates with the size and structure of the network. The capital model of exploitation can be perceived as one component of a socio-ecological framework of exploitation, as illustrated in Fig. 1. According to this view, to exercise agency is to mobilise resources to negotiate the risk factors in operation at different socio-ecological levels. A clear risk factor at the intersection of relationship and community levels is related to the power imbalances between an individual lacking the necessary capital to work independently, and having to rely on someone in a comparatively more powerful position. The synthesised findings from this case study inspired the *facilitator-ratio hypothesis*: the ratio of facilitators to sex workers is proposed to be positively correlated with the risk of exploitation. This hypothesis is premised upon the following observations from the previous chapters:

1. Exploitation is fundamentally relational and minimally requires one party to exploit the other.
2. Sex workers who need to rely on a facilitator to engage in sexual labour are likely to possess less human and social capital than the facilitator.
3. Power imbalances in the relationship between sex workers and facilitators create situations conducive to exploitation, especially in situations

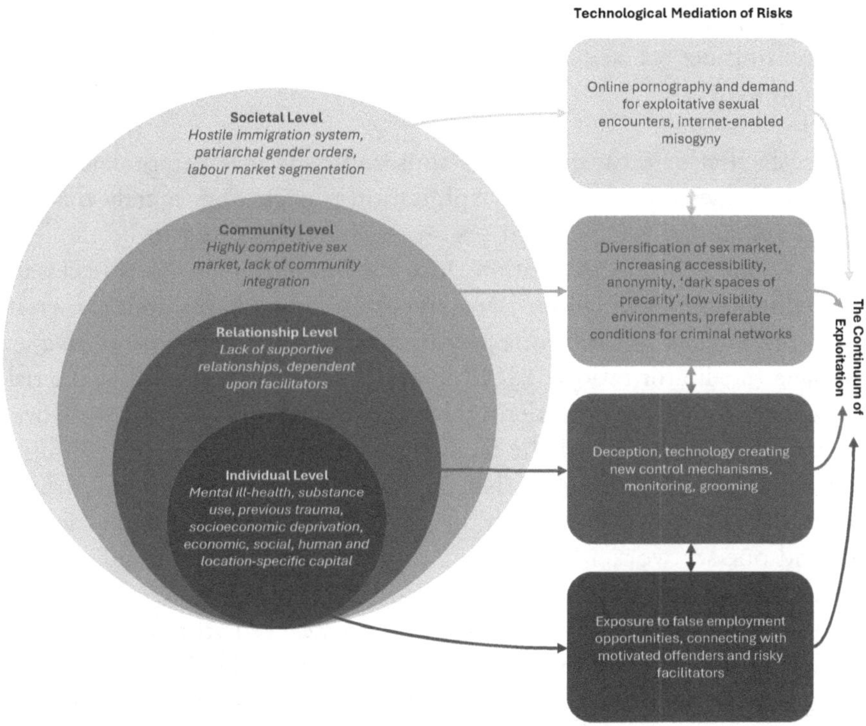

Fig. 1 Socio-ecological model of interplay between technology and exploitation

where sex workers must repay large debts accumulated through migration.

4. Facilitators take risks in facilitating the sexual labour of sex workers (due to the quasi-criminalised nature of sex work), and increased financial incentives, at the expense of working conditions, may be considered necessary to outweigh the risks.
5. Increasing the scale of sexual labour, by recruiting more women, increases profits, but also risks, as it becomes increasingly difficult to facilitate sexual labour on a larger scale.
6. Larger networks may depend upon a greater number of facilitators to operate effectively, and there is therefore an increased need to generate more revenue.

7. If the ratio of facilitators to sex workers increases disproportionately to the number of sex workers, the risks of exploitation may grow exponentially.

The facilitator-ratio hypothesis thus contends that the presence of a facilitator does not imply that exploitation is occurring, merely that the risk is *increasing*. Independent sex workers are suggested to be the least likely to suffer from exploitation since they have the resources necessary to facilitate their own labour.[2] This hypothesised relationship is shown in Fig. 2. In a scenario where one person is facilitating the labour of five sex workers (facilitator ratio = 0.20),[3] it would be hypothesised that the risk of exploitation is low, considering that the pooled capital of the sex workers may outweigh that of the facilitator. However, a ratio of 1.0 might potentially involve a higher risk. A 'loverboy' scenario would perhaps exemplify this, and even though the network only consists of one facilitator and one sex worker, chances are that the latter person is already in a vulnerable situation and has to rely on the facilitator to generate an income. When the proportion of facilitators exceeds the proportion of sex workers, the risk of exploitation may be extremely high. Arguably, it can be considered *inherently* exploitative since a numerical minority must generate income for the larger group. This idea of exploitation as a result of unequal access to different forms of capital and power imbalances is, of course, not unique to the sex market; the music industry offers another example where the number of facilitators may be involved in managing the career of an artist. Indeed, it has been reported how pre-existing, gendered power imbalances in the UK's music industry mean that women are at an increased risk of experiencing discrimination, sexual harassment, assault and sexual exploitation (Women and Equalities Committee 2024).

[2] Note that this does not imply independent that sex workers do not experience serious harm or risk being exploited by a client; on the contrary, independent sex workers are still at risk of serious violence or exploitation from clients, which, in part, is a result of the quasi-criminalised nature of sex work in the UK.

[3] This scenario might, according to this research, be quite plausible in the context of migrant networks; one person may have superior communication skills, be business savvy and make an excellent admin, which means that they may serve the network best from such a position.

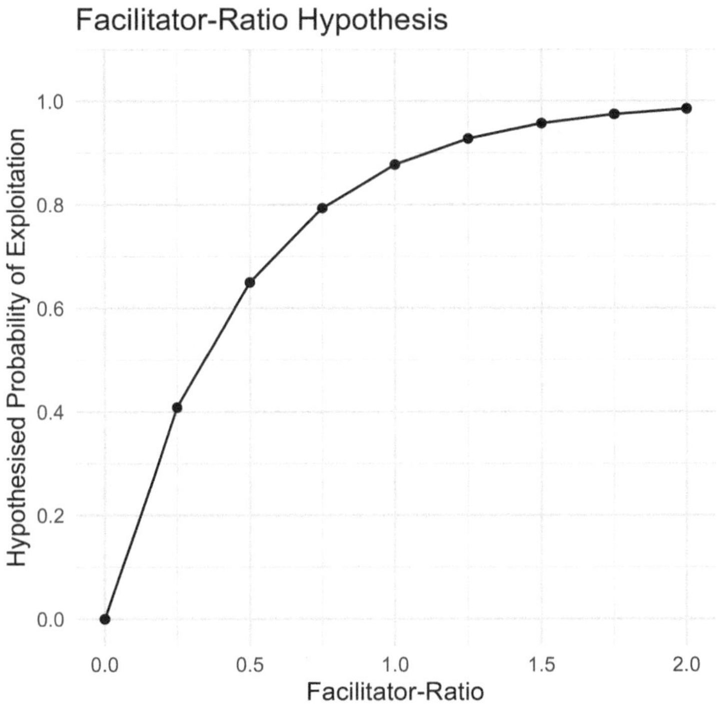

Fig. 2 The facilitator-ratio hypothesis

Whilst the facilitator-ratio hypothesis may be helpful in examining risks, the realities of exploitation are likely to be more nuanced; the relationship between the risk of exploitation and the ratio between facilitators and sex workers is likely mediated by other relational factors. For instance, consider the role of gatekeepers in exploitative networks, which police respondents referred to as 'alpha females' in the discussions from chapter "Exploitation and the Policing of Contemporary Sex Markets in Scotland". A sex worker loosely integrated within a network, with few connections to others, is arguably at an increased risk of exploitation when a gatekeeper facilitates communication with the outside world. In such a scenario, it is not necessarily the ratio of facilitators to sex workers that is the most important feature, but the internal structures of the network itself. In other words, whilst an increased facilitator-ratio can increase risk, this effect will be variable and contingent upon the internal dynamics of the network, where a more connected and integrated sex worker might more successfully negotiate the risks of exploitation.

If we accept the supposition that the digital traces of online networks *approximate*—albeit imperfectly—the structure and scale of offline networks, then vulnerability towards exploitation would be hypothesised to primarily be located within larger and more complex online networks. This, however, does not mean that vulnerability to exploitation is exclusive to larger networks; on the contrary, the qualitative findings from this research clearly suggest the size of criminal networks to be highly variable. It may, nevertheless, be more realistic to identify vulnerability towards exploitation in larger and more complex online networks, rather than in scenarios where a single perpetrator exploits one victim. Furthermore, it is also conceivable that network complexity is positively correlated to the number of facilitators involved in the offline network; this again reinforces the notion that the combination of network size and complexity may be the most useful attributes in evaluating vulnerability to exploitation. The crucial question, then, is the extent to which other empirically identified patterns map onto this hypothesis.

Network structure, operationalised by the network complexity scale, was demonstrated to predict advert-level outcomes. What is commonly referred to as 'extreme services' varies by network complexity. More complex networks tend to have higher rates of extreme services, and they are also more likely to *specifically* offer extreme services. It is important to note that advert networks across the complexity spectrum offer extreme services, but more complex networks do so at a significantly higher rate, and this association remains whilst controlling for other factors. The tendency to offer extreme services can perhaps be attributed to a marketing strategy of trying to maximise advert visibility, as suggested by Holt et al. (2021). Alternatively, if the sex market has become more diversified due to online technologies, wage penalties may be imposed upon sex workers who do not offer more specialised services (Adriaenssens and Hendrickx 2012). Whatever the true cause of these observed differences is, it is nevertheless important to note that the findings are consistent with the idea that extreme services correlate with networks hypothesised to be more likely to involve risks of exploitation.

This research was also the first of its kind that examined factors predicting the formation of ties between online adverts, and the extent to which advert networks are structured around certain characteristics. An important finding in this context is that group embeddedness correlates with network complexity. Simpler networks tend to be more homogeneous—both in terms of advert characteristics and textual similarity—whereas larger networks display a stronger tendency for heterogeneity. This is consistent with the idea that the digital footprints associated with simpler networks may be more likely to represent independent sex workers, whereas a broader diversity in marketing strategies and advert characteristics may suggest a certain degree of third-party facilitation. This has strong implications for our understanding of online networks in the sex market. Primarily, it reinforces the notion that identifying trafficking from adverts themselves, as often suggested by previous research (e.g., Alvari et al. 2017), is likely to be misguided; the true value of this source of data can only be appreciated when accounting for its relational nature.

From the qualitative interviews, police respondents reported that adverts part of their investigations did not substantially differ from other adverts, which were not suspected of involving exploitation. This supports the notion that the characteristics *within* adverts are neither reliable nor especially informative in the context of identifying trafficking. It appears that underlying processes, which cannot be observed through digital traces, shape the structure of these networks and contribute to observed differences in advert homophily. In turn, variations in advert homophily may imply the presence or absence of facilitators. Marketing strategies are naturally likely to evolve and change throughout time to address fluctuating market demands; however, large and heterophilous networks structured around specific marketing strategies may suggest the presence of multiple persons posting the adverts.

This research found evidence to suggest that the more complex a network is, the more likely it is to be similar to other complex networks. This has clear implications for policing, in that semantic similarity may not be a particularly strong indicator of trafficking, as suggested by others (Giommoni and Ikwu 2024; L'Hoiry et al. 2024). In fact, the findings from this case study would suggest that complex networks become increasingly similar to one another as they grow in complexity. If law enforcement insists upon highlighting one or more adverts as indicative of trafficking, without understanding the full extent to which they are connected to other adverts, they are likely to make a very limited assessment.

Relying on advert-level characteristics and variables to assess the presence of trafficking is highly susceptible to generating false positives; this is largely due to the fact that there are no indicators available that can convincingly distinguish between exploitation and other forms of organised sexual labour. However, examining the networks posting these adverts can, at the very least, provide a more satisfactory account of the complexity and scale of a network's digital footprints. In turn, and consistent with the hypothesis that the risk of exploitation increases with the scale and structure of a network, it is perhaps more plausible to identify *where* vulnerability can be considered most prominent. This is not to say that such an approach is not sensitive to generating false positives; it most certainly is. This reinforces the notion that the proactive identification of victims from online data can be problematic, even though the methodology used in this research project is more sophisticated and robust than previously suggested approaches (e.g., Skidmore et al. 2018; Giommoni and Ikwu 2024; L'Hoiry et al. 2024). These insights have very important implications for how the online dimension of the sex market can best be policed, and this will be discussed next.

Policing the Continuum

Perhaps some of the most important findings emerging from this research relate to the precise role that open-source intelligence (OSINT) plays in contemporary sex trafficking investigations in Scotland. Whereas it has previously been suggested that technologies capable of generating OSINT are the supposed silver bullet to sex trafficking (e.g., DeliverFund XE "DeliverFund" 2020; Marinus Analytics 2021; Tech Against Trafficking 2021), the findings from this research suggest a more mundane reality. Indeed, according to the perspectives of respondents from this research, there tend to be more systemic policing issues, such as a lack of resources, coupled with the often ambiguous situations victims find themselves in, which makes trafficking investigations particularly challenging. OSINT is important—in very specific stages of an investigation—and with limited resources—there is a need for highly targeted and precise approaches to policing sex trafficking.

Investigative Barriers

This research proposes that the most significant barriers to successful sex trafficking investigations have little to do with a lack of technical capabilities to generate OSINT from adult services websites (ASWs), as others have proposed (Petter et al. 2020). The findings are similar to what has previously been highlighted by Pajón and Walsh (2018), namely, that what truly makes trafficking difficult to investigate is that it is likely to involve a multitude of perpetrators and victims, who often experience ambivalence concerning their victimisation, and the tremendous amount of resources required to investigate such a complex crime. Bearing in mind that intelligence on potential exploitation comes from a wide variety of sources, including routine policing activities, responses to calls, or suspicious activity reports, it is an incredibly resource-intensive process to adequately develop the multitude of intelligence. The current research suggests it is uncommon, in this specific research context, for investigations to be opened solely based on OSINT. This goes contrary to what others have argued, such as that proactive screening for adverts suspicious of trafficking is a viable approach (Skidmore et al. 2018; L'Hoiry et al. 2024), and that the key barrier is that the police do not have the technology necessary to do so effectively (Deeb-Swihart et al. 2019). The findings from this case study would rather suggest there is a problem with the quality of intelligence that can be derived from online escort adverts, rather than the quantity that it could generate. To be more concrete, there are not sufficient resources to adequately and appropriately investigate all adverts that can be labelled suspicious.

The Function of Open-Source Intelligence

A considerable contribution from this research is the finding that OSINT plays a modest but important role in sex trafficking investigations. In contrast to the contention that the use of web scraping technologies and data analytics will revolutionise the policing of sex trafficking (Deeb-Swihart et al. 2019; DeliverFund XE "DeliverFund" 2020; Petter et al. 2020; Marinus Analytics 2021), the findings from this research would rather suggest that OSINT is important at particular stages throughout an investigation. Rather than proactive forms of monitoring and instigating investigations, it is perhaps more realistic, and indeed appropriate, to conceive of OSINT as providing a digital overlay to ongoing investigations. From the perspective of law enforcement respondents in this research, concerns regarding the safety and wellbeing of victims are usually what guide decision-making in evaluating incoming intelligence, and the capacity to evaluate safeguarding concerns is very limited in OSINT generated from escort adverts. The findings from this research suggest that OSINT can be particularly effective when used in triangulation with more robust forms of intelligence, indicating safeguarding concerns. The chief function in this context is to estimate the scale and extent of an offline network based on the digital traces available online. This is especially important in the early stages of an investigation, and OSINT on the structure of the criminal network can support the senior investigating officer in developing an investigative strategy.

It has previously been noted that there is a lack of proactive intelligence gathering relating to sex trafficking across police forces in the UK, and also at more divisional or regional levels (HMICFRS 2017). In addition to the role of OSINT in the course of investigations, findings from this research would also suggest benefits to using the methodology to proactively gather intelligence. Whilst the proposed methodology would not be able to directly identify sex trafficking or exploitation, it could provide valuable intelligence on the scale and structure of networks trying to penetrate local sex markets. An influx of larger and more complex networks could indicate the *risk* of exploitation to have increased locally, even if the presence of sex trafficking or exploitation cannot be confirmed through OSINT. Local police leaders would therefore better understand where risks and threats relating to the local sex market conceivably could be more likely to occur. Incoming intelligence from other sources could be triangulated against the OSINT networks to evaluate potential safeguarding concerns. As others have already pointed out (Scoular et al. 2019), such an approach is not unproblematic, and concerns related to this will be discussed in the next section.

Targeted and Proactive Approaches

What is often neglected in research on using technology to identify sex trafficking are the ethical implications. Indeed, this case study has highlighted the complexities associated with using technology to police the sex market, and that it is far from unproblematic to utilise technology in anti-trafficking efforts (see also Kjellgren 2022). Of particular importance, and as has been noted both in this research and elsewhere, is that brothel raids and the proactive identification of victims can have severely negative consequences (Mai 2009; Holt et al. 2021). Sex workers may inadvertently be criminalised for working together (Scoular et al. 2019), and those with a more precarious legal status always risk being detained and deported (Malloch 2016). Using technology to harvest and analyse escort adverts is inevitably a form of surveillance of populations within the sex market, and it is neither in the interest of the police nor the sex worker community to surveil individuals who are working out of their own volition. In a similar vein, a serious ethical concern raised by investigators in this research is that the police themselves do not want to hoard data on individuals where there is no suspicion of any criminality occurring. With the aforementioned complexities in mind, namely, that OSINT is incapable of distinguishing between individuals working out of their own volition vis-à-vis those in exploitative conditions, the proactive identification of trafficking from online data substantially increases the risk of generating false positives. In other words, relying only on OSINT to evaluate the working conditions will likely lead to conflating independent sex workers—particularly migrant sex workers—with trafficking victims.

The contention that the proactive use of technology to monitor the sex market can be harmful may appear to be in juxtaposition to the notion that intelligence proactively generated from online data is *also* useful for local police leaders. There is a very delicate balance between using OSINT strategically whilst also reducing the harms that can stem from over-policing vulnerable populations. To relate back to what was discussed earlier, the principal barrier to effective investigations, according to respondents from this research, is a combination of the resources required in large-scale investigations, and the complex role of agency in relation to sex trafficking. This, coupled with the notion that the proactive identification of victims is prone to generate false positives, which could lead to serious unintended consequences, suggests a highly targeted approach may be most viable. In such an approach, OSINT is used reactively to evaluate the online dimension of networks that have already been identified offline; this effectively eliminates the possibility of making incorrect assumptions about the offline conditions behind the adverts that are being posted. It should still be recognised that a more proactive use of online data could be viable, but only in very specific contexts. Using the data to examine the number of large and complex networks would increase the overall intelligence picture of local sex markets, whilst also shifting the focus from the adverts themselves to focus on the overall structure of advert networks. Incoming intelligence from more robust sources should continuously be triangulated against the online networks, and overt action may be appropriate only if safeguarding concerns can be identified from more substantial intelligence.

Partnership Working and Intelligence Sharing

A final point of consideration, and indeed of importance in improving the policing of the sex market, relates to the important role of partnership working and intelligence sharing. The findings that have been discussed would suggest that a potentially effective way to undermine the influence of criminal networks would be to increase the human and social capital of sex workers. This may be particularly imperative in relation to migrant sex workers. The key challenge is that the police are tasked with enforcing laws that prevent sex workers from drawing upon their social capital to work more safely, which is the case concerning current brothel-keeping legislation; strong ties to fellow sex workers may go a long way in terms of improving wellbeing and safety.

Positive examples were identified throughout this research, such as police forces working in partnership with groups supporting sex workers, suggesting there may be much to gain by working more closely with the sex worker community. This is important for several reasons. Sex workers, and the organisations that represent their interests, have unique knowledge pertaining to local sex markets and are crucial for developing both human and social capital. The sex worker community is undoubtedly in the best position to build trust with the most vulnerable populations of the sex market, including victims of exploitation, since further criminalisation is always a risk in law enforcement interactions. Policing approaches informed by the lived realities of sexual labour and exploitation will likely be more successful in identifying the most pressing threats on the sex market.

As noted by Pajón and Walsh (2023), effective partnership working and multi-agency collaboration are critical to ensure successful responses to human trafficking. The findings from this research support this conclusion; however, they also suggest it is crucial to include organisations supporting and advocating for sex workers in such partnerships. Doing so would contribute to a more nuanced understanding of the needs and threats associated with the sex market. In turn, the inclusion of sex worker-led groups into such partnerships could also provide intelligence on exploitation. Nevertheless, it must also be recognised that such an aspiration may not be feasible in practice due to how strained the relationship between the police and sex worker-led organisations currently is. As long as brothels are raided by the police, and sex workers are criminalised or migrants detained and deported, it is doubtful that organisations representing the rights of such groups would be inclined to cooperate. Indeed, what is urgently needed is for policymakers and practitioners to fundamentally reconfigure their approach to sexual labour and the policing of sex markets. Perhaps then, if trust can be established, more inclusive partnerships may be a possibility.

Ethical Challenges

Researching complex social phenomena, such as sexual labour, exploitation and policing, is always difficult. Conducting rigorous and robust research on these phenomena should include the input and expertise of the individuals affected by these issues—such as sex workers and those who consider themselves victims of exploitation and/or trafficking. The absence of such voices is by far the greatest limitation of this research, and particularly acute given the ethical challenges associated with policing the sex market. Whereas I have tried to integrate more critical understandings of sex work and exploitation in this research, the quality of this case study would have been significantly increased by including more non-police perspectives, particularly in relation to the interpretation of online data. Inevitably, the reliance on police perspectives means that the understanding of risks, consequences, and implications of policing the sex market is only partial.

Policing alone cannot prevent exploitation. The risk of focusing on improving policing is that the structural factors—which operates at the societal levelsuch as the criminalisation of migration and lack of opportunities, are neglected. Disrupting networks engaging in exploitation is important, but only a small fragment of what needs to be done to reduce the risks of exploitation. Nevertheless, with regard to how the policing of the UK's sex markets is currently conducted, there is ample room for improvement, to reduce the harms that can stem from policing itself, including the confiscation of sex workers' earnings, criminalisation for illegal brothel-keeping, the detention and deportation of migrant sex workers, or criminalisation of those that have, in various ways, been victimised. The findings from this case study are not definitive, but a starting point, for law enforcement, policymakers, tech entrepreneurs, and academics alike, to more carefully consider the implications of policing the sex market with online data.

Methodological Implications

The methodological contributions of this research are threefold. First, the combination of methods from the data sciences, including web scraping, text mining and automated workflows, with methods from the social sciences, such as multilevel modelling, MRQAP and social network analysis, has demonstrated the viability of interdisciplinary methodology in pushing the boundaries of computational criminology. The combination of such methods, as part of a comprehensive case study, may be particularly useful for studying complex social phenomena mediated by both offline and online spaces.

Second, the focus and analysis of advert networks, as opposed to online adverts alone, have provided a novel contribution to how we can better understand and measure the scale and complexity of online networks within the sex market. It offers a significantly more robust approach to understanding empirical networks and how we understand the overall structure of the online sex market itself. In this context, it allows us to conceive of the sex market as a constellation of components, part of a greater whole, which renders the notion of individual adverts as the primary unit of analysis limited in how we understand both networks and the structure of the sex market. Some of these methodological insights can conceivably be transferred to other research contexts where there is a need to estimate the scale and complexity of online networks.

Finally, the automated methodology developed for this research, which is focused on automatically identifying networks based on empirical variables and evaluating their structural characteristics, has clear applicability in researching the sex market and other internet-mediated contexts. Primarily, it will be highly relevant to research contexts where large quantities of data are likely to be nested within empirical networks. It may be particularly pertinent in criminological contexts, where we are often interested in studying networks that actively try to conceal their organised nature. The sex market, of course, is one such example, but it is likely also to be relevant to other criminal markets enabled by the internet and communication technologies, such as puppy trafficking, labour trafficking, the online drug trade, or networks facilitating the distribution and supply of child sexual exploitation materials.

Policing, Practitioner and Policy Implications

This section will briefly highlight the key implications for policing and practitioners and, more broadly, policy recommendations. It is important to note that there are considerable differences between the numerous police forces across the UK, and some of the recommendations highlighted here may already align with what has already been implemented. The recommendations should be conceived of as the best practices according to the findings and insights generated from this case study.

Utilise OSINT as Part of Targeted Approaches to Exploitation.

Resources are limited and must be focused on where the need is greatest. The credibility and quality of OSINT in this context are ambiguous, and investigations instigated solely based on OSINT are unlikely to capture the most pressing risks and threats accurately, and are likely to undermine relations between the police and sex worker and migrant communities. The use of OSINT will be most successful when used to provide a digital overlay of ongoing investigations, to appreciate the scale and extent of the networks under investigation.

If OSINT Is Used Proactively to Improve Local Intelligence Pictures, It Needs To Be Applied Cautiously and Used in Triangulation with Other Intelligence Sources.

OSINT provides limited information on what is actually going on offline, and whereas it can be useful to understand the presence of networks in local sex markets, overt action is best limited to circumstances where other intelligence suggests safeguarding concerns. The principal merit of proactive OSINT generation would be to continuously review incoming offline intelligence against OSINT pertaining to known online networks.

Indicator-Based Risk Matrices and Similar Approaches to OSINT Are Inefficient and Likely to Lead to Biased Estimations and Predictions.

Current methods based on the proactive identification of indicators of trafficking are highly susceptible to generating false positives and conflating sex workers, particularly migrant sex workers, with trafficking victims. More manual approaches, such as reviewing individual escort adverts to evaluate risks, are highly inefficient and will never be able to grasp the full complexity and extent of networks in the sex market. Automated methods engineered to evaluate the presence of indicators are similarly susceptible to generating false positives, albeit, on a larger scale. The network complexity scale offers a superior method to quantitatively assess networks based on their empirical characteristics rather than decision-making based on uncertain and spurious indicators.

The Implementation of Automated Tools and Web Scraping Is Not Unproblematic, and Caution Must be Exercised in Evaluating the Potential Harms and Gains Associated with Such Approaches.

Web scraping and collection of data from online escort adverts is inevitably a form of surveillance of the sex market. Increasing the capabilities of processing online data also increases the number of consenting adults who will be subjected to surveillance. Artificial intelligence and machine learning approaches used to evaluate the presence of trafficking are based on dubious assumptions and at serious risk of generating false positives. If automated data collection and analytical methods are employed, it is beneficial to focus on the network structures rather than the individual adverts; this ensures better information whilst also reducing the visibility of independent sex workers.

The Methodology Developed for this Case Study Is Capable of Addressing Law Enforcement Needs and Could Form the Basis of Further Evaluations of Digital Policing Efforts.

The proposed methodology maps well onto current law enforcement needs; however, it should be reviewed and improved by including and consulting sex workers and migrant sex workers, and organisations representing their interests to guide the design and implementation processes. Whereas the code is available and can be applied in practice, further work to formalise it into scalable software would be required. Importantly, it would need to be piloted during live investigations to evaluate its efficacy, and it would need to be carefully implemented to conform with current police regulations regarding surveillance and data collection.

Continue to Build and Strengthen Inclusive Partnerships at Local and National Levels.

Multi-agency collaboration and partnership working are key to addressing exploitation, especially since criminal justice responses may not be sufficient to identify, respond to and disrupt exploitation within the sex market. Local stakeholders are ideally placed to identify emerging threats in local communities, and national units and stakeholders should work jointly to collate local intelligence and identify nationwide patterns. Exploitation is a transient crime likely to span significant geographical areas. There needs to be a bidirectional flow of intelligence, with local intelligence being shared with national stakeholders who would review and evaluate patterns and feed that back to a local level. Partnerships need to be inclusive of groups representing and supporting sex workers. Human and social capital act as barriers against exploitation, and sex worker-led groups are important in providing the knowledge, tools, and social connections necessary to work more safely and autonomously. This would ensure that sex workers—and again, particularly migrant sex workers, who may already have reduced capital—are less likely to rely on third-parties to facilitate their labour, thereby reducing the risks of exploitation. In addition, the inclusion of sex worker-led groups in such responses will likely provide a much more comprehensive intelligence picture.

Legislation to Criminalise the Online Advertisement of Sexual Services is Misguided.

Current discussions and propositions of laws to ban the online advertisement of sexual services, in order to reduce exploitation, are unlikely to have positive effects. Such laws would make sexual labour even more precarious and dangerous; advertising online is important for the safety of sex workers. The criminalisation of online spaces may push sex workers to either work on the streets or rely on third-parties to facilitate their labour. The criminalisation of online spaces is also unlikely to actually curb the demand for sexual services nor reduce exploitation, and is more likely to displace online advertisement to even more precarious online spaces (e.g., the dark web). This would also deprive law enforcement of an important source of intelligence and make investigations more complicated.

Future Directions

Rather than perceiving this case study as offering definitive answers to the complexities of exploitation, the results should be perceived as a starting point for more robust and thoughtful research into the sex market, which encapsulates both its offline and online dimensions. This research was exploratory and sought to both extend our knowledge of the sex market, and the methodologies we can apply to study it.

At the heart of research into the online dimension of the sex market (including this case study) is a conspicuous absence of strong validity. Chiefly, this is the result of failures to effectively triangulate the online and offline dimensions of the sex market. Indeed, most research is either providing macro-level overviews of the online sex market, or qualitative accounts of the offline dimension. Attempts to harmonise these two dimensions, as has been the aim of this case study, often include limitations inherent to the data.

To successfully continue this line of inquiry, the most fruitful approach would be to work in direct partnership with police forces across the UK and sex worker-led organisations to examine the online presence of various networks collaboratively. This should ideally include an assessment of past or live investigative cases with contextual details regarding the presence of identifiable criminality. UK police forces and the NCA could contribute to the construction of a database of online adverts that have previously been part of investigations; such a database could provide the infrastructure for more thorough social scientific research. Moreover, sex workers, or the organisations that represent them, would be invaluable in interpreting and narrating the online patterns pertaining to sex workers, collectives and other forms of organised labour in the sex market. Together, a database of empirical networks could be constructed, and the conclusions drawn from such work could substantially improve the policing of the sex market. Such an approach would also mean that sex worker voices—as the true experts of the sex market—were central and that the research was beneficial to the overall working conditions of the sex market.

There is scope to further examine the facilitator-ratio hypothesis. This would ideally include a research design which compared (offline) networks with known elements of exploitation, with networks consisting of sex workers and migrant sex worker collectives. The former could be collected with the support of police forces, and the latter would ideally include peer-led research in the sex worker community. The key would be to identify a set of networks and obtain data pertaining to both the offline and online structures. The structure of online and offline networks, and the number of facilitators in criminal vis-à-vis non-criminal networks in the sex markets, could be compared. There is ample room to apply social network analysis in this context, and a promising line of inquiry would entail examining the extent to which offline connections correlate with online connections between escort adverts. This would make a significant contribution to the field by addressing some questions raised by this case study.

Concluding Remarks

Technology has likely led to continuous reconfigurations of the sex market, with the latest stage being the introduction of online and networked technologies. Sex trafficking, or more broadly, exploitation in the sex market, has potentially also changed as a result of this. There is a dearth of empirical data on sex trafficking, including how technology is used and the extent to which it facilitates this particular crime, especially in the UK. The aim of this case study was to explore the role of technology within Scotland's sex market, and more specifically, how criminal networks use technology in their operations, and what the consequences of this are. It also sought to examine the extent to which we can empirically identify networks and patterns of vulnerability and exploitation from online data about the sex market. Throughout this book, the feasibility of using computational criminology has been demonstrated, and the methodological design can provide a template for future studies into internet-mediated phenomena requiring a scalable approach to the collection of online data.

Indeed, this case study included a unique approach to the gathering, analysis and synthesis of data, which necessitated the development of a novel methodology. The fusion of insights from previous literature and qualitative fieldwork was distilled into a theoretical model of internet-mediated exploitation within the UK's off-street sex market, which formed the substantive foundation of the methodology. The complexity of translating the methodology into a practical tool to be used in case study, for purposes of data collection and analysis, required the programming of an automated workflow. This work had to be capable of identifying distinct networks from noisy open-source data and calculating key statistics related to their structure and scale. With a unique multilevel and relational dataset, social network analysis, MRQAP and multilevel modelling were used to identify and examine patterns, which were then evaluated in light of the qualitative findings.

With the application of the combined methods and triangulation, this research has addressed a key gap in the literature by advancing our understanding of the role of technology within the sex market, how criminal networks use it, the extent to which patterns of vulnerability and exploitation can be identified, and the subsequent value and utility of such patterns in practitioner contexts. More specifically, human and social capital were theorised as mediating the risks of exploitation, and a socio-ecological framework can be useful in disentangling how risk factors to exploitation operating on different levels are related. Sex workers with lower levels of capital were argued to be more likely to need to rely on third-parties to facilitate their labour. The findings suggest that the widespread adoption of online technologies may paradoxically have contributed to safer and more precarious working conditions; in general, sexual labour tends to have become safer due to the more advantageous working conditions offered by technology. However, technology has also created online spaces which are highly beneficial to those seeking to exploit others while operating outwith the periphery of routine policing activities.

Criminal networks were described by research participants to use technology extensively, but the extent to which the use of technology can be considered sophisticated is highly variable. In essence, technology may increase the permutations available within the sex trafficking crime script. In other words, from recruitment and transportation to exploitation, technology has the potential to offer novel ways of carrying out the logistical steps of the crime commission process. As such, technology has the potential to increase the logistical and administrative capacities of criminal networks; it allows them to streamline their operations whilst drawing less attention to their operations.

The empirical networks identified in this research were demonstrated to fall along a continuum of complexity, in terms of their scale and digital footprint. There appears to be a broader tendency towards organisation within the sex market, and the online sex market is possibly more organised than what was previously assumed. One of the most important contributions of this case study was the finding that network structure predicts advert-level outcomes. The actual structure of the networks themselves was demonstrated to vary based on a network's complexity: larger networks tend to be more heterogeneous and diverse, whereas simpler networks—which may be more likely to represent independent sex workers—are largely homogeneous in terms of the advertised characteristics. As such, the notion that networks are structured around characteristics such as age, location and ethnicity may imply that a certain degree of brokerage may be present in the offline networks, with some people controlling clusters of adverts. Relatedly, complex networks tend to leave digital footprints similar to other complex networks; simpler networks appear more unique.

The synthesis of qualitative data and the identified patterns and networks allowed for a nuanced discussion around the extent to which we can conceivably identify patterns related to vulnerability and exploitation. It was argued that the ability to identify vulnerability and exploitation from online data accurately is very limited. The primary reason for this is that online escort adverts are a highly ambiguous source of data—they represent the digital traces of different marketing strategies—and the information required to inform such judgements is absent within this data source. However, coupled with the notion that the risk of exploitation is likely to increase in larger networks, we can conceivably assess *vulnerability to exploitation*, by examining a network's complexity. This hypothesis received further support by multilevel modelling, in which it was demonstrated that more complex networks are more likely to advertise what some may consider 'extreme' or 'risky' services. In addition to this, an emergent hypothesis from the synthesis of findings from this case study is the proposition that the ratio between facilitators and sex workers may be positively correlated with the risk of exploitation.

This case study also evaluated the usefulness of the identified networks and patterns in practitioner contexts and, more broadly, the most appropriate and advantageous use of OSINT in the policing of sex trafficking. It was concluded that given the inherent limitations of open-source data, the methodology developed for this case study is best used reactively as part of targeted policing approaches. The key applicability of the methodology lies in its ability to augment ongoing investigations with a digital overlay, since it will enable investigators to better capture the extent, structure and geography of criminal networks. Whereas the methodology has clear applicability in proactive intelligence gathering, such efforts are prone to generate false positives. Using the methodology on divisional levels to improve local intelligence pictures would be advantageous, if incoming intelligence from other sources were continuously reviewed in light of the known online networks operating in the area. However, caution should be exercised, and overt action should be limited to credible intelligence suggesting safeguarding concerns, so as not to over-police sex workers.

Whilst a series of recommendations for policy and practice based on the findings from this case study have also been suggested, it is also recognised that policing alone cannot prevent exploitation: addressing inequalities and punitive laws, providing opportunities and supporting sex workers in developing social and human capital is critical. Disrupting criminal networks is extremely important, but it is far from sufficient to *end* exploitation.

To conclude, technology is important for sex workers to work more safely, but also for criminal networks seeking to exploit others. Technology paradoxically allows for safer working conditions and increasingly precarious online spaces. Online technologies have the potential to enhance the logistical and administrative capabilities of criminal networks, thereby rendering these groups more flexible in their modus operandi. Policing sex trafficking is incredibly challenging, and whereas OSINT is very useful in investigations, the epistemologically dubious qualities of escort adverts mean law enforcement cannot necessarily use them to identify vulnerability or exploitation directly. OSINT can, however, provide a digital overlay to ongoing sex trafficking investigations, and targeted policing and intelligence triangulation are critical to disrupting criminal networks operating within the sex market. Computational criminology can, and will, play a pivotal part in advancing our understanding in future research on crime and behaviour spanning the boundaries of the online and the offline.

References

Adriaenssens S, Hendrickx J (2012) Sex, Price and Preferences: Accounting for Unsafe Sexual Practices in Prostitution Markets. Sociol Health Illn 34(5):665–680

Agustín LM (2006) The Disappearing of a Migration Category: Migrants Who Sell Sex. J Ethn Migr Stud 32(1):29–47. https://doi.org/10.1080/13691830500335325

Albanese J, Broad R, Gadd D (2022) Consent, Coercion, and Fraud in Human Trafficking Relationships. J Hum Traffick 8(1):13–32. https://doi.org/10.1080/23322705.2021.2019529

Alvari H, Shakarian P, Snyder JEK (2017) Semi-supervised Learning for Detecting Human Trafficking. Secur Inform 6(1):1–24. https://doi.org/10.1186/s13388-017-0029-8

Antonopoulos GA, Baratto G, Di Nicola A, Diba P, Martini E, Papanicolaou G, Terenghi F (2020) Technology in Human Smuggling and Trafficking: Case Studies from Italy and the United Kingdom, 1st edn. Springer, Cham

Barlow C, Kidd A, Green ST, Darby B (2022) Circles of Analysis: A Systemic Model of Child Criminal Exploitation. JCS 17(3):158–174. https://doi.org/10.1108/JCS-04-2021-0016

Barner JR, Okech D, Camp MA (2018) "One Size Does Not Fit All:" A Proposed Ecological Model for Human Trafficking Intervention. J Evid Inf Soc Work 15(2):137–150. https://doi.org/10.1080/23761407.2017.1420514

Bjelland HF (2016) Identifying Human Trafficking in Norway: A Register-based Study of Cases, Outcomes and Police Practices. Eur J Criminol 14(5):522–542. https://doi.org/10.1177/1477370816677619

Campbell R, Teela S, Scoular J, Pitcher J, Cunningham S (2019) Risking Safety and Rights: Online Sex Work, Crimes and 'Blended Safety Repertoires'. Br J Sociol 70(4):1539–1560. https://doi.org/10.1111/1468-4446.12493

Chimienti M (2009) Selling Sex in Order to Migrate: The End of the Migratory Dream? J Ethn Migr Stud 36(1):27–45. https://doi.org/10.1080/13691830903266101

Christie N (1986) The Ideal Victim. In: Fattah EA (ed) From Crime Policy to Victim Policy. Macmillan, London

Cornish DB (1994) The Procedural Analysis of Offending and Its Relevance for Situational Prevention. In: Clarke RV (ed) Crime Prevention Studies, 2nd edn. Criminal Justice Press, New York, pp 151–196

Crocker R, Webb S, Garner S, Skidmore M (2017) The Impact of Organised Crime in Local Communities. The Police Foundation, London

Cunningham S, Sanders T, Platt L, Grenfell P, Macioti PG (2018) Sex Work and Occupational Homicide: Analysis of a U.K. Murder Database. Homicide Stud 22(3):321–338. https://doi.org/10.1177/1088767918754306

Dahlberg LL, Krug EG (2006) Violence a Global Public Health Problem. Cien Saude Colet 11(2):277–292. https://doi.org/10.1590/S1413-81232006000200007

Deeb-Swihart J, Endert A, Bruckman A (2019) Understanding Law Enforcement Strategies and Needs for Combating Human Trafficking. In: Proceedings of the 2019 CHI Conference on Human Factors in Computing Systems, Chicago, pp 1–14

DeliverFund (2020) Where We Are. https://deliverfund.org/how-deliverfund-is-fighting-human-trafficking-in-america/

Di Nicola A, Baratto G, Martini E (2017) The Role of the Internet in People Smuggling and Human Trafficking. Directorate-General Migration and Home Affairs, European Commission, Trento

Doezema J (1999) Loose Women or Lost Women? The Re-emergence of the Myth of White Slavery in Contemporary Discourses of Trafficking in Women. Gend Issues 18(1):23–50

Englund C, Viuhko M, Jokinen A, Aromaa K, Resetnikova A, Markina A, Söderström U, Nilsen M (2008) The Organisation of Human Trafficking: A Study of Criminal Involvement in Sexual Exploitation in Sweden, Finland and Estonia. Swedish National Council for Crime Prevention, Stockholm

Europol (2011) Trafficking in Human Beings in the European Union. Europol, Hague

Europol (2020) The Challenges of Countering Human Trafficking in the Digital Era. Europol Operations Directorate, Hague

Farley M, Franzblau K, Kennedy MA (2014) Online Prostitution and Trafficking. Albany Law Rev 77(3):1039–1094

Finn MA, Stalans LJ (2016) How Targeted Enforcement Shapes Marketing Decisions of Pimps: Evidence of Displacement and Innovation. Vict Offenders 11(4):578–599. https://doi.org/10.1080/15564886.2016.1187694

Giommoni L (2024) Why We Cannot Identify Human Trafficking from Online Advertisements. J Hum Traffick:1–15. https://doi.org/10.1080/23322705.2024.2435198

Giommoni L, Ikwu R (2024) Identifying Human Trafficking Indicators in the UK Online Sex Market. Trends Organ Crim 27(1):10–33. https://doi.org/10.1007/s12117-021-09431-0

HMICFRS (2017) Stolen Freedom: The Policing Response to Modern Slavery and Human Trafficking. Her Majesty's Inspectorate of Constabulary and Fire & Rescue Services, London

Holt V, Kenway E, Berry A (2021) Sex Workers As Collateral Damage, Once Again: A Critique Of The New 'Sex Trafficking Identification Matrix' Tool. SWARM. https://www.swarmcollective.org/sex-workers-as-collateral-damage-once-again-a-critique-of-the-new-sex-trafficking-identification-matrix-tool/. Accessed 24 Aug 2025.

Hughes DM (2002) The Use of New Communications and Information Technologies for Sexual Exploitation of Women and Children. Hastings Women's L J 13(1):127–146

Hughes DM (2004) Prostitution Online. Journal of Trauma. Practice 2(3–4):115–131. https://doi.org/10.1300/J189v02n03_06

Ibanez M, Suthers DD (2014) Detection of Domestic Human Trafficking Indicators and Movement Trends Using Content Available on Open Internet Sources. In: HICSS '14: Proceedings of the 2014 47th Hawaii International Conference on System Sciences, pp 1556–1565

Kempadoo K (2004) Sexing the Caribbean: Gender, Race and Sexual Labor, 1st edn. Routledge, Oxon

Kjellgren R (2022) Good Tech, Bad Tech: Policing Sex Trafficking with Big Data. Int J Crime Justice Soc Democr 11(1):149–166. https://doi.org/10.3316/agispt.20220412065553

Konrad RA, Trapp AC, Palmbach TM, Blom JS (2017) Overcoming Human Trafficking via Operations Research and Analytics: Opportunities for Methods, Models, and Applications. Eur J Oper Res 259(2):733–745. https://doi.org/10.1016/j.ejor.2016.10.049

L'Hoiry X, Moretti A, Antonopoulos GA (2024) Identifying Sex Trafficking in Adult Services Websites: An Exploratory Study with a British Police Force.

Trends Organ Crim 27(1):34–55. https://doi.org/10.1007/s12117-021-09414-1

Lainez N (2017) Social Structure, Relationships and Reproduction in Quasi-family Networks: Brokering Circular Migration of Vietnamese Sex Workers to Singapore. J Ethn Migr Stud 45(9):1631–1649. https://doi.org/10.1080/1369183x.2017.1417028

Latonero M (2011) Human Trafficking Online: The Role of Social Networking Sites and Online Classifieds. University of Southern California, Los Angeles

Latonero M (2012) The Rise of Mobile and the Diffusion of Technology-Facilitated Trafficking. University of Southern California, Los Angeles

Li L, Simek O, Lai A, Daggett M, Dagli CK, Jones C (2018) Detection and Characterization of Human Trafficking Networks Using Unsupervised Scalable Text Template Matching. In: 2018 IEEE International Conference on Big Data (Big Data), Seattle, WA

Mai N (2009) Migrant Workers in the UK Sex Industry: Full Research Report. Economic Social and Research Council, Swindon

Malloch M (2016) Criminalising Victims of Human Trafficking: State Responses and Punitive Practices. In: Malloch M, Rigby P (eds) Human Trafficking: The Complexities of Exploitation. Edinburgh University Press, Edinburgh, pp 175–193

Marinus Analytics (2021) Traffic Jam. Marinus Analytics

McKinley N (2017) Our Generation and the Fight Against Slavery. Huffpost, 6 December. https://www.huffpost.com/entry/our-generation-and-the-fi_b_9996634

Morselli C, Weitzer R, Zhang SX, Savoie-Gargiso I (2014) Coercion, Control, and Cooperation in a Prostitution Ring. Ann Am Acad Pol Soc Sci 653(1):247–265. https://doi.org/10.1177/0002716214521995

O'Connell Davidson J (2006) Will the Real Sex Slave Please Stand Up? Fem Rev 83(1):4–22

Pajón L, Walsh D (2018) Proposing a Theoretical Framework for the Criminal Investigation of Human Trafficking Crimes. Policing 14(2):493–511. https://doi.org/10.1093/police/pay031

Pajón L, Walsh D (2023) The Importance of Multi-agency Collaborations During Human Trafficking Criminal Investigations. Polic Soc 33(3):296–314. https://doi.org/10.1080/10439463.2022.2106984

Petter S, Giddens L, Fullilove M (2020) The Challenges of Using of Information Technology to Counter Human Trafficking. Association for Information Systems, pp 1–10

Plambech S (2017) Sex, Deportation and Rescue: Economies of Migration among Nigerian Sex Workers. Fem Econ 23(3):134–159. https://doi.org/10.1080/13545701.2016.1181272

Sanchez RV, Pacquiao DF (2018) An Ecological Approach toward the Prevention and Care of Victims of Domestic Minor Sex Trafficking. J Forensic Nurs 14(2):98–105. https://doi.org/10.1097/JFN.0000000000000205

Sanders T, Connelly L, King LJ (2016) On Our Own Terms: The Working Conditions of Internet-Based Sex Workers in the UK. Sociol Res Online 21(4):1–14. https://doi.org/10.5153/sro.4152

Sanders T, Scoular J, Campbell R, Pitcher J, Cunningham S (2018) Internet Sex Work: Beyond the Gaze, 1st edn. Springer Nature, Cham

Scoular J, Pitcher J, Sanders T, Cunningham S, Campbell R (2019) Beyond the Gaze and Well Beyond Wolfenden: The Practices and Rationalities of Regulating and Policing Sex Work in the Digital Age. J Law Soc 46(2):211–239

Skidmore M, Garner S, Desroches C, Saggu N (2018) The Threat of Exploitation in the Adult Sex Market: A Pilot Study of Online Sex Worker Advertisements. Policing 12(2):210–218. https://doi.org/10.1093/police/pax007

Such E, Laurent C, Jaipaul R, Salway S (2020) Modern Slavery and Public Health: A Rapid Evidence Assessment and an Emergent Public Health Approach. Public Health 180:168–179. https://doi.org/10.1016/j.puhe.2019.10.018

Tech Against Trafficking (2021) How We Work. Tech Against Trafficking

Volodko A, Cockbain E, Kleinberg B (2019) "Spotting the Signs" of Trafficking Recruitment Online: Exploring the Characteristics of Advertisements Targeted at Migrant Job-seekers. Trends Organ Crime 23:7–35. https://doi.org/10.1007/s12117-019-09376-5

Walby S, Apitzsch B, Armstrong J, Balderston S, Follis K, Francis B, Kelly L, May-Chahal C, Rashid A, Shire K, Towers J, Tunte M (2016) Study on the Gender Dimension of Trafficking in Human Beings: Final Report. European Commission, Luxembourg

Whitney J, Jennex M, Elkins A, Frost E (2018) Don't Want to Get Caught? Don't Say It: The Use of EMOJIS in Online Human Sex Trafficking Ads. In: Proceedings of the 51st Hawaii International Conference on System Sciences, pp 4273–4282

Wijkman M, Kleemans E (2019) Female Offenders of Human Trafficking and Sexual Exploitation. Crime Law Soc Chang 72(1):53–72. https://doi.org/10.1007/s10611-019-09840-x

Women and Equalities Committee (2024) Misogyny in Music: Second Report of Session 2023–24. House of Commons, London

Zimmermann C, Hossain M, Yun K, Roche B, Morison L, Watts C (2006) Stolen Smiles: A Summary Report on the Physical and Psychological Health Consequences of Women and Adolescents Trafficked in Europe. The London School of Hygiene & Tropical Medicine, London

Index[1]

[1] Note: Page numbers followed by 'n' refer to notes.

R. Kjellgren, *Internet-Mediated Exploitation in the Scottish Online Sex Market*, Transnational Crime, Crime Control and Security,
https://doi.org/10.1007/978-3-032-09275-5

Kolibri 360 GmbH
Ferdinand-Jühlke-Straße 7
99095 Erfurt, Deutschland
produktsicherheit@kolibri360.de